How Trump and the Christian Right Saved LGBTI Human Rights

SUNY series in Queer Politics and Cultures

Cynthia Burack and Jyl J. Josephson, editors

How Trump and the Christian Right Saved LGBTI Human Rights

A Religious Freedom Mystery

CYNTHIA BURACK

SUNY
PRESS

For information, contact State University of New York Press, Albany, NY
www.sunypress.edu

Library of Congress Cataloging-in-Publication Data

Name: Burack, Cynthia, 1958– author.
Title: How Trump and the Christian right saved LGBTI human rights : a
    religious freedom mystery / Cynthia Burack.
Description: Albany : State University of New York Press, [2022] | Series:
    SUNY series in queer politics and cultures | Includes bibliographical
    references and index.
Identifiers: LCCN 2022005504 | ISBN 9781438488837 (hardcover : alk. paper) |
    ISBN 9781438488844 (ebook) | ISBN 9781438488820 (pbk. : alk. paper)
Subjects: LCSH: Sexual minorities—Civil rights. | Sexual minorities—Civil rights—
    United States. | Sexual orientation—Religious aspects—Christianity. | Gay rights—
    Religious aspects—Christianity | Sexual minorities—Government policy—
    United States—History—21st century. | United States—Politics and government—
    2017–2021. | United States—Foreign relations—2017–2021.
Classification: LCC HQ76.5 B88 2022 | DDC 323.3/264—dc23/eng/20220406
LC record available at https://lccn.loc.gov/2022005504

10 9 8 7 6 5 4 3 2 1

In memory of my mother,
Dwanda Byrle Simmons Burack

Contents

Acknowledgments

First, I would like to thank colleagues and loved ones who read all or part of this project and offered their suggestions for improvement: Dennis Altman, Emil Edenborg, Lee Evans, Jyl Josephson, Laree Martin, Zein Murib, Julie Novkov, Michael Simrak, Elise Stephenson, Markus Thiel, and Franke Wilmer. Thanks to John Ross for technological support and to Felon for artistic consultation. The Mershon Center for International Security Studies at Ohio State provided funding for research travel to Africa in 2019. Looking back, I'm grateful for all the reviewers—some beloved pals—who have improved some piece of writing before I sent it out into the world. You've performed yeo(wo)man's service, and I appreciate the ways in which you've made me better. Also crucial to my well-being are the friends who sustain me, both when times are tough and when they're a blast. If I haven't bought you a cocktail recently, let me know, and I'll make it up to you. Finally, I'd like to thank Ohio State University undergraduates who provided research assistance as I mulled this project: Cara Clark, Samantha Turk, and Meredith Whitaker.

I'm grateful to Nick Romerhausen and the Equality Knowledge Project at Eastern Michigan University for a Knowledge Equality Project Award for 2016–18 and the opportunity to discuss this study in Ypsilanti. Because of Covid-19, I was unable to present some of this research at Montana State University and at the joint international human rights conference that was scheduled to be held at the University of London in June 2020. I missed opportunities to hear colleagues talk about their work in person and to mudlark along the Thames.

Part of chapter 4 was published as "Sexual Orientation and Gender Identity Human Rights Assistance in the Time of Trump," *Politics and Gender* 14, no. 4 (2018): 561–80. Copyright © The Women and Politics Research

Section of the American Political Science Association 2018. Reprinted with permission.

Whatever other categories this book belongs in, it also fits into the mystery genre. When I was growing up, I loved Arthur Conan Doyle's Sherlock Holmes, and as an adult I'm drawn to forensic analyses of crime. The crimes in question are puzzles that need to be solved, and this means investigators must collect and analyze data, make connections, and consider unlikely, as well as likely, solutions. The central mystery I take up here is this: considering how consistently the Christian right has pressed to reverse human rights protections for LGBT people, charging that human rights for gender and sexual minorities are responsible for jeopardizing religious freedom, why didn't the administration and its Christian conservative allies assail US support for LGBTI human rights during Trump's term in office? Many people had hunches or convictions about what the Trump administration was doing in this arena (note: some of these, however firmly held, were inaccurate) as well as why the administration was doing what it did. After researching the question diligently, I've come to some conclusions about who, what, and why.

Not everyone will recognize "Silver Blaze" as the title of one of Arthur Conan Doyle's Sherlock Holmes stories. However, one element of the tale has passed into common cultural use to denote the significance of an event that doesn't occur: the dog that didn't bark. In Conan Doyle's story, Holmes is close to completing his famed, fictional process of deduction to solve two related crimes—a murder and the theft of a racehorse—when he engages in a cryptic exchange with the local inspector on the case. Asked if he wishes to "draw [the inspector's] attention" to any other information he'd uncovered, Holmes responds, "To the curious incident of the dog in the night-time." When the inspector remonstrates that "the dog did nothing in the night-time," Holmes replies, "That was the curious incident." Determining the meaning of the dog's failure to bark enables Holmes to solve the case and retreat to his study.

I find myself fascinated not only by what did happen during Trump's tumultuous turn as president but also, like Holmes, by what didn't. In spite of what I and many other students of the Christian right would have expected, neither Trump nor the Christian right made a vigorous effort to dismantle US support for sexual orientation and gender identity (SOGI) human rights abroad. From where I sit, the Christian right—in this case, especially those I'll eventually get around to calling first-string Christian right elites—is the dog that didn't bark. And the movement's lack of interest in barking at one of its main preoccupations certainly warrants a closer investigative look.

I also appreciate Holmes's reflections on method. Noting that the case of Silver Blaze "suffer[ed] from a plethora of surmise, conjecture, and hypothesis," Holmes cautions Watson that the "art of the reasoner" may not require "fresh evidence" so much as "the sifting of details" already acquired. And he warns against "the embellishments of theorists and reporters." Like Holmes, I've done my best to establish a framework of "undeniable fact" and resolve the case of the missing saboteurs of SOGI. I wasn't led to these conclusions by the irresistible force of theory; rather, I arrived at them the old-fashioned way, through low-tech detective work. Sometimes I was surprised by what I found or deduced. Now that I've reached the end of this quest, I'm happy to hang up my Inverness coat, light a pipe, sit in front of the fire, and wait for another challenge.

Introduction

Setting the Table for SOGI Human Rights

From Obama to Trump

In this book, I tell the story of official support and assistance for sexual orientation and gender identity (SOGI) human rights in the Trump administration through the lens of domestic US politics and social movements. To be more specific, I place the orientation of the administration toward SOGI human rights in the context of the Christian conservative movement that helped to create the conditions for such an administration. I ask and answer this question: Has the Christian conservative movement that vehemently opposes LGBTQ civil rights in the US and LGBTQ human rights abroad used its influence to encourage the US government to revoke its advocacy for international SOGI human rights?

Lesbian, gay, bisexual, transgender, queer, and intersex (LGBTQI) communities continue to be disfavored and persecuted in many parts of the world. While conditions for LGBTI people have improved in some places since the turn of the millennium, conditions have deteriorated in other parts of the world, creating a situation of LGBTI safety and flourishing that has become more bifurcated over time.[1] One dimension of this bifurcation pertains in Europe, where instead of an iron curtain, "a rainbow curtain now divides the continent."[2] Indeed, there's evidence that "a transnational network of anti-LGBT actors . . . [is] co-opting the structures and mechanisms within the international system to coordinate the transnational diffusion of LGBT backlash and resistance."[3] During the Obama administration, the US came out in support of SOGI human rights.[4] But in 2016, Donald Trump's victory over Hillary Clinton aroused anxieties for many proponents of LGBTQ human rights who feared that under Trump the US government would rescind its progress toward full equality for gender and sexual minorities.

Between 2013 and 2016, I heard LGBTQ, and human rights advocates in formal and informal settings in the US, Europe, Africa, and Southeast Asia pose a question: What will happen to US support for sexual orientation and gender identity human rights after the US presidential election? These interlocutors believed that SOGI human rights advocacy and assistance they received or administered would be safe in a Hillary Clinton administration. However, grassroots and international activists alike wondered openly whether US commitments to SOGI human rights might be reversed under a Republican administration.

Candidate Trump made many right-wing populist claims and promises. In his most evident feint in the direction of targeting LGBTQ people during the campaign, Trump secured Christian conservative electoral support in part by promising to protect Christian conservatives' "religious freedom" to discriminate against gender and sexual minorities. This promise was freighted with Christian conservative expectations about what would have to happen to LGBTQ rights in order for religious freedom to be properly protected. However, it's significant that in the course of a campaign in which Trump persistently identified immigrants as threats to America and Americans, he notably didn't scapegoat and demonize gender and sexual minorities, as many populist, authoritarian leaders do.[5] His ostensible lack of interest in reversing the recent legal and social gains of LGBTQ movements puzzled some observers. For example, Trump disapproved of North Carolina's HB2, the "bathroom law," and promised that Caitlyn Jenner could use the women's room at Trump Tower whenever she wished.[6]

After the 2016 election, and even before Donald Trump took office, SOGI human rights advocates were tendering perspectives and strategies to deal with possible global consequences for SOGI human rights of the US election. Human rights advocates, implementing partners, grantees, and beneficiaries of US State Department human rights programs were anything but indifferent to the consequence of the presidential election for US human rights assistance. It was clear in these conversations that many grassroots and international human rights advocates were concerned about the possibility that US SOGI advocacy might come to a halt, or even that the US government might begin to amplify the anti-LGBTQ, anti-SOGI commitments of Trump's Christian conservative or white nationalist voting blocs.

What did anti-LGBT Christian conservatives expect from the election of Donald Trump? We can reconstruct an answer to that question from the outpouring of movement messaging that addressed itself specifically to the SOGI-related hopes and demands of the Christian right. I'll get to some of that messaging in the chapters to come, but for the moment I introduce a particular missive that differentiated Trump's personal views on LGBTQ people and issues from the likely effects of the policies of a Trump administration for a Christian conservative audience. Anti-LGBTQ pastor and attorney Scott Lively is a Christian conservative who has engaged in high-profile international efforts to lobby, amplify, and praise anti-LGBTQ civil and human rights projects. Lively is coauthor (with Kevin Abrams) of *The Pink Swastika: Homosexuality in the Nazi Party* and has personally been involved with influential anti-LGBTQ campaigns in Uganda, Russia, and Eastern Europe.[7]

Just after Trump's election, Lively published an article online in *BarbWire*—"politics and culture from a biblical worldview"—in which he acknowledged Trump's "obvious lack of support for the pro-family side of the Christian vs LGBT cultural showdown." There, he predicted success from the "populist power" of the "global uprising against the elites" that had emerged to fight "gay marriage" and the "Third World 'immigrant' invasion of the US and EU." In the column, Lively counsels Christian conservatives that "irrespective of Mr. Trump's personal views," two factors would weaken and rout " 'gay' supremacy" in the US. One was Trump's control of court nominations, especially his ability to appoint Christian conservatives to the Supreme Court and the pressure from Christian conservatives that would assure those selections. A second was consistent with Lively's professed admiration for Vladimir Putin as the world's "greatest defender of true human rights": that "if Mr. Trump simply emulates Mr. Putin and defers to the church to repair the damage caused by long-term Marxist rule, we'll be able to clean up the mess in relatively short order." In this chilling suggestion, Lively alludes to the kind of officially-sanctioned discrimination, harassment, and violence that has driven LGBTQI people underground and from their countries as refugees, and resulted in many egregious human rights violations. Such violence is often performed by nonstate actors who are rewarded for their efforts with impunity from prosecution.[8] Lively didn't get his wish during Trump's term as president, but he was onto something I return to in the conclusion.

In the course of this book, I assess the impact of the Christian right on US government SOGI policies and programs using two themes. The first theme is a rhetorical social movement frame developed and disseminated by the Christian right that counterposes US government support for SOGI human rights under the Obama administration with the charge that when it came to LGBTI rights, Obama and Hillary Clinton exposed their enmity to faith and religious freedom. Frames are a form of "meaning construction" social movements engage in to create and fix interpretations of issues "for constituents, antagonists . . . bystanders or observers."[9] This frame has performed crucial social movement work to link LGBTQ/SOGI rights with religious persecution and to link the fate of US Christians to those persecuted because of faith in other lands.

The second theme is an assessment of both the "supply" and "demand" sides of US SOGI human rights assistance in the Trump administration. By this, I mean I provide evidence of how Obama administration SOGI policies fared under Trump: the supply side of SOGI human rights assistance. I'll also show the continuity of the demand side of the SOGI human rights equation from Obama to Trump: SOGI human rights grantees and implementing partners who continued to coordinate with US officials to design and provide human rights assistance. An investigation of these two themes reveals the following realities: what happened with regard to US support for SOGI from 2017 to January, 2021; how the administration used religious freedom to cultivate its Christian conservative base; how the Christian right used administration support for religious freedom to defend the administration against its critics; and how the Christian right cynically ignored the SOGI human rights they had long argued constituted the most potent threat to religious freedom around the world.

In this introduction, I provide a brief overview of the Obama administration's SOGI policy that riled Christian conservatives and—in a formulation I've now heard many times on the SOGI trail—made the US the "biggest player" in international SOGI human rights. I also introduce readers to the dramatis personae of this story: the president, a key Christian right producer of political messaging, the Christian conservative US officials involved in SOGI and religious freedom during Trump's term in office, and the small team of officials in the State Department's Bureau of Democracy, Human Rights, and Labor who manage SOGI foreign assistance. Finally, I explain the terms I use in this book and sketch a roadmap of the argument to come.

This book is not primarily a work of theory. In addition to reporting on the administration from mainstream media, I've relied on scholarly sources, government documents, Christian right sources, and material derived from participant observation. I attended meetings at the State Department and US Capitol, LGBTQ/SOGI meetings in the US and abroad, and Christian right events. Instead of approaching the interplay of religious freedom and

SOGI human rights from theoretical perspectives, I employ a somewhat journalistic, "tick-tock," account of what transpired during the years in which Trump occupied the White House and Christian conservatives occupied a "privileged position" among domestic interest groups.[10]

SOGI Yesterday

US support for SOGI human rights didn't begin only when the Obama administration announced its SOGI human rights foreign policy. Before 2012, SOGI human rights assistance abroad originated within the State Department in the form of extensions to LGBTQ people of support for other vulnerable or marginalized populations. Thus, at first, SOGI was incorporated into longtime programs and policies such as Country Reports on Human Rights Practices and the President's Emergency Plan for AIDS Relief (PEPFAR), and into newer programs such as the State Department's Lifeline: Embattled Civil Society Organizations Assistance Fund. Perhaps the earliest cases of US support for SOGI human rights abroad involved allocations in the final years of the Clinton administration from a fund set up to pursue concealed Holocaust-era assets, compensate survivors of Nazi persecution and their heirs, and memorialize victims of Nazi persecution. State Department officials directed a percentage of the funds allocated by Congress for these purposes to gay Holocaust survivors and to projects related to commemorating gay and lesbian victims of Nazi persecution.[11]

Then, in December 2011, the Obama administration publicly declared its support for SOGI human rights through two coordinated mechanisms: Secretary of State Hillary Clinton's "Remarks on International Human Rights Day," delivered in Geneva, Switzerland, and Barack Obama's "Presidential Memorandum—International Initiatives to Advance the Human Rights of Lesbian, Gay, Bisexual, and Transgender Persons," directed to US government foreign affairs agencies. Even in 2011, the US government was a relatively late adopter of support and advocacy for international SOGI human rights. Indeed, the US followed private charities, LGBTQ and mainstream human rights civil society organizations; nations such as Sweden and the Netherlands; and multinational organizations such as the European Union and the Council of Europe in such international advocacy. Phillip Ayoub contributes an important analysis of norm diffusion in European support for LGBT human rights in *When States Come Out: Europe's Sexual Minorities and the Politics of Visibility*.[12] The integration of SOGI human rights into

US foreign policy was reflected in US participation in multilateral efforts to secure human rights protections for LGBTQ people and activists and in Secretary of State John Kerry's appointment in early 2015 of foreign service officer Randy Berry to serve as the first special envoy for the human rights of LGBTI persons. Before Obama left office, the US had achieved "unprecedented leadership in promoting LGBT rights abroad."[13]

What is meant by "SOGI human rights" has been contested, especially, but not only, from perspectives of diverse cultures, traditions, and religious beliefs. The fact that Secretary of State Hillary Clinton proclaimed in 2011 in Geneva, Switzerland, that "gay rights are human rights, and human rights are gay rights" hasn't settled the question of whether SOGI is a legitimate category of human rights. Indeed, noting two years after Clinton announced US support for SOGI that "international human rights law has been developed by consensus" and that "there is nothing even close to a consensus on positive protections for gender or sexual minorities," Jack Donnelly argued in 2013 that "advocacy for LGBT rights is *not* advocacy for internationally recognized human rights." However, Donnelly clarifies that even if there's no international consensus to, for example, prohibit the criminalization of same-sex relations, denying LGBTI people the protection of laws and internationally recognized human rights, and condoning violence against them are prohibited under international law.[14]

Later in this book, I address false Christian right claims that the Obama administration tried to coerce LGBTI-unfriendly nations to accept same-sex marriage. But what were the Obama administration's goals with regard to SOGI human rights? When I talked with State Department and USAID officials between 2013 and 2016, their descriptions of their work—and the human rights concerns and jeopardy that motivated it—revolved, first and foremost, around egregious human rights violations such as torture, murder, execution, and impunity for violations committed against LGBTI people by their governments or fellow citizens. Second, US human rights officials talked about the importance of upholding the application to LGBTI people of human rights outlined in international agreements such as the Universal Declaration of Human Rights: rights to, for example, equal protection of the law, a fair trial, privacy, freedom of movement, asylum, freedom of religion, freedom of expression, freedom to assemble, and freedom to associate with others, including in pursuit of political recognition and equality.

Essentially, SOGI human rights policy and practices have operated on a foundational understanding that human rights that apply to non-LGBTI people also belong to LGBTI people, or that LGBTI people shouldn't be singled out, as individuals or in groups, for stigma, harassment, discrimination, or violence. Decriminalization of same-sex sexuality, a goal to which the Trump administration gave occasional lip service, was one goal of US SOGI policy during the Obama administration, as indicated in Obama's presidential memorandum. However, although the US has provided some support for legal advocacy for decriminalization, State Department human rights officials have treated decriminalization efforts as contingent on circumstances in individual countries, and always requiring the judgment and leadership of local grassroots activists. As we shall see, this approach would have put State Department officials at odds with Ambassador Ric Grenell and his campaign for decriminalization of same-sex sexuality.

In Geneva, Clinton announced the formation of the Global Equality Fund (GEF), which over time has become the most significant global source for SOGI human rights funding and assistance.[15] The GEF is an umbrella fund with seventeen country partners that supports three kinds of assistance programs. These programs were constructed to perform different functions, and the officials who administer them use a variety of mechanisms to solicit and receive feedback from LGBTQI activists in order to try to make programs more responsive to the needs of LGBTQI people in different geographic spaces.

In addition to the GEF, international SOGI human rights advocacy also takes place in settings such as regular multilateral conferences as well as in a variety of other forums that represent different tracks of diplomacy, and diverse networks of advocates, civil society organizations, and government representatives.[16] During the Obama administration, it wasn't uncommon for SOGI activists to travel to Washington, DC, or locations outside the US where they could meet with US officials, and in many cases US officials went to the activists. My case study in chapter 5, which focuses on an activist organization I call ASOGIHRO, illustrates both of these varieties of collaboration between US officials and SOGI advocates abroad. Many such meetings are not publicized or reported in press accounts of SOGI human rights advocacy. Of course, researchers don't often observe meetings between US officials and LGBTQ people and activists. And researchers rarely participate in quiet diplomacy that consists of interactions between US officials and representatives of regimes and civil society in places where people face discrimination or violence on the basis of SOGI.

Given the prominent position of Christian conservatives and their issues in the 2016 presidential campaign, US-based and international LGBTQ and human rights advocates assumed that a Trump presidency would stem US support for SOGI human rights advocacy and, possibly, impair international progress on SOGI. Indeed, the US Christian conservative movement, the Christian right, had been the major source of opposition to LGBTQ civil rights since the 1970s and had been a major player in anti-LGBTQ international "family values" advocacy since the 1990s.[17] During the Obama administration, the movement began to link government support for SOGI human rights to the problem of international religious persecution and used support for SOGI as a rhetorical weapon against the Obama administration.

In this introduction, I briefly introduce the cast of players in the drama of Trump, religious freedom, and SOGI human rights. The key players are: Trump (elucidating especially his alliance with Christian conservatives); the Family Research Council and its president, Tony Perkins; and the cast of Christian conservatives who served the forty-fifth president in some role adjacent to SOGI human rights or religious freedom. Behind the scenes, a set of State Department officials continued to carry out the SOGI human rights assistance programs of the US government. In surveying the Christian conservative sector of the cast, I also introduce the rhetorical frame the Christian right used to tie threats to international religious freedom to US support for SOGI human rights: SOGI human rights vs. religious freedom.

The Players

TRUMP AND "HIS" CHRISTIAN CONSERVATIVES

One feature of Trump's leadership style was his habit of claiming a personal, indeed possessive, connection with subordinates and others he understood as properly related to him by fealty. As research confirms, there is no denying that Christian conservatives belonged to Donald Trump before, during, and after his term. However, it's useful to remind ourselves that the Christian right was not in Trump's corner from the beginning of his quest for the White House. In the autumn of 2015, not long after Trump declared himself a candidate for president, he addressed the Values Voter Summit at the Omni Shoreham Hotel in Washington, DC. There, Trump worked to ingratiate himself with the Christian conservative attendees and many others who would view the proceedings remotely. Trump carried a bible his mother had given him to the podium and announced, to scattered applause, "I brought my bible." Neither Marco Rubio nor Ted Cruz brought his childhood bible to the summit that year. Trump's bible clearly struck some in the audience, of which I was a member, as a prop intended to influence their perception of him. Indeed, in the early months of the primary season, Donald Trump's personal reputation and his awkward attempts to bond with Christian conservatives persuaded some political pundits that he'd be unlikely to attract the support of "values voters." As we know, those pundits were wrong. Even though researchers found that Christian conservative voters didn't identify Trump as a religious person, he soon consolidated his support with this essential Republican constituency.[18]

Christian conservative enthusiasm for Trump has been a source of incredulity for many on the left. Since 2017, I've heard variations on this question: "I don't agree with Christian conservatives, but how can they call themselves Christian and endorse someone as amoral as Trump? It doesn't make any sense." Christian right support for Trump does make sense, however. Or, rather, sense can be made of it, and many thoughtful observers have contributed pieces of that puzzle. Indeed, the messaging of Christian conservative media and elites is replete with a variety of arguments for the close relationship that came to prevail between Trump and Christian conservatives. One of these explanations—Trump's evolving personal morality as a function of his maturing Christian identity—was proffered early by Christian right eminence James Dobson when he dubbed Trump a "baby Christian."[19] Another genre of justification can reasonably be understood, especially by outsiders, as intended to bind Christian conservatives to Trump by interpreting him through the lens of scripture. Multiple identifications of Trump with biblical figures explain and justify him to believers while also mobilizing them to the mission of protecting him from his political adversaries.[20]

One of the key identities projected onto Trump by Christian conservative leaders is King Cyrus, or Cyrus the Great, whose story is related in the Book of Isaiah.[21] The reference is common enough that Rebecca Barrett-Fox describes Trump as a "King Cyrus president," and Trump's Christian right followers have been called "King Cyrus Christians."[22] Trump has also been identified as Nebuchadnezzar, another ungodly king used by god for his purposes.[23] Both allusions to Cyrus and Nebuchadnezzar had the virtue of operating as prophetic wisdom after Christian conservative elites could no longer ignore the investigation of the Trump campaign's and administration's ties to Russia and obstruction of justice in attempts to obscure those ties.

Another identification of Trump with a biblical figure was particularly useful when news broke that Trump and his associates were compromised not only by financial and political misconduct but also by the claims of

Karen McDougal and Stephanie Clifford (aka Stormy Daniels) to have had sexual relationships with him and been paid for their silence about the affairs just before the election.[24] This figure is King David. To refresh the reader's memory, the books of 1 and 2 Samuel provide accounts of David's relationship with God and his emergence as a leader of the people of Israel. A number of prominent Christian conservatives echoed the identification of Trump with David. But they didn't do so on the basis of Trump's victory over great odds in the presidential administration (David and Goliath) or even on the basis of Trump's womanizing (David and Bathsheba) alone. No, one dimension of the identification of Trump with/as David was predicated on the King's sexual attraction to Bathsheba and his willingness to use his office to assure the death in battle of Bathsheba's husband so she could become one of his wives.

There are moments that help to illuminate specific elements of Christian right values and politics. So, picture it: the Values Voter Summit in the autumn of 2017. On the last day of the conference, I attend a breakout session featuring George Barna, the Christian conservative movement's survey researcher, who provides the movement with data and conclusions about Americans' beliefs, and religious and political behavior.[25] Barna is an enthusiastic Trump supporter, and on this day he is talking about and offering to sign copies of his new book: *The Day Christians Changed America: How Christian Conservatives Put Trump in the White House and Redirected America's Future.*[26] A member of the audience, an elderly man in a wheelchair who seems more skeptical toward the president than other values voters in attendance, interrupts the presentation to ask Barna to explain Christian conservative support for Trump. Barna's terse reply, before returning to his presentation, is "David killed someone." That spontaneous utterance is informative: Barna didn't say that David, with his many wives and concubines, was beloved by God, and so Trump may be, even though he hasn't excelled at the biblical monogamy contemporary Christian conservatives embrace.[27] Instead, what Barna said was that David was guilty of murder. The unspoken surmise of anticipatory absolution was clear: any crime short of murder would not stimulate Christian conservatives to reconsider their commitment to the president. And if Trump were to commit murder for personal gain, only then would he be in David's unimpeachable company.

What of Trump's response toward diligent Christian right efforts to identify him with or as biblical figures? Perhaps Trump decided he was being disrespected by being compared with a set of obscure, ancient rulers. Whatever the motivation, nothing less than an affirmation that he was

Jesus Christ would suffice to shore up his fragile, yet belligerent, ego. In August, 2019, Trump approvingly quoted Wayne Allyn Root, a messianic Jewish supporter, who had declared Trump to be the "King of Israel." *Washington Post* reporter Sarah Pulliam Bailey provides biblical context for this unusual claim: "In the Bible, Jewish leaders call Jesus the 'king of Israel' in a mocking way when he was put on the cross, according to Matthew 27:42: 'He's the king of Israel! Let him come down now from the cross, and we will believe in him.'" On the same day, the president followed up this apparent blasphemy by looking skyward and proclaiming himself to be "the chosen one."[28] Trump's apologists have sometimes cast him as a gifted comic conveniently misinterpreted by his malign critics on the left. Given the accumulated evidence of Trump's self-regard, I believe it makes more sense to say that Trump understood and publicly demonstrated the extent of his Christian conservative followers' devotion to him.

However we conceptualize the passionate attachment of Christian conservative elites and grassroots followers to Trump, it is undeniable that he gave those believers hope, even if that hope was tinged with pessimism. Writing in the *Washington Post*, Elizabeth Bruenig relies on conversations she had with Christian conservative Texans to explain "what happened" to persuade Christian conservatives to back Trump. Bruenig comes away from these meetings with a sense that Trump has provided a "respite"—or perhaps "a bitter, brief victory amidst creeping defeat" from Christian conservatives' losses in the culture wars.[29] The idea of Trump as an indispensable immoral, even non-Christian, figure to protect Christian conservatives from stigma and cultural change is consistent with John Fea's case that the Christian right found in Trump their "strongman" as well as Thomas J. Main's case that the Alt-Right found in him their "American Caesar."[30] Chip Berlet and his colleagues have provided cogent analyses of the connections between these Trump constituencies.[31]

One aspect of Christian conservative support for Trump that for some people deepens the mystery and for others resolves it is Trump's history of racist positions and propositions. From adamant support for the enslavement of African Americans to opposition to the civil rights movement, white Christian conservatism has frequently made common cause with racism as consistent with scripture and God's will. Because Christian conservativism is a broad coalition, it is also accurate that some white Christian conservatives have striven to practice an antiracism that demands love, coworship, and reparation (though not financial reparations) with African Americans.[32]

There are many explanations for the historical linkage of racism with Christian conservatism, past and present. One I find persuasive is Fea's argument that Christian conservative support for Trump can't be explained without taking into account a durable conservative evangelical fear of outsiders and otherness that Fea connects historically to racial othering and racism.[33] In 2020, anxieties about race and racism became evident in a statement by six white presidents of Baptist seminaries that repudiated critical race theory and the analytical tool of intersectionality as incompatible with the Baptist Faith and Message and biblical truth. As a result of the statement, many African American pastors—already a minority in the Southern Baptist Convention—made the decision to leave the SBC.[34]

A common explanation for the bond between Trump and Christian conservatives has been that their support—frequently justified in other terms—is purely transactional. I agree with Sarah Posner, who rejects this account, arguing that the relationship is better explained as an "intense meeting of the minds" of "starstruck" supporters who "idolize" a leader who openly and relentlessly "articulates their shared grievances."[35] Of course, such an intense bond may have multiple causes and enabling conditions. Empirical studies of closely related explanations such as "cultural backlash" and "status threat" identify demographics that are more receptive to appeals rooted in these reactions to social, political, and economic change. These groups—including "the Interwar generation, non-college graduates, the working class, white Europeans, the more religious, men, and residents of rural communities"—overlap considerably with Christian conservative believers.[36] However we conceptualize the meeting of the minds between Trump and his supporters, moral entrepreneurs devised messaging and scriptural touchstones as resources to facilitate both the bond with Trump and its ex post facto justifications.[37]

THE FRAME AND A FRAMER

Before he announced that he was running for president in 2015, Donald Trump had no discernable interest in religious freedom, including the freedom of conservative American believers to be exempted from laws intended to protect LGBT people from discrimination. However, during the campaign, Trump secured the endorsements of many Christian conservative elites. And he assured conservative believers that he would protect their right to dissent from and refuse to obey laws they understood as encroaching on the freedom to practice their faith. Since the state of Massachusetts legalized same-sex marriages in 2004 and the handwriting on the wall indicated that other victories for LGBT equality would likely follow, the Christian right has pursued consistent strategies. These include a legal and political strategy of carving out exemptions for believers and a communicative strategy of claiming that LGBTQ people and their cultural allies are victimizing ordinary people for their belief. In fact, I agree with Andrew Koppelman that "in a free society . . . radical disagreement about moral fundamentals is inevitable" and that, in the kinds of conflicts that have become common between LGBT people and conservative believers, we'd all be better off seeking possible compromises and "accommodating religious dissenters" than trying to defeat them utterly and "eradicate [their] ideas."[38]

Because debates about the scope of religious freedom so often pit conservative believers against proponents of LGBTQ rights, many on both sides probably assume that religious freedom is self-evidently a value that only serves the interests of orthodox believers. Understanding religious freedom as "synonymous with the right of individual conscience and freedom of mind," Frederick Clarkson points out that it liberates and protects citizens who hold a "progressive vision of religious liberty" and, thus, supports pluralism against theocracy.[39] Rather than focusing here on the ways in which these debates and legal strategies have played out in the US in recent years, in this book I focus on a particular messaging strategy that Christian conservative elites adopted during Obama's second term in office and continued to use throughout most of Trump's term. The strategy extended to the international arena a domestic US frame that contrasted religious freedom in the US with LGBT civil rights.

After the Obama administration announced its commitment to SOGI human rights, the Christian right enthusiastically engaged in the systematic strategy of linking the administration's support for LGBTQ civil and SOGI human rights to its putative lack of interest in both religious freedom in the US and threats to religious minorities—especially Christians—abroad. The Christian right's *SOGI human rights vs. religious freedom* social movement frame that links SOGI to the persecution of Christians abroad has two prongs. The first prong of this frame is that Obama and his administration were indifferent or actively hostile to persecution of Christians outside the US (just as they were indifferent or hostile to the persecution of American Christians). The second prong is that the Obama administration consistently elevated LGBTQ people, identity, and human rights claims over the persecution of Christians abroad. By persistently deploying this frame, Christian right elites disparaged Obama, Hillary Clinton, and Democrats, and primed

Christian conservatives to support Trump and his administration across a range of policies they deemed essential to religious freedom.

Many important figures constitute the ecosystem of Christian conservative opinion in the US, including prominent pastors, leaders of Christian conservative organizations, elected officials, and media personalities. Some of these figures have a national profile; others' leadership is local or regional. Some elites rely on diverse media technologies and platforms to reach their audiences. Some have connections to party politics or have served in Republican administrations; others are relatively "apolitical." Some have achieved some renown for their role in nonprofits and legal efforts. Not all elites are equal in the authority they wield with Christian conservative constituencies. However, even in the fragmented realm of Christian conservative movement leadership, there's a remarkable degree of cooperation, coordination, and something of an interlocking directorate of elites—most of them men—across boards, ministries, networks, and organizations.[40]

Acknowledging the difficulty of ascribing leadership in the Christian right to a particular person or organization, I argue that the Washington, DC–based 501(c)(3) nonprofit Family Research Council (FRC) plays a particularly central role in setting and reflecting the agenda of the Christian conservative movement, formulating political messaging—what FRC calls "shaping the narrative"—networking key movement figures and organizations, lobbying Congress, helping to elect amenable policymakers, and influencing the agenda of the Trump White House.[41] Formed in 1983 after Focus on the Family founder, James Dobson, convened a meeting of pro-family Christian conservatives in Washington, DC, the FRC describes its earliest agenda as "counter[ing] the credentialed voices arrayed against life and family with equally capable men and women of faith."[42] Today, the FRC describes itself as a

> nonprofit research and educational organization dedicated to articulating and advancing a family-centered philosophy of public life. In addition to providing policy research and analysis for the legislative, executive, and judicial branches of the federal government, FRC seeks to inform the news media, the academic community, business leaders, and the general public about family issues that affect the nation from a biblical worldview.[43]

FRC Action, the "legislative affiliate" of the FRC, is a 501(c)(4) nonprofit and the sponsor of the annual Values Voter Summit, held every year since 2006 at the Omni Shoreham Hotel in Washington, DC.[44] A blow to the

FRC's reputation was the group's designation as an anti-LGBTQ hate group by the Southern Poverty Law Center (SPLC) in 2010.[45] The designation rankled the FRC, which in turn responded gleefully to later revelations about discrimination and financial irregularities at the SPLC.[46]

In his account of the bond between Trump and conservative Christians, John Fea refers to the elites who are drawn to political power, provide Trump moral cover, and justify him to Christian conservative followers as "court evangelicals."[47] Both because evangelicals aren't all politically conservative and because the category, "Christian conservative," contains adherents of other Christian faith traditions, I could call the moral entrepreneurs I discuss in this book, "court Christian conservatives." Generally speaking, however, I'll refer to them as movement elites, leaders, or moral entrepreneurs.[48] Whatever appellation we use, the Family Research Council's president, Tony Perkins, qualifies as such a figure, and in what follows I focus on messaging produced and disseminated by the FRC, most of which is attributed to Perkins.

Tony Perkins became the FRC's fourth president in 2003. A former Marine and Republican Louisiana state legislator, Perkins has a well-documented history of anti-LGBTQ advocacy. Perkins wasn't one of Trump's earliest court Christian conservative endorsers. However, as it became clear that Trump had the best shot of uniting Republicans and clinching the nomination, Perkins and the FRC moved to consolidate movement support for Trump. Perkins's fingerprints on Trump's campaign were evident as early as January 2016, after Trump spoke at Liberty University and, citing a verse from Paul's second epistle to the Corinthians, said "two Corinthians," as written, instead of pronouncing "two" as "second."

Defending himself to CNN's Don Lemon against the scorn that greeted his biblical illiteracy, Trump said, "Tony Perkins wrote that out for me—he actually wrote out 2, he wrote out the number 2 Corinthians. . . . I took exactly what Tony said, and I said, 'Well Tony has to know better than anybody.' "[49] Perkins was a close ally of President Trump as well as of key Trump administration officials such as Sam Brownback and Mike Pompeo. In May 2018, Perkins was appointed by Mitch McConnell to a two-year term on the US Commission on International Religious Freedom, an independent, bipartisan commission created by the International Religious Freedom Act of 1998. He was elected by the commission as its chair for a one-year term in 2019. During Trump's term, Perkins stepped up to neutralize criticisms of the president by Democrats and other Christian conservatives, most notably former George W. Bush speechwriter and *Washington Post* columnist, Michael Gerson.[50]

Christian conservative moral entrepreneurs—elected and appointed officials, movement intellectuals, high-profile pastors, and media personalities—carefully craft theopolitical arguments to movement followers. These communiques build on preexisting attitudes of believers and followers to directly or indirectly instruct them about what policies and political leaders to support.[51] So pro-Trump messaging focused on a diverse set of policy and political domains: the Supreme Court and federal courts; the abomination of abortion and the need to defund Planned Parenthood; conscience protections for a wide range of medical professionals; rolling back undeserved civil rights protections for LGBTQ people; stemming illegal immigration; and securing "law and order" in the streets. Christian conservative elites also provide reasons to support these policies and politicians, constructing social movement frames using various kinds of evidence. Some of the facts, claims, and narratives that constitute this evidence would be recognizable to those outside Christian conservatism as political, while other evidence is doctrinal, theological, or prophetic. The frames, evidence, and even the biblical justifications (or absence thereof) can, and do, change over time to meet new political challenges. I have more to say about the central social movement frame the Christian right used to delegitimize Obama, Clinton, and SOGI in chapter 1.

PERSONNEL AS POLICY

In 2019, Secretary of State Mike Pompeo delivered a speech, "Being a Christian Leader," to the American Association of Christian Counselors in Nashville, Tennessee. Controversy ensued over Pompeo giving the speech in his official role as secretary of state and having it posted to the State Department website.[52] Addressing the controversy, Tony Perkins forcefully defended Pompeo by deploying the predictable comparison between the Obama administration's hostility to religion and believers and the Trump administration's passionate endorsement of Christianity.

> After eight years of an administration that didn't just marginalize faith, but punished it, it's no wonder the far-Left has trouble coming to grips with Obama's successor. As one insider joked, "President Trump may not be a Sunday school teacher, but he sure knows how to hire them." Thanks to that, Americans are starting to see the pendulum of policies start to swing back to what the Framers intended.

Perkins closes the essay: "Personnel is policy, the old adage goes. Under this president, we're grateful for both."[53]

Government policies don't administer themselves or shut themselves down, and it can matter what individuals hold key positions in an administration. When the Trump administration launched, many politically appointed positions were staffed with people who held traditional establishment credentials. Some of these were affiliated with the Christian conservative movement, but many—including James Mattis, John Kelly, Rex Tillerson, and Dan Coats—were not. Over time, however, the president shed many of these obstacles to his personal interests and elevated a set of officials who, whatever their professional credentials, shared a particular qualification for public service in the Trump administration: personal loyalty to Trump and whatever public policy agenda he announced. Here, I offer a quick overview of Trump appointees who ended up in key SOGI human rights–adjacent positions, many of whom I return to later in the book.

Besides their conservative commitments and loyalty to Trump, many political appointees and elected officials had anti-LGBT bona fides in common. I offer brief biographies of Mike Pence, Pam Pryor, Mick Mulvaney, Sam Brownback, Mike Pompeo, Kiron Skinner, and Robert Destro. I include Richard "Ric" Grenell's bio in spite of the fact that he isn't a Christian conservative because of his high-profile efforts to use the levers of US foreign policy to pressure countries that have continued to criminalize same-sex sexual relations to decriminalize. I list these bios in roughly the order in which these figures joined the Trump campaign or administration, or were appointed to positions with influence over US SOGI human rights.

Before she joined the Trump campaign, **Pam Pryor** held a number of positions that included political organizations and service to Republican elected officials. Her last position before the campaign was as a senior advisor for Governor Sarah Palin—a role John Hudson, writing for *Foreign Policy*, referred to as Palin's "go-to girl." Pryor served as director of "faith and Christian outreach" for the Trump campaign, where she helped "evangelical women 'speak up' for Donald Trump."[54] She was a member of the Trump transition team for the State Department, including the Bureau of Democracy, Human Rights, and Labor (DRL). She went on to serve as senior advisor on global justice issues, senior advisor to the under secretary for civilian security, democracy, and human rights, and, in March 2020, acting assistant secretary for the Bureau of International Organization Affairs.

Foreign policy experts expressed concern about Pryor's lack of expertise.[55] At State, she was tasked with advancing the Trump administration's efforts on "protecting and promoting religious freedom."[56] According to Equity Forward, a watchdog group of lawyers, researchers, and communications specialists who monitor anti-reproductive health forces, opposition to abortion has been a focus of much of Pryor's career. After joining the State Department, she worked to reverse "the underrepresentation of anti-abortion groups at international conferences" such as the United Nation's Commission on the Status of Women. Pryor didn't have a public record of anti-LGBTQ advocacy, but she had long worked closely with organizations that oppose LGBTQ human rights.[57]

Mike Pence, a former member of Congress and governor from Indiana, wasn't Trump's first choice as a running mate. Ultimately, Trump's selection of Pence for his pull with Christian conservatives in July 2016 "felt a lot like the medicine Trump didn't want to choke down." According to Tom LoBianco, Trump worried that Pence "carried the whiff of a loser" because of the battle over a Religious Freedom Restoration Act (RFRA) Pence had signed into law in March 2015.[58] The RFRA, backed by the Christian right, was widely understood to have been crafted to protect businesses that refused to serve LGBTQ people, and at first Pence defended it. Before long, however, the law became a national story. The controversy polarized Indiana residents and subjected the state and Pence to scathing criticism from LGBTQ people and their allies, members of the business community, and—when he backed down and signed an amendment that clarified the law couldn't be used to discriminate against LGBT people—Christian conservatives. However, even before this episode, Pence had a long history of anti-LGBT positions repudiating the idea of "sexual preference as a source of civil rights."[59]

Richard "Ric" Grenell is a former Republican Party operative and, throughout most of Trump's term, was US ambassador to Germany. He's also a gay man who, in February 2019, spearheaded what quickly came to be understood as the Trump administration's campaign for the decriminalization of same-sex sexuality worldwide. The decriminalization campaign wasn't Grenell's first moment of celebrity as ambassador. After Grenell assumed his post in Berlin in April 2018, he made headlines for comments in an interview with "alt-lite" internet media outlet *Breitbart* about seeking "to 'empower' anti-establishment rightwing forces throughout Europe."[60] Despite fierce criticisms about Grenell's conception of his role as ambassador from German government officials and former US diplomats, Grenell was neither recalled nor openly disciplined. While continuing to serve as US ambassador to Germany, in 2020, Grenell was appointed to the position of acting director of national intelligence. Soon after Trump replaced him as DNI with former Texas Congressman John Ratcliffe, Grenell also resigned his position as US ambassador. Grenell reemerged after the 2020 election to denounce what Trump and his loyal retinue characterized as a stolen election and to agitate for a reversal of the election's verdict.

Mick Mulvaney was confirmed as the director of the Office of Management and Budget (OMB) in February 2017 and, on the departure of John Kelly, was named as Trump's acting White House chief of staff in January 2019. As director of OMB, Mulvaney attempted to enact budget rescissions in the late summers of 2018 and 2019 that would have retracted billions of dollars in foreign assistance funding appropriated by Congress but not yet obligated to particular programs by the State Department and USAID. The plan, which would have starved many human rights programs of resources, was protested by Republican and Democratic members of Congress and other officials, including Mike Pompeo.[61]

When Mulvaney was appointed to his post at the White House, LGBT media reported on Mulvaney's anti-LGBTQ record. As a state representative in South Carolina, Mulvaney cosponsored a bill to ban same-sex marriage in his state. Later, as a member of Congress, Mulvaney supported a Constitutional amendment to ban same-sex marriage, advocated for the Obama administration to defend the Defense of Marriage Act in court and, after the Supreme Court decision in *Obergefell v. Hodges*, endorsed religious exemptions for citizens who wanted to refuse to acknowledge the validity of these marriages.[62] After Mulvaney inadvertently confirmed during the impeachment process that Trump had demanded a quid pro quo from the president of Ukraine, Trump replaced him as acting chief of staff with Congressman Mark Meadows. Mulvaney was named special envoy to Northern Ireland.[63]

Former Kansas governor **Sam Brownback**, a prominent Christian conservative, was appointed by Trump and confirmed by the Senate to serve as the ambassador at large for international religious freedom. Brownback served in the House of Representatives and in the Senate before becoming governor of Kansas. As governor, Brownback instituted a series of economic policies and reforms that made him one of the most unpopular governors in the US.[64] Brownback has been an opponent of LGBT civil rights throughout his career, opposing same-sex marriage as well as nondiscrimination policies, and LGBTQ organizations opposed his confirmation to serve as ambassador. One of Brownback's most significant accomplishments as ambassador is the International Religious Freedom Alliance and International Religious Freedom (IRF) Fund, first announced during the 2019 Ministerial to Advance Religious

Freedom and launched in early 2020.[65] In its structure and function, the IRF Fund is the religious freedom version of the Global Equality Fund.[66] An irony of such a global alliance is that Christian conservatives have frequently repudiated international organizations and multilateral cooperation between governments that conservatives cast as undermining national sovereignty.

The intensity and consistency of Brownback's opposition to LGBT rights was on display in 2006 when he blocked the nomination of Michigan Court of Appeals judge Janet Neff to be a US district judge because she had attended the same-sex wedding ceremony of a family friend. As the *New York Times* put it in an editorial on the standoff, "Whether someone has attended a same-sex commitment ceremony is not a worthy litmus test to impose on someone seeking an important office. Whether someone holds hateful views toward gay people certainly is."[67] During his confirmation hearing in 2017, Democratic senator Tim Kaine, who had been Hillary Clinton's running mate in 2016, was unable to elicit a clear response when Kaine asked Brownback whether he could imagine a "circumstance under which religious freedom can justify criminalizing, imprisoning or executing people based on their LGBT status."[68]

Trump fired his first secretary of state, Rex Tillerson, and the Senate confirmed Trump's next choice, **Michael (Mike) Pompeo**, on May 1, 2018. A former member of Congress from Kansas and director of the Central Intelligence Agency, Pompeo had spoken publicly about his faith with Christian conservative media outlets and was welcomed by the Christian right as Tillerson's replacement.[69] Before heading the State Department, Pompeo had developed a reputation as an anti-LGBTQ policymaker. After the Supreme Court decision in *Obergefell v. Hodges*, he issued a statement characterizing the ruling as a "shocking abuse of power":

> I am deeply saddened by the Supreme Court's ruling that imposes legalized gay marriage on the 70% of Kansans who voted to honor and protect the traditional definition of marriage as the union between one man and one woman. Creating, out of nowhere, a federal right to marry, flies in the face of centuries of shared understanding of our constitution. It is a shocking abuse of power. It is wrong. I will continue to fight to protect our most sacred institutions; Kansans and our nation deserve no less.[70]

During his confirmation hearing, Pompeo was "grilled" by New Jersey senator Cory Booker about his views on gay people and identity. Citing comments

Pompeo delivered at a God and Country rally in Kansas in 2015, when he called being gay a "perversion," Booker questioned whether Pompeo could protect the civil rights of LGBT personnel at the State Department. Booker also wondered whether, given his views, Pompeo could represent a US commitment to equality for LGBT people on the international stage.[71]

Kiron Skinner is a professor at Carnegie Mellon University whose teaching and research fields are international relations, international security, US foreign policy, and political strategy. She is a prolific scholar, public intellectual, foreign policy advisor to Republican political candidates, and research fellow at the Hoover Institution. Skinner took leave from her faculty position to serve as the director for policy planning and senior advisor to the secretary of state from September 2018 until her firing in August 2019. During her tenure as a member of Secretary Pompeo's leadership team, Skinner attracted criticism for a talk she gave at a "Future Security Forum" of the New America Foundation about US policy toward China. There, Skinner posited that US-China relations are characterized by "unavoidable civilizational conflict" in large measure because the Chinese are non-Caucasians who don't share Western commitments to human rights.[72] In the summer of 2019, Skinner also became a public face of the Unalienable Human Rights Commission, which critics immediately saw as a possible means of extirpating support for SOGI human rights from US foreign policy. Skinner was fired from her State Department position for allegedly having an abusive management style that included homophobic comments in the workplace.[73]

The Bureau of Democracy, Human Rights, and Labor (DRL) is tasked with executing foreign policy goals of "promoting freedom and democracy and protecting human rights around the world."[74] Congress mandated DRL to administer the Human Rights and Democracy Fund (HRDF) and the US contribution to the Global Equality Fund (GEF) comes from the HRDF. During Tillerson's tenure as secretary, no assistant secretary for DRL was nominated. In June 2018, the Trump administration finally nominated Catholic University law professor **Robert Destro** to serve as assistant secretary for Democracy, Human Rights, and Labor. Founder of the Program in Law and Religion at Catholic, Destro has advocated against abortion rights and for religious freedom. He rhetorically defended a Catholic high school in Charlotte, North Carolina, after the diocese fired a teacher—a former teacher of the year—who announced his intention to marry his same-sex partner on Facebook.[75] GLAAD documented a more complete set of anti-LGBTQ statements and affiliations.[76]

Destro's nomination was applauded by Christian conservative media and criticized by Democrats and human rights groups. Like Pompeo, his record on LGBT people and rights was scrutinized, including in a March 22, 2019, letter signed by forty-six human rights and civil society organizations. The letter, addressed to the chair (Jim Risch, R-ID) and ranking minority member (Bob Menendez, D-NJ) of the Senate Foreign Relations Committee, noted that "the Bureau of Democracy, Human Rights, and Labor is responsible for promoting democracy and protecting human rights, including the reproductive rights of women and girls, as well as the rights of LGBTI individuals, around the world." On the basis of evidence documented in the letter, the signatories asserted that the Senate should decline to confirm him.[77]

LGBTQ organizations also opposed the nomination. One such organization was the Council for Global Equality (CGE), a coalition of thirty human rights and LGBTQ civil society organizations that focuses on SOGI human rights in US foreign policy. CGE opposed Destro's nomination because of "the gap between Destro's [anti-LGBT] record and the requirements of" the position of assistant secretary of DRL.[78] Responding to Destro's record, Senator Menendez placed a hold on the nomination. Destro was finally confirmed as assistant secretary in September 2019. With Destro's confirmation, Trump's human rights team of appointees at the State Department was in place.

Team "Deep State"

I have more to say about the Christian right's embrace of the "deep state" calumny to describe federal civil servants in the next chapter. Here, I want to acknowledge the State Department officials who kept SOGI human rights foreign assistance running in the State Department during Trump's term. Deputy assistant secretary Scott Busby served as acting special envoy for the human rights of LGBTI persons during the Trump administration. Patricia Davis is the director of global programs in the Bureau of Democracy, Human Rights, and Labor. Deputy directors of DRL's Office of Global Programs are Jeff Bell and Doreen Mullady. Jessica Huber is team lead for marginalized populations, which includes LGBTI (under the Biden administration, now LGBTQI+), gender, and disability.[79] During the Trump administration, the Global Equality Fund programs were managed by Huber, Keisha Adams, and Taylor Brown, who worked directly on SOGI human rights assistance. The work carried out by these officials is far less visible than that of high-ranking political appointees, elected officials, and high-profile moral entrepreneurs. Nonetheless, they are important actors in the drama of SOGI human rights and religious freedom in the Trump administration.

Defining My Terms

To the confusion of outsiders, over time, social and political movements change the signifiers by which ascriptive or affinity groups want to be identified. At times, these revisions are performed because new groups are inducted into movements or identify themselves as having been there all along, even if their presence wasn't acknowledged. At times, groups reclaim stigmatizing terms or revise existing terminology to better express group members' self-understanding or presentation. Academics who write about groups usually want to get these signifiers right, even if our work eventually falls behind the latest terminology or we decide to resist some linguistic shift for reasons we're willing to explain.

In this book, I use a set of terms to denote the coalitional identity and human rights category on which I focus. In discussions of US-based civil or human rights, I use LGBT (for lesbian, gay, bisexual, and transgender) or LGBTQ (for queer). If academic research has focused on a particular subset of that coalitional identity, I use whatever term is appropriate.[80] When I focus on the international situation for the human rights of gender and sexual minorities or on US programs and policies to support gender and sexual minorities abroad, I use the term that has been most widely used in international law and human rights: sexual orientation and gender identity, or SOGI.[81]

In the international arena more than in domestic US political thought and practice, LGBTI, the last letter standing for "intersex," is a common way to identify the coalitional identity of gender and sexual minorities who risk systematic discrimination and persecution in many parts of the world. During the Obama administration, LGBTI became the term of choice in pro-SOGI policy within the State Department. Randy Berry was first appointed to serve as the special envoy for the human rights of LGBT persons, but soon after his appointment the title of the post was modified to refer to "LGBTI persons." The State Department's Bureau of Democracy, Human Rights, and Labor (DRL), which manages human rights programs, was consistent in using the designation "LGBTI" during the Obama and Trump administrations.

As a scholar, I strive to be as accurate as possible in denoting groups and their rhetoric, goals, and acts. I also prefer when possible to use the language that groups—including, perhaps especially, groups of which I'm critical—have chosen for themselves. In the chapters that follow, I use the terms "Christian conservative" and "Christian right" to denote the movement that advocates against the civil and human rights of LGBTQ people in the US and abroad. Other scholars have used different terms to refer to the movement and roughly similar sets of believers, including religious right, evangelical, dominionist/ism, and Christian nationalist/ism. All of these categories can be applied usefully to convey either particular information or an interpretive perspective. For a variety of reasons, I have chosen "Christian conservative" to designate people of different denominations or doctrines who are theologically and politically conservative, and who share collective political goals.

I will often refer to US Christian conservative opposition to, rhetoric toward, messaging about, and strategies regarding LGBT people's domestic civil rights, and US government SOGI policies. Although the Christian right has been a foe of civil rights for gender and sexual minorities since the advent of the gay liberation movement in the 1970s, it's not accurate to suggest, as we often do for simplicity, that the Christian right movement has always positioned itself against each of these identities equally. For example, Christian right opposition against gay men and lesbians has manifested in meaningfully different ways.[82] Christian conservative public rhetoric and political strategy has had little to say about bisexual identity, probably because Christian conservative moral entrepreneurs have collapsed bisexuality into homosexuality, ignoring bisexuals' self-identification and attending only to homosexual behavior and the potential for same-sex sexuality implied by the label.

Until recent years, the Christian right also largely ignored transgender identity and identification, collapsing trans identity and nonnormative gender expression into same-sex sexuality. That disinterest in nonnormative gender and transgender identity *except* as a manifestation of homosexuality changed quickly and dramatically during the Obama administration as Christian right elites suddenly focused on transgender identity as a specific threat to Christians.[83] Finally, there are intersex people, the group denoted by the "I" in the coalition of vulnerable gender and sexual minorities that SOGI human rights programs and policies are meant to support. I've seen no evidence that the US Christian right targets intersex people for discrimination or opposes policies that might serve their interests.[84] Thus, when

I refer to the group of gender and sexual minorities whose interests the Christian right has mobilized to preclude or reverse, I generally use LGBT or LGBTQ, but not LGBTI.

A Map of the Book

Throughout this book, I address a number of questions: As a key coalition partner in Trump's election and public support, did the Christian right commit its resources and attention to revoking SOGI human rights policies and practices? Did Christian conservatives in the Trump administration succeed in revoking SOGI human rights policies and practices during the Trump administration? Do Christian right elites believe the central misrepresentation of the SOGI human rights vs. religious freedom frame—that the Obama administration refused to support religious freedom and oppose religious persecution while committing to demanding SOGI human rights recognition, including recognition of same-sex marriage? Those of us who care about the ways in which gender identity and sexuality shape and scourge the lives of many people throughout the world want to know the answers to these questions.

In chapter 1, I survey the Christian conservative movement as an anti-LGBT/SOGI interest group. I unpack the Christian conservative movement's ingroup anti-SOGI messaging to believers and activists. Throughout the Obama administration, the Christian conservative movement consistently packaged and delivered messaging to Christian conservatives that linked international human rights violations against Christians to purported violations of American Christians' civil and human rights and, in turn, linked this domestic anti-Christian discrimination to LGBT people, an LGBT social and political agenda, and pro-LGBT elites. President Barack Obama and his administration emerged in this rhetoric as key advocates for an LGBTQ hegemony that threatened Christians in the US and abroad. Christian conservative elites framed their outreach, resourcing, and assistance to global peoples and leaders as measures intended to prevent vulnerable peoples from suffering the devastation of their faith, families, and moral traditions at the hands of LGBT people and their allies. In this chapter, I focus on the Family Research Council (FRC) and its president, tracing the evolution of the group's rhetoric on US support for SOGI human rights from 2015 through 2020. As a counterpoint to the rhetoric and strategy of the Christian right (in general) and the FRC (in particular), I elucidate some of the contradictions the movement has to negotiate in order to mobilize its constituents and target SOGI human rights.

In chapter 2, I turn to the ways in which the Trump administration cultivated and responded to the Christian right as an interest group whose support was essential to Trump's election and his political survival. Just as Christian conservatives lobbied and pressured the administration, the administration courted the movement with outreach explicitly articulated in terms of religious freedom, in the US and abroad. Central to cultivating Christian conservative support has been a set of State Department initiatives intended to focus the agency's efforts—and Christian conservatives' perceptions—on priorities of religious freedom and the urgent resurrection of an eighteenth-century American understanding of human rights. Thus, in this chapter, I analyze the two Trump administration Ministerials to Advance Religious Freedom and the controversial Commission on Unalienable Human Rights for their implications for US SOGI human rights policy and practices.[85]

In the course of the Trump administration, there were two secretaries of state: Rex Tillerson and Mike Pompeo. In his brief leadership of the State Department, Rex Tillerson approached the mission of the agency from a corporatist perspective, and he made downsizing and reorganization the centerpiece of his brief tenure. By the time the president fired Tillerson in early 2018, the Christian right was campaigning against him, and the movement was buoyed when Trump selected Pompeo to replace him. Christian right leaders perceived Pompeo to be one of their own. Recognizing the importance of leadership in institutions and political movements, in chapter 3, I use the secretaries' speeches and other sources to discern and analyze both some differences between Tillerson's and Pompeo's orientations toward human rights and the different ways in which support for human rights, including SOGI, can be rendered precarious.

In chapter 4, I provide a timeline and analysis of events, public statements, and government deliberations that I argue constitute indicators or, loosely, "data points" to gauge the stability of US commitment to SOGI during the Trump administration. Barring unanticipated tweets from the president, most scholars and human rights professionals wouldn't have expected the administration to rescind official US advocacy on LGBTQ/SOGI in a public statement. Instead, we would expect a policy that dismantled US support for SOGI human rights to become visible gradually as a consequence of many acts and failures (or refusals) to act—what Elise Carlson Rainer has referred to as the process of SOGI human rights policy "go[ing] dormant."[86] Just as the administration signaled to congenial autocrats and dictators around the world that while Trump was president the US wouldn't condemn human rights violations they committed, the administration could easily signal to those who would abuse the human rights of LGBTQI people that the US no longer took an interest in such abuses. What signals did the administration send on SOGI, and what do these signals and policy moves say collectively about a US commitment to SOGI human rights?

Although I didn't begin writing this book in earnest until early 2018, I formed the idea for the project and began to type up my initial thoughts after the 2016 election, during a trip that took me to Bangkok, Thailand, and Phnom Penh, Cambodia. In Bangkok, I attended sessions of the International Lesbian, Gay, Bisexual, Transgender, and Intersex Association's (ILGA) World conference and encountered considerable anxiety in that space about the future of funding and assistance for SOGI human rights. At that time, nobody could predict how Trump's election might reshape, and possibly disrupt, the US commitment to SOGI human rights abroad, but a number of participants speculated, and tendered perspectives and strategies to deal with possible global consequences for SOGI human rights of the US election. It was clear that many—human rights advocates; grantees and implementing partners of the US State Department and the State Department–administered Global Equality Fund; and other donors—were anything but indifferent to the consequence of the presidential election for US human rights support.

With that anxiety among SOGI human rights defenders in mind, I embarked on this second study of US government SOGI human rights assistance and its discontents. In chapter 5, I turn to a question that is urgent to scholars and activists of SOGI human rights alike: Did grassroots activists in places where LGBTI people are imperiled welcome US support, even under the Trump administration? And did they continue to rely on the assistance made possible by a US commitment to SOGI, even under the Trump administration? Essential to answering this question is a case study that takes me back to Africa to a second meeting of a grassroots LGBTQI human rights advocacy organization that I wrote about in *Because We Are Human*, this one convening in the time of Trump.

One question academics are trained to answer with regard to our intellectual projects is the "so what?" question. Even if we regard a subject as the most compelling one we can imagine spending a few years researching, we must still explain why this is an important subject and encourage others to come along for the journey. In the case of SOGI human rights and the Trump administration, I think the question of how resilient US support was is important in and of itself. This is so because, relying on its own contributions and pooled resources from partner countries, the US government has become the biggest donor of LGBTI movements in the world. But a study like this makes other contributions. I closely examine a central set of claims of the most influential faction in our country's conservative party and demonstrate the cynicism behind their deployment. I trace SOGI human rights advocacy across multiple sites in the US government during the Trump administration, providing a careful empirical survey of the complexity of SOGI under threat of retrenchment. I also offer readers an inside, grounded look at US human rights advocacy, and the interactions and intersections between US officials and LGBTI human rights advocates.[87]

As we'll see, Christian conservative elites, including Mike Pompeo and Sam Brownback, did little or nothing to defund, revoke, or otherwise undermine SOGI human rights policies and practices when they were in a position to do so. It's also clear that when the Christian right movement was in a position to publicize the Trump administration's SOGI policies and practices and use the rhetorical tools at its disposal to demand that US officials do everything in their power to terminate them, they demurred. These failures to act constitute a religious freedom mystery.

Chapter 1

The Christian Right as Anti-SOGI Interest Group

Losing in the US and Looking Abroad

In the face of numerous declarations of its death as a political force since the 1980s, the Christian right "romanc[ed]" and became integrated into the Republican Party.[1] Ralph Reed, who served as executive director of the now-defunct Christian Coalition, survived a scandal linked to Jack Abramoff, and founded the Faith and Freedom Coalition, noted the institutionalizing of the Christian right when he described the movement during the Bush years in these terms: "You're no longer throwing rocks at the building; you're in the building."[2] Christian conservatives are a minority of the US electorate, but in terms of the influence on US politics of the movement that represents their beliefs and interests, the Christian right punches above its weight, especially in Republican states and under Republican administrations.[3] Now an established political movement and interest group, the Christian right has continued to innovate, institutionalize, and transnationalize its influence.[4]

However, in the years before the 2016 election, the Christian right suffered a number of LGBTQ policy and political blows. These included the Supreme Court decision in *Lawrence v. Texas* (2003), in which the court overturned state sodomy laws, and Supreme Court decisions in *United States v. Windsor* (2013) and *Obergefell v. Hodges* (2015), which together ruled the Defense of Marriage Act unconstitutional. A surprising victory for LGBTQ rights in 2020 was *Bostock v. Clayton County, Georgia*, in which the court held that employment discrimination against LGBT people violated Title VII of the Civil Rights Act of 1964. Throughout the 2000s, public support for LGB rights claims rose until, in 2010, a national poll found that a majority of Americans supported same-sex marriage for the first time.[5] By contrast, LGBT political scientists have confirmed that "the public is less likely to support discrimination protections for transgender people in comparison with gay men and lesbians."[6]

After the 2016 election, some pro-LGBT public policies, such as the Obama administration's guidance on accommodation of transgender students in public schools, and the decision that the US government interpret sex discrimination in court decisions to include sexual orientation and gender identity, were reversed. But the nullification of sodomy laws, the demise of the Defense of Marriage Act, and rising public tolerance or support for same-sex sexuality were blows the Christian right struggled to incorporate into a public narrative of a return to morality. Even so, Christian right moral entrepreneurs found ways to turn losses in US culture wars to their advantage.

Increasing public support for LGBTQ people in the US accelerated two trends in Christian right politics: first, the construction and deployment of new religious freedom arguments and legal strategies; and, second, the intensification of anti-LGBT Christian right networks, lobbying, and ministries in postsocialist and developing countries. In this chapter, I focus on a particular sector of the internationalized Christian right: the movement's domestic strategic advocacy against US government support for SOGI human rights abroad as a function of its advocacy for international religious freedom. The claim that religious freedom is threatened in the US wasn't a central feature of Christian conservative public discourse in the movement's early decades of prominence in US politics. Indeed, for much of the Christian right's history as the largest faction in the Republican coalition, Christian right discourse touted the morality of most Americans (the "moral majority") and even, especially under Republican presidents, the moral responsibilities of the US government.

As long as most Americans disapproved of same-sex relations and government institutions didn't protect the rights of LGBTQ people, Christian conservative discourse foregrounded the threat to America, Christianity, and orthodox believers posed by gender and sexual minorities. The religious freedom social movement frame emerged in part as a response to increasing support for or indifference to gender and sexuality civil rights. The frame appears at first glance to posit a zero-sum logic: recognition and protection of civil or human rights for a disfavored minority (LGBT people) leaves less recognition or protection available for other groups ("biblical" Christian conservatives). I think it's more accurate to say that for Christian conservatives, LGBT rights enact harm, even if the harm they conceptualize doesn't comport with a standard such as John Stuart Mill's harm principle.[7] Specifically, LGBT rights preclude believers from inhabiting a traditionally moral society and a moral public square in which to exercise their faith. Such rights also guarantee that conservative believers cannot live under the authority of a civil government that imposes Christian conservative moral standards and punishes immorality.

Christian conservatives have long argued that public policy should privilege the demands of conservative religious believers on issues involving public education, family policy, reproductive rights, and other domains. They continue to make these claims even if they sometimes make them in less biblical and more democratic, rights-based terms of public discourse. Even though I don't fully subscribe to the idea that Christian conservative elites believe that human rights are zero sum, I use this formulation at times in this book as a shortcut way of expressing the core message of the SOGI human rights vs. religious freedom social movement frame.

During the Obama administration, the Christian right made common cause with traditional Christian believers and other anti-LGBT actors and institutions abroad, especially in poor and developing countries and regions. A central feature of these alliances has been the frame of religious freedom threatened specifically by LGBT people and the demand for recognition of their human rights. The Christian right exports this frame to anti-LGBTI cultures, regimes, and people outside the US and reinforces the frame as allies articulate it in the contexts of their own cultures.

In *Sin, Sex, and Democracy* and *Tough Love*, I analyzed the distinct antigay (and, in *Tough Love*, antiabortion) frames intended for ingroup believers and those outside the Christian conservative movement. One characteristic of both antigay and antiabortion Christian right rhetoric is its differentiation into messaging meant to be mastered by Christian conservative followers to be used for public consumption and that intended to circulate only within a Christian conservative ingroup. A second feature of this rhetoric has been its differentiation into discourse appropriate to diverse sociopolitical contexts, especially compassionate therapeutic discourse and political discourse.[8]

Maintaining liberal democracy isn't a principal goal of Christian conservative politics. Even so, antigay frames evolved over time from less mature public appeals to enact god's will for public policy to more sophisticated appeals to democratic discourses, rights, and liberty. Meanwhile, denunciations of same-sex sexuality inside the Christian right continue to reflect conceptions of sexual minorities as unrepentant sinners committing acts of moral abomination that threaten Christians, Christianity, and the nation. Between the Supreme Court decision in *Lawrence* and the end of Obama's first term in office, the democratic rhetorical strategy manifested in campaigns against same-sex marriage organized around a simple demand to let the people vote. However, the limit of a majoritarian democratic strategy is obvious: as public support for LGBTQ civil rights increases, opponents can no longer count on majorities to reject LGBTQ rights measures and to support anti-LGBTQ initiatives, statutes, and state constitutional amendments. In contrast with the democratic antigay frame, the SOGI human rights vs. religious freedom frame doesn't rely on democratic majoritarianism.

In this chapter, I trace the Christian right's deployment of the SOGI human rights vs. religious freedom frame from late 2015 to 2020, showing Christian right elites' use of the frame to vilify Obama, the left, and the federal government civil service. A crucial element of the story of Christian right opposition to US support for SOGI human rights is that Christian conservatives who had some leverage over SOGI foreign policy signaled adherence to the frame to ingroup Christian right audiences. However, these elites then either moderated their hostility to SOGI in more public forums or carefully adjusted ingroup messaging to direct attention away from the Trump administration and back toward Obama, Hillary Clinton, Democrats, and liberals. In this chapter, we'll see this switch between ingroup and public modes of rhetoric in operation.

Besides tracing the trajectory of the SOGI human rights vs. religious freedom frame during the Trump administration, I excavate underlying tactics the Christian conservative movement has used to delegitimize US support for SOGI human rights, both inside the Christian right and in collaboration with allies abroad. Communicating as it does an immediate threat to Christians and Christianity, the frame has been productive in many ways. However, the tactics used to implement the frame reveal internal contradictions and empirical discrepancies that movement rhetoric must elide or suppress. These contradictions and discrepancies matter; they point to rhetorical work elites have to do to keep the discourse about the unique threat to religious faith posed by LGBTI people from unraveling.

Finally, a single example of backlash against the Trump administration based on its continued advocacy for SOGI shows what Christian right rhetoric might have looked like if movement elites and institutions had been serious about the conviction that SOGI human rights threatened religious freedom. Instead of subjecting Trump and Pompeo to the same scrutiny they turned on Obama and Clinton, the movement was careful to spare their allies. As we'll see in the next chapter, the Trump administration reciprocated the Christian right's goodwill and reinforced its alliance with the movement by rhetorically and programmatically emphasizing international religious freedom. The Christian right praised Trump and his administration for placing religious freedom at the heart of US foreign policy. Yet the movement protected Trump and Pompeo from allegations that they were sacrificing Christian believers abroad by continuing SOGI diplomacy and foreign assistance. Let's look more closely at Christian right messaging about US support for SOGI human rights and international religious freedom.

SOGI Human Rights vs. Religious Freedom

The Christian right consistently misrepresented the goals of US advocacy for LGBTI human rights abroad under the Obama administration to include advocacy for same-sex marriage and draconian US penalties on countries for opposing same-sex marriage. It was never the policy of the Obama administration to demand international compliance with same-sex marriage. Indeed, even the Biden administration, which quickly affirmed support for SOGI human rights in US foreign policy, didn't mandate same-sex marriage in other nations or threaten sanctions for noncompliance. On June 24, 2021, this position was affirmed by Scott Busby, deputy assistant secretary of the Bureau of Democracy, Human Rights, and Labor (DRL) during a US House of Representatives Committee on Foreign Affairs hearing on the subject of advancing and protecting LGBTQI+ rights abroad. In light of the SOGI human rights vs. religious freedom frame, it's particularly interesting that in the hearing Busby also affirmed the position of the Biden administration and the State Department that LGBTQI human rights and religious freedom, including the religious freedom of gender and sexual minorities, are not mutually exclusive.[9] Busby served as de facto special envoy for LGBTI human rights in the Trump administration, which never appointed anyone to succeed Randy Berry, the first State Department official in the role. The day after Busby's testimony before the House committee, Jessica Stern was appointed to the post, renamed Special Envoy to Advance the Human Rights of LGBTQI+ Persons.[10]

Christian conservative misrepresentation on US advocacy for same-sex marriage abroad during the Obama and Trump administration has served multiple movement goals. The first goal is establishing and reinforcing the idea that liberals/progressives/Democrats are, at best, indifferent to religious persecution and, at worst, hostile to religious freedom—that is, only conservatives and the Republican Party can serve the movement's religious freedom expectations. Second, misrepresentations of a SOGI agenda continue to stimulate mobilization by Christian conservative American citizens against domestic US policies that serve LGBTQ equality in a time when some might accommodate themselves to such changes. A third goal is encouraging American Christian conservatives to understand themselves sharing an abject condition and fate with Christians persecuted for their faith in other lands, thus eliding the differences between, for example, Chinese government persecution of Uighurs and nondiscrimination laws in the US.

Fourth, the misrepresentations not only shape negative perceptions of the Obama administration but warn conservative believers about the future threat that Democratic administrations or Democratic-majority institutions would pose to orthodox religious believers, both in the US and abroad. And, finally, a misrepresentation such as that the US under Obama used its fiscal or (the threat of) military leverage to force same-sex marriage on Christian peoples in other countries strengthens the reliance of Christian conservatives on the Christian right movement and movement elites. After all, only Christian conservatives' trusted moral entrepreneurs expose these hidden and malevolent practices, and exercise the political clout to undo them.

Christian right movement elites may exercise political influence by holding key offices themselves, as some did in the Trump administration, but they also exercise influence by shaping the narrative: creating and directing political messaging to Christian right followers. For example, in response to a concern that political gains for the LGBTQ movement can incite backlash against anti-LGBTQ people and rights, political scientists Benjamin G. Bishin, Thomas J. Hayes, Matthew B. Incantalupo, and Charles Anthony Smith argue that movement elites mobilize existing supporters to push back against the disrupted status quo. Thus, the phenomenon we may see during divisive debates over LGBTQ rights is the intensification of "existing negative opinion" as anti-LGBT elites work to mobilize their constituencies to oppose challenges to bias and discrimination.[11]

I've received many examples of the SOGI human rights vs. religious freedom frame in Christian right messaging since the 2016 presidential campaign began in 2015. Most of the rhetoric from FRC is disseminated by way of brief daily articles packaged in sets of two or three on different topics emailed to subscribers and posted to the FRC website. The majority of FRC messaging is on domestic US topics; however, FRC also blasts out articles on international issues for consumption by US Christian conservatives. This messaging "informs" believers, shaping their convictions and mobilizing them on the issues. Generally speaking, relevant messaging before the election started by emphasizing Obama's indifference or hostility to the scourge of religious persecution abroad, moving, in Obama's second term, to add Hillary Clinton to that indictment. Articles occasionally mentioned the Obama administration's prioritizing of SOGI rights and LGBT-friendly displays abroad and the administration's punitive reactions to anti-LGBT cultures and values abroad. For example, in 2015, as the Christian right mobilized its supporters for the election, Tony Perkins and the Family Research Council (FRC) sent these messages:[12]

> [Obama] shrugs off the persecution of Christians in other countries. (FRC Action fundraising letter, February 2015)

> If the President won't talk about religious persecution, Congress will. Today, at a Senate subcommittee hearing, members turned the floodlights on the dark world of religious hostility—an international crisis this administration continues to ignore. ("Religious Liberty Gets a Witness," subscriber email, March 11, 2015)

> The Obama administration has engaged in an aggressive effort to force recipients of American foreign aid to accept the President's pro-homosexual agenda. ("Cultural Imperialism and the Obama Administration," event invitation, May 27, 2015)

> When the President travels abroad, there's one thing he never leaves at home: his radical social agenda. . . . The White House has dispatched an army of liberal ambassadors—all with strict instructions to use their influence to force acceptance of the President's extreme sexual priorities. ("Kenya Take a Step Back, Mr. President?," subscriber email, July 8, 2015)

Besides the content of this rhetoric, two things are significant about these messages. First, they evince the construction of an identification between US Christian conservatives and persecuted Christians abroad that Melani

McAlister calls "victim identification."[13] Second, they demonstrate how the conflict between LGBT rights and religious freedom in the US, a staple of Christian right rhetoric and legal strategy throughout the Obama administration, expanded into the social movement frame of international SOGI human rights vs. religious freedom.

The apprehensiveness of the movement and its leaders' sense of what was at stake was on display only days before the 2016 presidential election when the FRC offered its subscribers "Rainbow Blight: Obama's LGBT Legacy." The article focuses attention on the Obama administration's global SOGI human rights efforts and, in particular, Hillary Clinton's role in supporting SOGI human rights. "Rainbow Blight" contains predictable elements of Christian conservative messaging on LGBTQ issues. First, the article identifies Obama, National Security Advisor Susan Rice, and former Secretary of State Hillary Clinton (the "Grand Marshall of the [pro-LGBT] celebration") with US "global bullying on homosexuality." Second, "Rainbow Blight" reinforces the ostensibly zero-sum logic of support for LGBTQ/ SOGI human rights common on the Christian right, arguing that commitment to the human rights of LGBTQ people inevitably comes at the expense of the human right to religious freedom. An unusual argument in "Rainbow Blight" is that US assistance to LGBT people indirectly harms more deserving—presumably non-LGBT—potential recipients by "depriv[ing] them] of some of the most effective, efficient, and compassionate [US] care in the world."[14] In other words, funding LGBT people diverts resources from deserving to undeserving (LGBT) recipients.

Tony Perkins also issued a more direct statement that seemed to affirm that the Christian right expected SOGI human rights policy and programs would be terminated under Trump. In December, 2016, Perkins issued a "letter to supporters" in which he excoriated Obama administration SOGI and reproductive rights policies and urged the president-elect "to expel State Department 'activists' promoting LGBT rights overseas." A spokesperson for the incoming administration responded to Perkins' demand by affirming that discrimination wouldn't be "condoned or tolerated." Nevertheless, news sources reported that

> LGBT employees worry that the State Department will scale back its overseas work on gay rights issues under Trump. The concern stems partly from the fact that although Trump himself appeared to be generally gay friendly during his presidential run, Vice President-elect Mike Pence is a staunch Christian conservative with a record of opposing gay rights.[15]

By the end of Trump's term in office, Perkins' statement had been removed from FRC's website.[16]

After Trump took office, the volume of FRC SOGI human rights vs. religious freedom messaging increased. In spite of the fact that Trump had won the election, messaging alleging that the Obama administration was indifferent or hostile to religious freedom abroad, and that the Democratic administration had pursued a SOGI human rights agenda instead of a religious freedom agenda, became *more* common from late 2016 through 2019 than it had been before the 2016 election.[17] Of course, in addition to FRC's messages to subscribers, believers were also being tutored on the relationship between religious persecution abroad and SOGI human rights advocacy by a host of other elites and platforms. In this chapter and the next, elements related to the frame—including evidence against its veracity—show up in a January 2020 interview of Mike Pompeo conducted by Tony Perkins; the January 2020 podcast of a conversation between *New York Times* reporter Wajahat Ali and Sam Brownback; the 2018 and 2019 Ministerials to Advance Religious Freedom; the defenses of the Commission on Unalienable Rights; and the July 2020 "Undeniable" conference call for pastors between Perkins and Pompeo.

By contrast with the period from the time Trump took office through the end of 2019, however, during the 2020 presidential campaign the FRC only clearly invoked the SOGI human rights vs. religious freedom frame twice in its regular messaging. The first instance was in response to the recall of Ambassador Daniel Foote from Zambia, and the second instance was in response to openly gay Ambassador Ric Grenell's gay decriminalization campaign, both of which I discuss in more detail in chapter 4. Responding to the contretemps over Foote's disagreement with the Zambian government over the arrest of gay Zambians, the FRC said:

> President Trump doesn't share a lot of Barack Obama's views—especially when it comes to the mission of the State Department. After eight years, it was obvious that the 44th president was more interested in domineering than diplomacy. Even now, pockets of his cultural imperialism live on, deep inside the agency that Trump has tried desperately to clean up. . . .
>
> The move was a shocking contrast to the last administration, which not only ignored—but mocked—their host country's beliefs in places like Latin America. In fact, Barack Obama's efforts to radicalize other nations was so offensive that citizens of other nations openly celebrated when Donald Trump was elected. Like

dozens of other countries on the receiving end of the president's extreme social agenda, people in the Caribbean were under enormous pressure from the bullies at the State Department to abandon ship on their traditional Christian beliefs.[18]

In response to Grenell's campaign to end the criminalization of same-sex sexuality worldwide, the FRC said:

> Richard Grenell never worked for Barack Obama—but he's using tactics near and dear to that administration's foreign policy. The acting director of national intelligence has decided that it's time for America to stop sharing information with countries who aren't as pro-LGBT as he is—a view that's eerily similar to Hillary Clinton's State Department, where ideological blackmail was the order of every day. . . .[19]
>
> Now, in addition to pushing a policy that cuts off intelligence sharing with countries who believe differently than he does, Grenell is also assembling an international group of "gay, lesbian, bisexual, and transgender" advocates to change "anti-gay" laws (which, we know from experience, is the Left's code for any policy that promotes religious liberty).[20]

It's possible that the near disappearance in 2020 of the SOGI human rights vs. religious freedom frame suggests that FRC determined they might not be as successful tarring Biden with the charge of hostility to religious freedom as they had been with the same charge against Obama and Trump's 2016 adversary, Clinton. One factor in this calculation was no doubt the salience and pervasiveness of Republicans' and Trump supporters' belief that Obama was a secret Muslim. A 2015 CNN/ORC (Opinion Research Corporation) International poll that found 29 percent of Americans, 43 percent of Republicans, and 54 percent of Trump supporters believed that Obama was a Muslim.[21]

Although the Christian right has tied Joe Biden to other Obama administration policies and progressive goals, including domestic LGBTQ rights, the FRC made no attempt to indict Trump's successor for Obama's putative hostility to religious freedom until after the 2020 presidential election. Trump had refused to concede, and the Christian right, prominent Republicans, and Pompeo amplified Trump's defiance and claims of election fraud.

Coy for FRC messaging, Pompeo's warning of the dangers to international religious freedom of a "new" administration doesn't castigate Biden directly:

> The Trump administration's foreign policy has become known for prioritizing religious freedom. But what will happen if a new presidential administration ends all that? Pompeo says, "it will just be an enormous reduction in the ability of human beings to live the way God wants us to live." When governments suppress the ability of individuals to practice their faith as they see fit, Pompeo stated, "the reduction in human dignity is of staggering proportions."[22]

Throughout the 2020 presidential contest, Perkins continued to praise Trump for his interest in, knowledge of, and commitment to religious freedom abroad.

The SOGI human rights vs. religious freedom frame applies the existing Christian right frame of ineluctable conflict between LGBT civil rights and religious freedom to the international arena. Many examples of the internationalized version of the frame blame the Obama administration, Hillary Clinton, Democratic "radicals," LGBT people, and—connected with the right-wing denunciation of the "deep state"—"liberal holdovers" in the civil service. The indictment that the US government sacrifices religious freedom when it advocates for the human rights of LGBTI people abroad seems straightforward, especially to Christian conservative believers who have been socialized to perceive that equality for gender and sexual minorities in the US always comes at a cost to religious believers. However, the SOGI human rights vs. religious freedom frame is more complicated than it first appears. I argue that the operationalization of the SOGI human rights vs. religious freedom frame rests on several tactics employed in the conflict between SOGI human rights and religious freedom. These tactics are potentially tricky for the Christian right because they contain internal contradictions or can expose uncomfortable questions for the movement.

What Lies Beneath

I address three of these tactics in *Because We Are Human*: first, informing believers that the US government is an agent of cultural imperialism when it supports SOGI human rights abroad (but the Christian right doesn't commit cultural imperialism when it advocates against SOGI human rights); second, arguing that it's moral for the Christian right to champion cultural relativism in developing countries (while vigorously opposing cultural relativism in the US); and, third, forming alliances with foreign governments and peoples for the struggle against LGBT human rights (including those that perpetrate religious persecution). For the Trump era, I add a fourth tactic: maintaining that a "deep state" undermined Trump policy and Trump's presidency, including by effectuating SOGI human rights programs and practices in secret and at cross purposes with Trump and his top officials. I briefly present the first three and then turn to the "deep state" that functioned as enemy, foil, and scapegoat for Trump and his followers.

Under Obama, the US Government Was an Agent of Cultural Imperialism

When the Christian right focuses on US support for gender and sexual minority human rights, it borrows a charge that has more often been leveled by the political left: (cultural) imperialism. Thus, when the US government promotes SOGI human rights in its foreign policy and advocates for the human rights of LGBTI people, the US commits cultural imperialism against countries that might prefer to stigmatize LGBTI people and not protect their human rights. One goal of such an indictment is to delegitimize rights discourses and advocacy that run counter to Christian conservative goals and beliefs. Another is to reinforce and influence anti-LGBTQ discourse, policies, and social practices outside the US to stem and, if possible, reverse global movements for SOGI human rights.

Many Christian conservative movement elites and groups have used the trope of imperialism or colonialism as a way to frame US commitments to LGBTI and women's human rights as duress against poorer, weaker states by an immoral geopolitical oppressor.[23] A wide variety of Christian conservative groups and moral entrepreneurs have taken up this analysis to explain the immorality of the US putatively forcing nations to abide by its conditions on SOGI or face ruinous consequences. Groups include, but aren't limited to, the World Congress of Families, Family Watch International, and the Family Research Council. Reporting on Senator Cory Booker's questioning of Mike Pompeo during Pompeo's confirmation hearing in 2018, the *Daily Signal* alleged that the US government had "gone far beyond standing for basic human rights" with its SOGI human rights policy and had "sought to advance a liberal LGBT agenda abroad." One element of this agenda, the appointment of Randy Berry to serve as the first special envoy for the human rights of LGBTI persons, constituted "a most egregious form of cultural imperialism."[24]

In January 2020, Tony Perkins interviewed Mike Pompeo about Trump foreign policy and its reversals of Obama policy, especially on "international pro-life efforts." Alluding to US imperialism practiced under Obama, Perkins specifically asks Pompeo about US "global policies":

> If I can, let me ask a—kind of a defining question or one that would draw a contrast between previous administrations. When you talk about this, you're essentially saying allow countries to make their own decisions based upon their religious conviction and cultural heritage and not force them through a form of cultural imperialism with our global policies to adhere to something that is an anathema to them.

Responding, "Yes, Tony, you nailed it," Pompeo continues:

> They have often had international organizations show up on their doorstep and tie resources, funding, support, commitment, all the things that some of these countries who aren't wealthy nations need—tie them to a set of policies that are inconsistent with what their culture and their heritage reflects and their religious beliefs in their particular country would reflect.
>
> We've talked about religious freedom. We want to make sure every country has the understanding how central that is to their nation's success and how they shouldn't let a bureaucrat somewhere sitting in an international organization interfere with their country's sovereign desire to allow their citizens to practice their—to practice religious freedom.

Pompeo refers here to coercive efforts of international organizations rather than the US government. However, Pompeo's reflection was provoked by Perkins's explicit allusions to the Trump administration "correct[ing] policies . . . that are inconsistent with America's founding values"—one of several clear references to the Commission on Unalienable Rights—and "correct[ing] America's stand internationally."[25]

Another figure who became significant in Trump administration support for religious freedom is Mary Ann Glendon, chair of the administration's

Commission on Unalienable Rights. In Rome in November 2018, Glendon delivered a talk entitled "Fundamental Rights and a Conflict among Rights" that was sponsored by the Joseph Ratzinger-Benedict XVI Foundation. In a post-speech interview with *Crux*, a Catholic news site, Glendon expressed a concern about "Western-funded human rights organizations . . . coming in and claiming universal human rights status for their agenda, treating people in those countries as if they are ignorant and they better get with the human rights program." She added that such human rights advocacy "smacks of neocolonialism, and makes people very angry."[26] Of course the "people in those countries" for whom Glendon and other Christian conservatives speak are not those whose fundamental human rights are in jeopardy because of their status as gender or sexual minorities. For the US Christian right movement, citizens endangered for those reasons aren't "the people."

Jan-Werner Müller lays out a parsimonious set of features characteristic of the populisms that currently threaten democracy and human rights in many parts of the world, including the US. In his analysis, populism insists "that a part of the people *is* the people"; moralizes politics and political conflict in a way that discredits and demonizes opponents and compromise with those opponents; and treats political opponents as "enemies of the people."[27] I've applied Müller's model of populism to a subset of Christian right political prayers "for" and about Obama, but the model applies to other dimensions of Christian conservative rhetoric.[28] Implicit in many Christian conservative commentaries about LGBTQ/SOGI rights is such a distinction between moral citizens and sinful, destructive others.

A distinction between "the people" and LGBTQI people often forces LGBTQI citizens to solicit "boomerang" advocacy from actors outside their countries or cultures and work with regional and international human rights actors to meet the social, political, and legal needs of their communities.[29] Christian conservative activists and intellectuals who advocate for "fundamental rights" against the superfluous rights they associate with SOGI tendentiously ignore that US human rights assistance to LGBTI people and religious minorities alike is constructed to support disfavored and marginalized groups in their quest to enjoy those fundamental human rights US Christian conservatives claim for themselves.

The irony of the Christian conservative movement deploying the charge of cultural imperialism against the US government on SOGI human rights is the US Christian right's history of international campaigns *against* human rights for LGBTQ people that might as easily be characterized as cultural imperialism. Roger Ross Williams depicts one discrete example of this campaign in his film, *God Loves Uganda*, which explores how American missionaries helped to produce what Williams calls the "noxious flower" of anti-LGBT sentiment and policy in Uganda.[30] In a unique twist on missionary interventions from developed countries on poor countries, the US-based Christian right reverses the historical logic of Christian missionary colonialism by praising the moral superiority of Christian believers and elites in poor countries as long as these believers are anti-LGBTQ.[31]

THE US SHOULD ADOPT CULTURAL RELATIVISM ABOUT LGBT RIGHTS ABROAD

Since the 1990s, SOGI human rights–respecting norms have spread to parts of the world where they didn't exist before, including the US. Closely following this norm diffusion, and in some places anticipating it, US Christian conservatives bolster SOGI human rights resistance abroad.[32] At times, the Christian right explicitly depicts opposition to SOGI as moral and Christian. However, the cultural imperialism tactic allows the movement to represent the opposition to SOGI human rights as a manifestation of organic beliefs that deserve to be respected. This call for respect for the people's beliefs can take a variety of forms but usually looks similar to Mike Pompeo's caution not to impose on people in other nations "a set of policies that are inconsistent with what their culture and their heritage reflects and their religious beliefs in their particular country would reflect."

Deferring to the culture, values, heritage, and beliefs of a people against SOGI human rights is different than merely commending diverse viewpoints. Indeed, it's a narrative of cultural relativism akin to saying, "The most important issue isn't whether this group agrees with me but that they are permitted to act in accordance with their long and deeply held beliefs, values, and cultural heritage; we should all respect those viewpoints regardless of whether they coincide with ours." I doubt that the Christian right would continue to champion the value of cultural relativism if the governments and cultures it now recognizes as avatars of traditional values became more tolerant of gender and sexual minorities. It seems that Christian right elites perceive a benefit to championing respect for cultural relativism as a public narrative that doesn't rely on biblical morality for its efficacy.

The irony of the Christian conservative movement valorizing cultural relativism abroad is that the movement has advanced its critique of sexual immorality by directly repudiating cultural relativism at home. For the movement, cultural relativism in the US has been the outcome of replacing

Christianity with immoral secularism in public institutions. And cultural relativism has, in turn, enabled a social climate and public policy that embraces LGBT rights. So the Christian conservative movement depicts cultural relativism as a social good in international relations and demands that the US government respect and abide by anti-LGBT beliefs in US foreign policy. However, the Christian right only recognizes the benefits of cultural relativism for those who adhere to their own anti-LGBT, antiabortion rights doctrine.

I describe this tendency of the US Christian right to champion anti-LGBT governments and movements abroad as "projective cultural relativism." Projective cultural relativism evinces concern to protect cultural difference but only to the extent that it enables the movement to designate as virtuous and authentic those societies and cultures that approve doctrines dear to the Christian right. That means denying human rights protections to LGBTQ people, inciting social disapprobation, and using public policy against them.

The US Should Ally with Anti-LGBT Governments and Peoples

For several decades, the US Christian right and transnational Christian conservative groups, many based in the US, have allied and partnered with conservative states and within multinational organizations to advance their anti-LGBT/anti–reproductive rights agenda. In some respects, these states and organizations are natural allies of a Christian right movement that has lost many major conflicts over policy and public opinion in the US. However, complicating US Christian right international alliances is the fact that many partners consistently persecute religious minorities, including Christians.

An example of the overlap between governments that persecute LGBTI people and those that persecute religious minorities was provided in 2016. Reporting for People for the American Way on a UN summit dedicated to "Uniting Nations for a Family Friendly World," held at UN headquarters in New York City, Peter Montgomery observed that the Group of Friends of the Family (GoFF), a 25-member organization of UN member states launched by Belarus, Egypt, and Qatar in 2015 included many members identified by the United States Commission on International Religious Freedom (USCIRF) as grave violators of religious freedom.[33] Today, several US-based Christian conservative civil society organizations ally with the GoFF, including the Center for Family and Human Rights (C-FAM), Family Watch International, Concerned Women for America, and the Family Research Council.[34]

In the USCIRF's 2020 report, the following members of the GoFF were recommended for designation as "countries of particular concern" because of conditions for religious freedom: Iran, Nigeria, Pakistan, the Russian Federation, Saudi Arabia, Tajikistan, and Turkmenistan. And these GoFF member countries were recommended for designation on the State Department's "special watch list": Egypt, Indonesia, Iraq, Malaysia, Nicaragua, and Sudan.[35] Hence, Christian conservative groups and elites—including the FRC and its president—often end up engaging in joint efforts to suppress LGBT civil and human rights with foreign elites and regimes that commit religious oppression they abhor. These collaborations constitute an international version of cobelligerence, a doctrine championed by theologian Francis Schaeffer. For Schaeffer, "a co-belligerent is a person with whom I do not agree on all sorts of vital issues, but who, for whatever reasons of their own, is on the same side in a fight for some specific issue of public justice."[36]

It's not surprising that, in global contexts, cobelligerents who agree on suppressing civil and political rights of gender and sexual minorities may also suppress religious pluralism. Nor is the empirical linkage between religious freedom and gender and sexual minority human rights unknown to Christian conservative elites. An illuminating example is found in a January 1, 2020, conversation between *New York Times* reporter Wajahat Ali and ambassador at large for international religious freedom Sam Brownback, podcasted by *Faith Angle*. Ali and Brownback discuss many issues, including domestic US conflicts over LGBT civil rights and the rights of religious believers. In the following exchange, which I quote at length, the conversation shifts suddenly from domestic US political conflict between Christian conservatives and LGBTQ people to the close empirical relationship between the protection of the rights of disfavored believers and disfavored gender and sexual minorities.

> **Ali:** How can you reconcile—or how do we reconcile as a country—the religious freedoms of some faith communities versus the desire of others—say LGBTQ—to be protected from discrimination? Is there a balance? Or does one group—let's be blunt—does one group have to cede?

> **Brownback:** The short answer is: I don't know. Because this has been going on for a while, and it's gonna go on for a while. That's why we have courts and why so many of these religious freedom cases are making their way up to the Supreme Court. Because that issue has to be resolved here in the United States.

One of the interesting things to point out globally, though, is that the countries that are the best on religious freedom also tend to be the best on LGBT rights.

Ali: Example, please.

Brownback: Western Europe, United States. Uh, if you compare us to much of the rest of the world—particularly, say, the Islamic regions of the world, a number of other developing countries—LGBT rights are not, are not, strong.

Ali: Right, Iran, for example.

Brownback: [Agrees with Ali on Iran] *But that's the foundational piece that we keep—I keep—harping about on religious freedom. You get this one right, your balance sheet goes up on freedom of assembly, freedom of speech, your basics. And it actually happens to get much better for you on the LGBT rights. Which is not what most people would think in this country.* But if you go abroad, there would be more people thinking in that category because it just means that you really are looking more at the dignity of the individual. You made a choice one way or the other, and I'm able to agree with it or disagree with it. There are people who look at me and they'd say: he made a choice to be a follower of Jesus; I don't agree with that. You know, I think it's too bad or this or that. But, look, he made a choice, and that's just the basis of freedom of religion is really the dignity of the individual to choose, whether people agree with you or not.

Ali: It's a reciprocity, right?

Brownback: Yes, it applies to you, it applies to me.

In this remarkable exchange, Brownback acknowledges an empirical correlation: that both Western Europe and the US have *relatively* high levels of support for religious and gender/sexuality self-determination, while countries that don't respect religious choice and autonomy often are also dangerous to gender and sexual minorities.[37] This acknowledgment undercuts the Christian right position that seems to provide most of the rationale for a vigorous

Christian conservative movement and interest group: that in the US and internationally, LGBTQ rights come at the expense of religious freedom.

In his conversation with Ali, Brownback describes the work of the International Religious Freedom office in the State Department as "mainly just trying to keep people from being killed and not getting thrown out of the country." In spite of the rhetoric disseminated by the Christian right about US support for SOGI human rights, this characterization is quite similar to the ways I've heard officials in DRL talk about their SOGI efforts. Somewhat later in the interview, Brownback recalls what seems like mild dismay at the Obama administration's commitment to SOGI human rights when he recounts wondering during a prayer breakfast

> if we weren't getting a little bit ahead of our skis with the strong impulse to advance LGBTQ rights abroad. I remember a speech by President Obama, and you just think about sort of the balance on this. . . . What are the ways that—remember they used to say in philanthropy you want to have less money to get great outcomes. You want your philanthropic investment to be more like a lubricant to help something that already wants to happen rather than being something that you're paying for everything.[38]

This brief comment misstates the nature of SOGI human rights policies and practices when it suggests that DRL officials didn't work closely with grassroots activists to achieve goals and that the US was paying for "everything" that constituted SOGI advocacy during Obama's terms in office. US leadership of the GEF, funded by seventeen countries and a set of other foundation and corporate donors, disproves this statement. But what's most striking about this rebuke is its tone of gentle disapproval. In these public comments, there's no moralizing about the wickedness of gender and sexual minorities and no effort to portray anti-LGBTQ people and governments as suffering the injury of US cultural imperialism. In this public conversation, Brownback betrays the reality that Christian right elites don't believe key aspects of movement messaging on SOGI and religious freedom.

SOGI HUMAN RIGHTS WAS PERPETRATED BY THE ANTI-TRUMP "DEEP STATE"

Conservative media and public discourse routinely excoriated the "deep state" as an obstacle to President Trump's agenda and an instrument in the plot to terminate his presidency. Despite its ubiquity, the term has only recently entered US political discourse, borrowed from descriptions of corrupt networks of state and nonstate actors in developing countries. In the US, former congressional staffer and author Mike Lofgren applies the term to the US, describing the deep state as "a hybrid association of elements of government and parts of top-level finance and industry that is effectively able to govern the United States without reference to the consent of the governed as expressed through the formal political process." The deep state, he argues, "operates according to its own compass heading regardless of who is formally in power."[39] Lofgren's and other accounts of deep states include state and nonstate elements, including bureaucrats, elected officials, military officers, defense and intelligence professionals, business leaders, and organized crime. But the conception of the deep state that right-wing media and Trump's allies, especially Steve Bannon, pushed after his inauguration was considerably narrower. This conception essentially redefined the administrative state—the agencies of the executive branch of government and the civil servants who staff them—as a counterdemocratic and specifically anti-Trump cabal.

When the populist, nationalist right reconceptualized the bureaucracy that assures continuity of government functioning as a lawless insurgency from within, Christian right moral entrepreneurs were receptive to this conceptualization. One feature of the Christian conservative movement has been its flexibility in allying with other conservative movements and reconfiguring its political language to conform to, use, and benefit from overlaps and association with these movements while interjecting its own issues and political goals into the resulting coalition.

The Christian right's alliance with Trump's populism and nationalism—including white nationalism—has followed a similar pattern to its alliance with the Tea Party. However, there is a key difference between the playbooks for allying with the Tea Party and Trump's MAGA movement. In 2009 and 2010, the Christian right consistently urged on the Tea Party a conceptualization of core principles that cast cultural conservatism as a necessary constituent of a program of fidelity to constitutional originalism and economic conservatism. That is, not only were Christian conservatives present at the creation of the Tea Party and throughout its political evolution, but the Christian right actively advocated for the incorporation of its agenda into the Tea Party.[40] By contrast, the Christian right has had to perform relatively little advocacy on behalf of the incorporation of its agenda into MAGA, presumably because there have been relatively few areas of disagreement. More troubling is the movement's silence on Trump's racism and racial politics. The Christian right's tacit approval of Trump's racism has been illuminated and dissected by dissenting Christian intellectuals such as Michael Gerson and John Fea as well as by critics outside the movement such as investigative journalist Sarah Posner.[41]

Under Obama, the "deep state" promulgated and executed many policies that, for Christian conservatives, reflected immoral liberal designs. In addition to SOGI human rights policies and practices, the Obama administration supported LGBT civil rights (including, over time, same-sex marriage and transgender inclusion); domestic and international policies to combat climate change; domestic and international reproductive rights; enforcement of racial minority civil rights laws that were neglected under the Bush administration; a national health law that aimed to use insurance markets to provide health insurance to millions of Americans; and a variety of policy responses to the Great Recession that conservative critics decried as socialism.

Like other tactics that underlie the operationalizing of the SOGI human rights vs. religious freedom frame, there are ironies in Trump and his networks defining the "deep state" as an entrenched cabal of anti-Trump actors who contravened the administration's and its Christian right movement allies' agenda. One is evident in the case Andrew Rudalevige makes that many of Trump's successes were achieved through administrative means. Rudalevige argues that Trump effectively "fell in love" with the deep state as he realized ways of accomplishing his ends through the use of executive branch agencies.[42] Another irony is that while officials in executive branch agencies were responsible for executing SOGI policies with bipartisan congressional support in both the Obama and Trump administrations, US officials were also responsible for executing longstanding US foreign policies that support religious freedom and counter religious persecution.

The Christian right depicts the Obama administration as having been a threat to international religious freedom through its advocacy for LGBTI human rights. However, the Obama administration continued established religious freedom foreign policy. Near the end of Obama's second term, a White House "Fact Sheet: Promoting and Protecting Religious Freedom Around the Globe" publicized the administration's "efforts to promote freedom of religion globally as a universal human right, a strategic national interest, and as a key foreign policy objective."[43]

Taking into account that administrations will publicize, and possibly even exaggerate, achievements for political purposes, it's clear that Obama and high-ranking officials in his administration raised the issue of persecution of religious minorities in public speeches as well as in diplomacy with foreign heads of state and government officials. The administration supported the State Department's Office of International Religious Freedom and appointed, first, Suzan Johnson Cook and, later, David N. Saperstein as ambassadors at large for international religious freedom. In 2016, Obama signed into law the Frank R. Wolf International Religious Freedom Act, which expanded the International Religious Freedom Act of 1998. In addition to providing additional resources and training to State Department officials, the law strengthened the Office of International Religious Freedom and explicitly included persecution against "non-theists, humanists, and atheists" as forms of religious persecution.[44]

Beginning in late 2016, FRC messaging emphasized the culpability of the State Department as the vehicle by which the Obama administration and the "deep state," pursued a SOGI foreign policy at the expense of believers abroad. Again, such messages appeared with greater frequency after Trump was elected and assumed office than they had during the 2016 presidential campaign:

> To carry out this extreme agenda, the Obama administration has systematically filled the ranks of State with LGBTQ and abortion activists. (Tony Perkins, "What Does the State Department Have to Do with Social Issues?," subscriber email, December 15, 2016)

> After eight years of watching the State Department operate as a global base for abortion and sexual activism, most Republicans are ready to get back to the real business of diplomacy. (Perkins, "Setting the Record State," subscriber email, January 3, 2017)

> Now on top of having to fight against the Obama holdovers who aren't representing the Trump administration, . . . (Perkins, "Libs Try to Bounce Conservatives from U.N.," subscriber email, March 17, 2017)

> As usual, the decisions [about assisting Christians and other religious minorities abroad] are being made by Obama holdovers. (Perkins, "State Department Errs on the Genocide," subscriber email, September 26, 2017)

> Donald Trump expected to fight plenty of liberals over his agenda, but his own administration? That's a challenge most

people never saw coming. But even now, deep into the president's first year, Barack Obama's footprint on offices like USAID still loom large. (Perkins, "U.S. Strayed by USAID," subscriber email, November 15, 2017)

Throughout most of Trump's term in office, the FRC continued to denounce the "deep state" of "liberal holdovers" and its agenda of sexual extremism while praising the religious freedom agenda of the same agency it was vilifying.

The Wages of Spin

Christian right elites are anything but naive about the propensity of elected officials to court Christian conservatives while sidelining their cultural issues. The movement often tries to hold Republican elected officials to account on issues of importance. However, discourse on accountability is often conducted in ways that don't attract public attention and may circulate only sporadically to followers within the movement. So, for example, Christian right leaders are mindful of the ways in which the Reagan and G. W. Bush administrations failed them on a variety of issues, including abortion rights and the inability to secure a constitutional amendment prohibiting same-sex marriage. Beyond these cultural issues, just as other conservative activists and policymakers recoiled from some emergency measures the Bush administration took in 2008 to diminish the impact of the housing market collapse that led to the Great Recession, many Christian conservatives also disapproved. Christian conservatives allied with other factions of the conservative coalition to foment a Tea Party movement that had roots in Bush's large government apostasy. However, the Tea Party's strategic messaging took place on Obama's watch and took aim at Democrats and Obama.[45]

This is to say that although Christian right elites don't usually air their disagreements with Republicans the movement has deemed to be allies in public, they do sometimes have these conversations "in private"—on media or in face-to-face settings where Christian conservatives talk among themselves. Thus, it's significant that for the period from 2017 to 2020, there are so few examples of Christian right ingroup messaging about Trump administration culpability for the continuation of Obama administration SOGI foreign policy. A rare example of Christian conservative ingroup advocacy against Trump administration support for SOGI occurred in September 2018, after Trump delivered a speech to the United Nations General Assembly. Trump's speech was followed quickly by an article published in *LifeSite News*, "Is the Trump Administration Serious about Refusing to Promote the LGBT Agenda?" Author Stephano Gennarini noted that the president "made assurances that he was not interested in using U.S. foreign policy as a tool for social engineering in other countries, as the Obama administration did to promote international acceptance of homosexuality and abortion rights."

Gennarini wanted to know why "just hours after Trump promised to honor countries' traditions and cultures, the U.S. backed an event promoting international LGBT rights in the conference room immediately under the General Assembly Hall." To underscore the outrage, the *LifeSite News* article is illustrated with a photo of the president on stage holding up a rainbow flag on which "LGBTs for Trump" has been written with a marker.[46] The event to which Gennarini alludes was a high-level side event of the LGBTI Core Group, an "informal cross regional group of United Nations Member States," of which the US is a member, established to "work within the United Nations framework on ensuring universal respect for the human rights and fundamental freedoms for all, specifically lesbian, gay bisexual, transgender and intersex (LGBTI) persons, with a particular focus on protection from violence and discrimination."[47] The panel, "Violence Against LGBTI Individuals: Extrajudicial, Summary, or Arbitrary Executions," was organized by the mission of Albania.[48]

The article accurately identifies a contradiction in Trump's address that was typical of some of his public speeches: promising that his administration will "honor countries' traditions and cultures" while also speaking out in favor of LGBT rights. In this case, Trump made the national values statement while US government officials participated in a multilateral event aimed at protecting LGBTI people from violence in some of the very countries that reject LGBTI human rights. Indeed, this internal contradiction would be on display in Trump's speech to the General Assembly a year later. However, it's shocking and informative that the relatively obscure source of Christian conservative news objected to this particular event: not a cosmopolitan celebration of same-sex marriage but an international effort to curb extrajudicial, summary, or arbitrary executions of gender and sexual minorities.

The *LifeSite News* rebuke stands out because the reality is that even though the administration continued to carry out the SOGI human rights policies of its predecessor, Christian right messaging on SOGI foreign policy after Trump's inauguration shifted dramatically. Rhetoric targeting US support for SOGI—sometimes specifically calling out the State Department—functioned as a marker of Obama administration perfidy and the necessity of electing Trump. However, if terminating SOGI policies such as assistance to human rights activists were a movement goal, we'd expect the movement to continue to pressure the administration on the issue. And we'd expect Christian right appointees in key positions in the administration to leverage their authority to undermine US support for SOGI.

Instead, movement messaging on SOGI during the Trump administration initially disparaged Trump's first secretary of state, Rex Tillerson, as a liberal and an unreliable ally to Trump. Referring to the federal civil service workforce, messaging on SOGI also highlighted the operations of a deep state of "liberal" or "Obama holdovers" in the State Department. After Tillerson departed and Pompeo was confirmed as secretary, rhetoric on SOGI focused on the rogue deep state of civil service "holdovers" that Christian right elites asserted could be routed by Pompeo and his loyalists. Hence, rather than calling unequivocally for the termination of SOGI policies, the movement seemed to tacitly acknowledge their continued existence and simultaneously absolve Pompeo and Trump of responsibility for them. As we'll see, high-ranking political appointees also don't seem to have worked hard to extirpate SOGI human rights policies and practices, and such a lack of interest requires explanation. In the chapters to come, I'll address the disparity between criticisms of Obama on SOGI and relative silence and disinterest on SOGI after Trump took office.

The Christian conservative movement represents Christians—especially Christian conservatives—as victimized and persecuted. In the international arena, this abjection can come at the hands of states and believers of other faith traditions, particularly Islam. But the narrative of a bullying LGBT minority that uses the levers of culture and government to impose its worldview on people of (Christian) faith has been profoundly productive, both within the US and in shaping US Christian conservatives' view of global politics and international religious persecution.

In chapter 2, I examine the ways in which the Trump administration engaged in outreach to Christian conservatives and signaled its receptiveness toward the Christian right's concern with the precarious state of religious freedom, in the US and globally. A signature intervention is the administration's international State Department Ministerials to Advance Religious Freedom, held in 2018 and 2019. Another is the creation of a Commission on Unalienable Rights that unnerved proponents of LGBTQ/SOGI rights. Trump also met with movement elites, addressed groups of Christian conservative activists on their issues, relayed his administration's commitment to religious freedom in other venues, and falsely presented support for religious freedom in US foreign policy as a Trump administration innovation. Often, it's not possible to determine what political movement elites know and to use that information to evaluate the sincerity or mendacity of internal movement claims and rhetoric. Fortunately, the ministerials provided opportunities to assess Christian right movement rhetoric on the social movement frame the Christian right used to delegitimize the Obama administration's efforts on both religious freedom and SOGI human rights.

Chapter 2

His Christian Conservatives

As president, Donald Trump disconcerted many Americans with his penchant for regarding particular groups and individuals possessively: "my generals," "my intelligence people," "my Wilbur [Ross]," and even, of a fan at a rally, "my African American."[1] As an empirical matter, though, it's undeniable both that Christian conservatives assertively and unapologetically allied themselves with Trump and that Trump cultivated the movement's fidelity. If the Obama administration putatively cared too little about religious freedom and religious persecution, and too much about LGBT people's civil and human rights, the Christian right seemed to demand and expect that the Trump administration would curtail LGBT rights advocacy and concentrate its resources and attention on people of faith. The movement wasn't disappointed by the administration's efforts to focus on the needs and interests of Christian conservatives and religious freedom.

The efforts were many, including forming an evangelical advisory board whose members the *Guardian* described as "a mix of radical born-again preachers, televangelists, and conservative political influencers";[2] moving the US embassy in Israel from Tel Aviv to Jerusalem; elevating the Office of International Religious Freedom from the authority of the assistant secretary of the Bureau of Democracy, Human Rights, and Labor (DRL) to the authority of the under secretary for civilian security, democracy, and human rights, a post never filled by the administration; appointing former Kansas governor Sam Brownback as US ambassador at large for international religious freedom; launching the administration's signature Ministerials to Advance Religious Freedom; creating the Faith and Opportunity Initiative, the successor to similar offices under the Bush and Obama administrations, and installing televangelist Paula White as its director; creating the State Department's Commission on Unalienable Rights; and periodically advocating for international religious freedom in secular and religious forums.

Beginning immediately after the 2016 election, I tracked US SOGI diplomacy, public diplomacy, and foreign assistance in real time. Given virtually monolithic support for Trump from Christian conservatives and Trump administration's vigorous outreach to the Christian right, I assumed that even if Trump had no personal interest in terminating SOGI foreign policy, Christian conservative government officials and policymakers would target SOGI. The Trump administration courted Christian conservatives, including with outreach that featured the cause of international religious freedom. To investigate this outreach and its possible relevance for SOGI, I attended the first and second international Ministerials to Advance Religious Freedom, sponsored by the Trump administration and held at the State Department in 2018 and 2019.

The third Ministerial to Advance Freedom of Religion or Belief was virtual, held November 16–17, 2020, and sponsored by the Polish Ministry of Foreign Affairs.[3] the decision to collaborate with the Polish government to put on the ministerial wasn't surprising in light of Trump's fondness for authoritarian political parties and leaders. The conference included a first day of speeches by and discussions among government representatives and featured Mike Pompeo and Sam Brownback. A second day, focused on civil society and religious organizations, was styled as the "Virtual International Religious Freedom Roundtable" and featured a US nonprofit, the International Religious Freedom (IRF) Roundtable, the IRF Secretariat (a "global coordination mechanism" for advancing international religious freedom), and the cochair/coexecutive of both entities, Greg Mitchell.[4] I return to the IRF Roundtable, IRF Secretariat, and Mitchell in the conclusion.

Used by the Trump administration in part to highlight the gulf between Obama's and Trump's concern about international and domestic religious freedom, the 2018 and 2019 ministerials also served as venues for the Christian right's assertion that the Obama administration supported and promoted SOGI human rights to the detriment of religious freedom and the human rights of religious minorities. As a bonus, the ministerials also provided information that calls into question the veracity of the SOGI human rights vs. religious freedom frame and reveals Christian right elites' indifference to the frame's veracity.

In what follows, I present some observations and analysis from the 2018 and 2019 ministerials that bear on the rhetoric, strategy, and aspirations of the

Christian right with regard to US support for SOGI human rights. Between these two ministerials, the State Department launched a new Commission on Unalienable Rights. The commission quickly became a Rorschach test in which proponents saw a reasonable—indeed, a necessary—opportunity to reassess US human rights policy, and critics saw a vehicle for removing human rights protections from women and LGBTQ people. My analysis of the commission's founding and operation emphasizes the political utility of Trump administration religious freedom projects. In addition to the ministerial and commission, I respond briefly to Trump's address to the annual National Prayer Breakfast in early 2020, which included a self-aggrandizing take on his role in promoting international religious freedom.

I think the evidence shows that prominent members and allies of the administration used religious freedom projects such as the ministerials and the Commission on Unalienable Rights to reap the political benefits of reinforcing the administration's alliance with the Christian conservative movement and its goals. My analysis demonstrates that Christian right leaders inside and outside the federal government used the movement frame of LGBTI human rights vs. religious freedom for their own purposes but don't actually believe the frame themselves. Thus, we can conclude with Angelia R. Wilson and Paul A. Djupe that on the issue of US support for SOGI, Christian right elites aren't "communicating in good faith."[5] We won't be surprised, then, to consider that foreign policy projects like the ministerials and the commission—ostensibly executed for lofty foreign policy purposes—served more mundane domestic political goals that were intended to benefit Christian right elites even after Trump left office.

Ministerial to Advance Religious Freedom, 2018

In the summer of 2018, the Trump administration and Secretary of State Pompeo hosted the first international Ministerial to Advance Religious Freedom. The meeting, organized by the Office of International Religious Freedom of the Bureau of Democracy, Human Rights, and Labor, convened on July 24 in the Loy Henderson Conference Room at the Department of State for one full day of plenary sessions. For the occasion, the lobby and public areas of the State Department building were festooned with posters that declared, "Religious Freedom Is: Opportunity, Growth, Liberty, Peace, Security."[6] Additional meetings for international guests were scheduled on July 25 (civil society organizations) and 26 (representatives of governments and international organizations) in a number of locations, including visits with policymakers and a US government grant workshop.[7]

The Trump administration framed the event as a ministerial-level acknowledgment of the precarious state of international religious freedom and a sign of the US government's global leadership on the issue under Trump. The State Department promised:

> This event will focus on concrete outcomes that reaffirm international commitments to promote religious freedom and produce real, positive change. The Ministerial will convene a broad range of stakeholders, including foreign ministers, international organization representatives, religious leaders, and civil society representatives, to discuss challenges, identify concrete ways to combat religious persecution and discrimination, and ensure greater respect for religious freedom for all.[8]

The organizers were successful in inviting and assembling an international and ecumenical group of participants for the conference. And the substance of the day's speeches and testimonies focused on global challenges and multiple faith traditions. However, the number of foreign ministers who attended the 2018 and 2019 meetings was lower than the State Department had hoped and expected.

During the 2018 ministerial, the State Department issued the Potomac Declaration, an official statement that presented the US government's position on religious freedom as a universal human right, and the related Potomac Plan of Action. Deriving its moral force from the Universal Declaration of Human Rights (UDHR), the declaration states that religious freedom is "universal and inalienable," that "a person's conscience is inviolable," that "religious freedom applies to all individuals as rights-holders," and that defending religious freedom is the "collective responsibility of the global community."[9] The plan of action provides a detailed set of recommendations under several categories that include "advocating for equal rights and protections for all, including members of religious minorities," "responding to genocide and other mass atrocities," "preserving cultural heritage," and "promoting and protecting religious freedom and tolerance in schools."[10]

The penultimate speech of the 2018 ministerial was delivered by Mick Mulvaney, Trump's director of the Office of Management and Budget (OMB) and, from late 2018 to early 2020, also the president's acting White House chief of staff. At the end of a day of addresses by US officials and others, this speech showcased both prongs of the SOGI human rights vs. religious freedom frame: Obama administration derogation of religious persecution and affirmation of LGBT civil and human rights to the detriment of faith and people of faith. Mulvaney opened by rhetorically raising the question of why the director of OMB was addressing an international audience of religious freedom advocates. He explained that, although he had "never been a victim of religious persecution," he was introduced to the experience of religious persecution when he attended gatherings of "Catholic lawmakers" from around the world and heard some speak about their experience of being terrorized by ISIS in the Middle East. After alluding to ISIS, however, Mulvaney pivoted to "persecution [that] stops well short of life and death matters." In this vein, Mulvaney reported that people in sub-Saharan Africa had revealed to him that "our US taxpayer dollars are used to discourage Christian values in other democratic countries."

As Mulvaney explained, the Obama administration committed this assault on Christian values because of LGBT rights and the elevation of SOGI over the human right to religious security and self-determination:

> It's stunning to me that my government under [a] previous administration would go to folks in Sub-Saharan Africa and say . . . We know you have a law against gay marriage, but if you enforce that law we're not going to give you any money. That's a different type of religious persecution, and I'm not trying to put them on a moral equivalency between death and that, but that is a different type of persecution that I never expected to see. I never expected to see that as an American Christian that we would be doing that to other folks.

The charge that the Obama administration imposed same-sex marriage on unwilling countries was commonplace among Christian conservatives both before and after Trump took office, but there is no evidence that the Obama administration ever conditioned US foreign assistance on same-sex marriage or punished governments because of their failure to embrace same-sex marriage. When Uganda passed the Anti-Homosexuality Bill—dubbed by critics the "Kill the Gays Bill"—in 2014, the Obama administration did respond by redirecting funds allocated to police training and other government functions to civil society groups and banning some government officials from entering the US.[11] After falsely making the case that the Obama administration pressured Christians in Africa to accept same-sex marriage, Mulvaney reassured the international attendees "that there are many, many people in our government in both parties" who care about religious freedom. But he also framed this concern as a repudiation of the Obama administration, gesturing to "a lot of people in this government who just want to see things done differently."[12]

Taken by itself, Mulvaney's speech might be dismissed as an artifact of Christian right political messaging by a political appointee who identifies with the movement. A more illuminating way of reading the speech is by comparison with a speech delivered earlier in the day. That speaker, whose remarks are not available on the State Department website, was Patricia Davis, director of global programs in DRL. Davis informed the international guests about opportunities to partner with the State Department to support religious freedom globally. Before getting to that practical information, however, she provided information about the history and policies of DRL related to religious freedom that directly contradicts one prong of the SOGI human rights vs. religious freedom frame that Mulvaney espoused in his speech.

First, Davis described having been involved in work on behalf of international religious freedom with strong bipartisan support under Democratic and Republican administrations. Second, she offered a few key pertinent policy indicators to orient international guests on the history of US advocacy for global religious freedom. These indicators included the establishment of the Human Rights and Democracy Fund (HRDF) the annual State Department Report on International Religious Freedom, and the Country Reports on Human Rights Practices.[13] Created in 1998, the HRDF is DRL's "flagship program," a fund that "allows the U.S. to respond rapidly and decisively to democratization and human rights crises and deficits."[14] The HRDF funds a variety of programs related to human rights violations against marginalized groups, including LGBTI people and religious minorities.

The annual report on international religious freedom is a product of the International Religious Freedom Act, signed into law in 1998 by Bill Clinton. According to the State Department, the law, "placed the promotion of religious freedom as a central element of America's foreign policy."[15] The Religious Freedom Act created both the State Department's Office of International Religious Freedom (IRF) and the US Commission on International Religious Freedom. Frank R. Wolf, a former Republican member of Congress from Virginia, and longtime proponent of religious freedom, offered concluding remarks at the 2018 ministerial, and he appeared on stage with Speaker of the House Nancy Pelosi during the 2019 ministerial for a conversation about their shared commitment to religious freedom as it is defined by the UDHR.

Finally, since the 1970s, the State Department has been required to compile reports on the human rights conditions in all United Nations member states and present these country reports to Congress. For most of their history, country reports haven't captured threats, violence, and discrimination based on SOGI. Before 2010, some harms perpetrated against LGBTQ people were listed under a miscellaneous category of "Other Societal Abuses and Discrimination" for each country, but there was no required category for assessing the human rights situation of LGBTQ people. A public sign of the increased salience of SOGI human rights in the Obama administration was a revision to the country reports produced in 2010 for conditions in 2009. With these reports, the targeting of LGBTQ people was denoted in a distinct category, "Societal Abuses, Discrimination, and Acts of Violence Based on Sexual Orientation and Gender Identity."[16]

Throughout their history, the country reports have documented violations of freedom of conscience and religion. Starting in 2011, for the reports on human rights conditions in 2010, these violations began to be documented separately in the annual international religious freedom report, compiled by the Office of International Religious Freedom instead of in the country reports. Under the category of religious freedom, the country reports refer readers to the IRF report. In 2019, Secretary of State Pompeo announced that the IRF office would no longer be located in DRL and would, instead, report to the under secretary of state for civilian security, democracy, and human rights. As the Congressional Research Service reported, Pompeo understood this transfer of function within the State Department to have "elevat[ed]" the significance of the office."[17] What this brief account of human rights reporting on LGBTI and religious freedom clarifies is that, for the State Department, there is no apparent conflict between these two categories of human rights values and advocacy.

Returning to the contrast between Mulvaney's and Davis's remarks on the history of US policy, Davis directly contradicted one of the two prongs of Christian right discourse about the Obama administration on religious persecution and LGBTQ rights: that the US government under Obama was indifferent to the persecution of Christians abroad. In fact, as she made clear, there was more continuity than discontinuity in the policies and practices of the Obama and Trump administration, because the underlying policies and most of the personnel who executed them had remained the same.[18]

Davis didn't explicitly address the second prong: the zero-sum linkage the Christian conservative movement makes between Christian religious freedom and LGBTQ civil or human rights. Instead, her remarks outlined some tools that Republican and Democratic administrations have used to fund and advocate for both religious freedom and SOGI human rights.

It makes sense to infer from Davis's remarks that human rights officials in DRL don't believe that human rights for vulnerable groups of religious minorities and LGBTI people are mutually exclusive. Indeed, the record of continuity and bipartisanship in the US commitment to and delivery of assistance to persecuted people of faith contradicts Mulvaney's account of the Obama administration's preference for LGBTI human rights and lack of interest in the human rights of religious minorities. Nevertheless, in publicizing the Christian right's mendacious account of the Obama administration's antipathy to faith, Mulvaney legitimized the SOGI human rights vs. religious freedom frame and its contrast between Obama and Trump. And his remarks seemed to signal the Trump administration's openness to SOGI human rights retrenchment.

Ministerial to Advance Religious Freedom, 2019

In 2019, the Ministerial to Advance Religious Freedom expanded from its inception in 2018. This time there were two full days of plenary and concurrent sessions in the Dean Acheson Auditorium and other spaces. Meetings off-site were also scheduled for civil society organizations (CSOs), government officials, and representatives of multilateral organizations. The meeting was so well subscribed that some sessions had to be held in the nearby US Institute of Peace. Tents were erected in the north and south courtyards of the main State building for breakfast, lunch, and coffee breaks.[19]

In 2018, the conflicting positions about the approach of the State Department to SOGI and religious human rights under the Obama and Trump administrations were presented in different sessions by different speakers: one, a career State Department official, and the other, a high-ranking Republican political appointee. In 2019, a workshop on the mechanics of human rights assistance was scheduled off-site, at the US Government Printing Office, rather than as a plenary session at the State Department. However, a State Department official did contradict the Christian right narrative of the Obama administration's fecklessness toward religious freedom and persecution. Ironically, the official did so while seated next to Tony Perkins, president of the FRC and a principal expositor of the SOGI human rights vs. religious freedom frame.

The session in which this telling information was conveyed was "Monitoring International Religious Freedom," and two of the panelists on the dais were Perkins, then chair of the US Commission on International Religious Freedom, and Daniel Nadel, director of the Office of International Religious Freedom at the State Department. Nadel moderated the panel, and just as the director of global programs had done in 2018, in his remarks he directly contradicted the frame's account of an Obama administration that catered to LGBTQ people and ignored affronts to religious freedom and Christians' human rights. Nadel spoke about the attention given to religious freedom and persecution by other governments in the five years before 2019, so approximately since 2014. Nadel recalled that at that point—during Obama's second term in office—he led a staff of thirty within the State Department and that this number was greater than the total number of officials working on issues related to international religious freedom in all other foreign ministries worldwide.

The contrast Nadel drew between the early period of his tenure (during the Obama administration) and the later period (the Trump administration) had nothing to do with a greater commitment to religious freedom under Trump. Instead, the contrast was that over the course of this period of approximately five years, many other countries had joined the US in committing resources and personnel to the struggle against international religious persecution. As Nadel explained the history of the US government's commitment to international religious freedom, Tony Perkins listened politely. In his remarks, Perkins didn't challenge Nadel or repeat the set of charges he has frequently aimed at Obama, Hillary Clinton, Democrats, liberals, or LGBTQ proponents in his missives to Christian conservatives. As a result, the contradictory narratives of the Christian right and US civil servants on display in 2018, albeit in different sessions, was not highlighted in 2019. Even so, it was informative to observe that Perkins didn't seem surprised or discomfited by the history of religious freedom advocacy within the State Department that Nadel presented. I can only conclude from Perkins' reaction that the claim that US foreign policy under Obama sacrificed religious freedom for LGBTI human rights is a fabrication produced for political purposes rather than a misunderstanding of, or disagreement with, foreign policy as it was practiced under a Democratic president.

In addition to noting the quite different positions of US civil servants and partisan Christian conservatives on the question of whether the Trump administration inaugurated a US government dedication to religious freedom, a few other observations are germane to my interest in US commitments to SOGI human rights. Although all who spoke at the ministerial were proponents of religious freedom, the meeting highlighted different conceptions of human rights that were not addressed explicitly. Indeed, the fundamental comity on religious freedom on display at this international gathering likely required a tacit agreement not to probe differences on such questions as the foundations of human rights, what rights specifically qualify as "human rights," and US Christian conservatives' zero-sum conception of LGBTQ/ SOGI and Christians' human rights.

One such difference is that human rights scholars, and at least some of the invited ministerial guests, agreed that to truly be *human* rights, such rights must be universal and inalienable, indivisible, interdependent, and interrelated. That is,

> They are universal because everyone is born with and possesses the same rights, regardless of where they live, their gender or race, or their religious, cultural or ethnic background. Inalienable because people's rights can never be taken away. Indivisible and interdependent because all rights—political, civil, social, cultural and economic—are equal in importance and none can be fully enjoyed without the others.[20]

This perspective on human rights was expressed during the ministerial by Markus Grübel, commissioner for global freedom of religion of the German Federal Ministry for Economic Cooperation and Development. Speaking through a translator, Grübel asserted that there are no first- or second-class human rights—that all human rights are important and must be defended. In a likely riposte to a Hungarian official on the same panel, Grübel noted that when the German government supports the human rights of members of a community, it "support[s] *all* the people there." Of course, not all proponents of human rights agree with this conception of human rights. As became clear when Pompeo introduced the report of the Commission on Unalienable Rights, orthodox religious believers who reject human rights claims that conflict with their beliefs fundamentally disagree.

A second difference arose sporadically during the ministerial: the question of whether the human right to freedom of belief encompasses the right *not to believe* in accordance with an individual's conscience. Often overlooked in debates about religious persecution are the ways in which people who do not believe, worship, or identify with a religious tradition—PEW's "religious nones" or David S. Gutterman and Andrew R. Murphy's "religious independents"[21]—face harassment in many parts of the world.[22] Indeed, the Frank R. Wolf International Religious Freedom Act, signed into law by Obama in 2016, addresses this challenge. Although all those who addressed the audience endorsed religious freedom, and many advocated for the right of conversion to another faith, fewer speakers directly endorsed a human right not to be persecuted for rejecting religious belief altogether. Indeed, those who directly spoke to nonbelief as a fundamental human right included representatives of international organizations such as the United Nations and European Union (Ahmed Shaheed, UN special rapporteur on freedom of religion or belief, and Ján Figel, EU special envoy for promotion of freedom of religion or belief), a UK cleric (Philip Mounstephen, bishop of Truro), and two Americans, Gayle Manchin (vice chair of the US Commission on International Religious Freedom and wife of Democratic West Virginia Senator Joe Manchin) and Mark Green (then the administrator of USAID).[23]

Although dozens of speakers spoke about religious freedom, and many recounted tragic personal experiences of religious persecution, only these four mentioned that religious freedom encompasses the right to freedom *from* religion. None of the survivors of religious persecution featured as speakers had been subjected to human rights violations based on their refusal to believe or worship (as distinguished from persecution as a result of a religious conversion). Thus, the human right to be free of persecution by believers as a "religious none" was marginalized as a concern of the ministerial even though the Potomac Declaration issued by the State Department in 2018 affirmed freedom of nonbelief as a fundamental human right associated with religious freedom. It is worth reminding ourselves that Christian conservatives have consistently denied that people who affirm LGBT identity or engage in behavior consistent with nonnormative sexuality or gender identity are authentic Christians. In the face of some LGBT peoples' (and their allies') self-identification as Christian, the Christian right repudiates that profession of faith, asserting that true Christians are theologically and political conservative.[24]

Third, of the ministerial speakers, few included LGBTI people as a class persecuted for exercising fundamental human rights. But some did raise this issue in a forum dedicated to religious freedom and persecution and a panel on monitoring international religious freedom. Those who mentioned the problem of violations of the human rights of LGBTI people included Aud Marit Wiig (Norwegian special envoy for religious freedom), Lord David Alton (Liberal Democrat member of the UK Parliament), and Monique Wubbenhorst (deputy assistant administrator in USAID's Bureau for Global Health). Only one speaker, Bishop Philip Mounstephen, referenced discrimination against women and gender-based violence.

Many participants spoke of the urgent need for interfaith cooperation on matters of common concern. Unfortunately, cooperation among different Christian denominations and across faith traditions in global venues has often reflected cobelligerence, even if the parties don't invoke this framework for their joint activities. Consistent with the doctrine of cobelligerence, people who can't agree on theology have often been able to agree on the sinfulness of gender and sexual minorities; the need to punish LGBT people and women who seek bodily and reproductive autonomy; and the virtue of constraining and stigmatizing advocacy for sexual and reproductive freedoms as civil and human rights.[25]

In addition to differences in conceptualizations of human rights, one difference between the two ministerials was the greater focus in 2019 on persecuted *Christians* and *Christianity*. The 2018 ministerial was genuinely ecumenical in its attention to multiple faith traditions. By contrast, in 2019, the centrality of Christianity was prefigured when Sam Brownback took the stage for his welcome address and awkwardly referred to feeling "like a kid on Christmas." A tense moment in the proceedings occurred when the American-Israeli author Joel Rosenberg, a Messianic Jew who promotes the conversion of Jews to Christianity, spoke.[26] After Rosenberg left the stage, Brownback took the microphone to concede that many attendees might not be pleased with every speaker and that all were free to agree or disagree. Unlike in 2018, several US speakers declared the persecution of Christians throughout the world to be the worst form of persecution suffered on the basis of religious faith, and one speaker supported this claim by referring to data and analysis by the Pew Research Center.

However, the data and analysis on global religious persecution in Pew reports complicate the picture presented by these American Christian religious freedom proponents. In 2017, Vice President Pence averred in a Christian right venue that "Christians faced widespread harassment in 2015" and that Christians had been "harassed in more countries than any other religious group." But Pew's 2017 analysis from which these facts were drawn clarified that widespread persecution of Christians is a function of "the huge size and broad geographic dispersion of Christians around the world." That is, Christians constitute the largest religious group in the world and Christian populations exist throughout most of the world. What's more, approximately two thirds of countries have Christian majorities, and much Christian persecution, often state-sanctioned, takes place in these countries.[27]

An additional inconvenient fact for pro-Trump proponents of religious freedom is also provided by Pew: that global restrictions on religious practice and identity increased in 2016, and that much of the increase was driven by the rise of nationalist parties and movements—parties and movements of which Trump explicitly approved—especially in Europe.[28] Pew also surveys kinds and sources of restrictions on religion and the changing climate for religious exercise across countries. In the category, "Individual and Social Group Harassment" for the US, the Pew analysis is worth quoting at length. After considering this source of harassment in Bangladesh and Pakistan, Pew explains that

> the U.S. also ranked among the highest-scoring countries in this category in 2017, in part because of the "Unite the Right" rally in Charlottesville, Virginia, where white supremacists were protesting the removal of a Confederate statue from a park. Protesters expressed anti-Semitic and racist sentiments, displaying swastika flags and chanting "Jews will not replace us!"[29]

Again, Pew reminds us that an administration that publicly committed itself to rectifying the undeniable scourge of religious persecution allied itself with movements and regimes that foster and commit religious persecution.

Also obvious to an observer at the ministerial were encomia by US officials to Trump's personal commitment to religious freedom and ending religious persecution. The irony of these accolades was obvious when survivors of religious persecution visited Trump in the Oval Office as part of their ministerial experience. Reporters documented the president's lack of knowledge about and interest in the survivors, including a testy exchange he had with Nadia Murad, who had addressed the ministerial as a survivor of religious persecution. Murad is a Yazidi, a persecuted minority religious community in Northern Iraq, who was victimized by ISIS. As the *Washington Post* reported, Trump noted in the meeting that Murad received a 2018 Nobel Peace Prize, a recognition he had expressed interest in being awarded, and asked, "they gave it to you for what reason?"[30] As Murad explained, she was the first woman who suffered the ISIS mass rapes of Yazidi girls and women to publicly advocate for victims. As the Nobel Prize Committee put it, Murad was honored for her "efforts to end the use of sexual violence as a weapon of war and armed conflict."[31]

On a linguistic and perhaps symbolic note, with the formation of the Commission on Unalienable Rights in mind, it wasn't difficult to observe who among the ministerial speakers used the archaic word, "unalienable," to refer to human rights that aren't dependent on the political community to which citizens belong. Indeed, in defending the formation of the commission, Pompeo would distinguish between "unalienable rights" and "ad hoc rights granted by governments."[32] At the ministerial, only Secretary Mike Pompeo and Ambassador Sam Brownback—both government officials who identify with the Christian conservative movement—modified "human rights" and references to the human right to religious freedom with the term, "unalienable." Linguistically, "unalienable" is merely a variant of "inalienable" that is no longer used in American English. The use of this archaic term likely reflects the founding of the Commission on Unalienable Rights and anticipates its operation.

Commission on Unalienable Rights, Part 1

In May 2019, shortly before the 2019 ministerial, the State Department announced its intention to form a committee to advise the Secretary of State on matters related to international human rights policy. Federal advisory committees such as the Commission on Unalienable Rights don't require congressional approval; they merely require "timely notice" in the Federal Register. Consistent with the law that provides for their formation, advisory committees may not make policy. And "membership of the advisory committee [should] be fairly balanced in terms of the points of view represented."[33] Although in the ceremony marking the end of the commission's labor Pompeo lauded the committee's "broad and diverse range of membership," numerous critics pointed out that the commission didn't meet this criterion.

The explanation for the commission given in the Federal Register— that contemporary human rights discourse "has departed from our nation's founding principles of natural law and natural rights"—confirms that the title of the commission is drawn from the Declaration of Independence, which famously lists the unalienable rights to which Americans lay claim as "Life, Liberty and the pursuit of Happiness." A more sinister reading of the committee's formation suggested itself immediately: that the point of the commission's "fresh thinking" was to turn back the clock for groups, such as gender and sexual minorities, whose rights were not acknowledged at the time of the founding of the American republic.

Listed as the notice's author was Kiron K. Skinner, an academic, political appointee and, at the time, director of policy planning for the agency.[34] It quickly became apparent that the commission would provide a platform for conservative believers. Selected as chair was Harvard University's Mary Ann Glendon, Learned Hand Professor of Law at Harvard University, a former professor of Mike Pompeo, a former ambassador to the Holy See, and the author of *A World Made New: Eleanor Roosevelt and the Universal Declaration of Human Rights*. Presaging the central justification of the Commission on Unalienable Rights, Glendon noted in 2018 that "when it comes to liberal democracies, the number of rights claims is now somewhere around 1,000, and this 'cheapens the currency' " of human rights. A journalist who covered Glendon's speech and later interviewed her characterized as Glendon's position that a proliferation of rights "trivialize[s] the meaning of a right" and "also takes attention away from legitimate causes such as slavery or torture."[35]

Other members of the commission were Kenneth Anderson (Lawfare), Russell A. Berman (Stanford, Hoover), Peter Berkowitz (Stanford, Hoover), Paolo Carozza (Notre Dame), Hamza Yusuf Hanson (Zaytuna College), Jacqueline Rivers (Harvard), Meir Soloveichik (Yeshiva University), Katrina Lantos Swett (Tom Lantos Foundation for Human Rights and Justice), Christopher Tollefsen (University of South Carolina), and David Tse-Chien Pan (California, Irvine). F. Cartwright Weiland, a political appointee in the State Department's Office of Policy Planning, served as rapporteur for the commission. Robert P. George, the Princeton political philosopher whom the *New York Times* has called "this country's most influential conservative Christian thinker," was not a member; however, when the commission debuted, critics pointed out his influence.[36]

George is first coauthor of the 2009 *Manhattan Declaration*, a Christian manifesto focused on abortion (and related issues of stem-cell research and euthanasia), same-sex marriage, and religious freedom: "Because the sanctity of human life, the dignity of marriage as a union of husband and wife, and the freedom of conscience and religion are foundational principles of justice and the common good, we are compelled by our Christian faith to speak and act in their defense."[37] As scholars have noted, in this manifesto, "religious liberty" encompasses a justification of civil disobedience when people of faith are compelled to follow laws regarding, for example, marriage that violate their consciences.[38]

Other conservative intellectuals also contributed to establishing the commission's rationale, including Peter C. Myers (University of Wisconsin–Eau Claire), who in 2017 produced *From Natural Rights to Human Rights—and Beyond* for the Heritage Foundation. Anticipating the formation of the Commission on Unalienable Rights, Myers makes a case against the transition from "natural rights" to "human rights," the proliferation of rights claims, and the reliance on more recent international covenants and agreements—including the Universal Declaration of Human Rights—instead of the Declaration of Independence.[39] And in 2018, during the first Ministerial to Advance Religious Freedom, the Heritage Foundation hosted a panel discussion on "How to Protect International Religious Freedom from the Politicization of Human Rights." As Sarah Posner relates, in that forum, Benjamin Bull of the First Liberty Institute echoed the concern with human rights inflation, arguing that progressive politics relied on " 'newly manufactured human rights' to 'crush' the 'traditional' and 'natural' rights recognized by Christians."[40]

In the midst of the uproar over the founding of the commission, Secretary Pompeo defended the need for such a body in a July op-ed in the *Wall Street Journal*, "Unalienable Rights and U.S. Foreign Policy." Intended to allay concerns about the new commission and defend it as a vehicle for strengthening liberal democracy globally, the essay raises many questions. Not surprisingly, Pompeo begins with the American founding and the Constitution's assertion of the unalienable rights to "life, liberty, and the pursuit of happiness." He positions the Commission on Unalienable Rights as the contemporary manifestation of constitutional language. The essay moves quickly from the founding to the period after the end of the Cold War—essentially since 1991—when, he argues, human rights claims and justifications began to diverge from founding constitutional principles.

For Pompeo, it is in the years since the early 1990s that "new categories of rights" promulgated by "politicians and bureaucrats" have "blur[red] the distinction between unalienable rights and ad hoc rights granted by governments." In the face of the "loose talk of rights" associated with these "new categories," the commission's mandate is to return to American "founding documents" and more recent statements of principles such as the Universal Declaration. Pompeo's essay suggests two quite different objects that generate the need for such a commission: first, identity group–related human rights claims, and, second, claims for second-generation social and economic rights.

Evidence for the first category of new rights claims in Pompeo's essay include, first, the Cold War dividing line Pompeo draws—that is, these divisive rights claims have arisen or are perceived to have arisen since the early 1990s; and, second, his assertion that these claims "are often aimed at rewarding interest groups and dividing humanity into subgroups." Evidence for the second category of new rights claims consists of Pompeo's conflation of deceptive Soviet and Cuban claims to champion economic rights with a contemporary human rights "industry" that "appeal[s] to contrived rights for political advantage." Besides clarifying the rationale for the commission, Pompeo outlines his ambition for the committee's findings in a way that seems tailored to an American, or "America First," audience. This ambition is that even though the commission begins with the understanding that a "moral [US] foreign policy" must be grounded in American founding documents—namely, the Declaration of Independence and the Constitution—the commission's work will be as influential as the UDHR, transcending "party lines and national borders."[41]

After the new commission was announced in the Federal Register, numerous critics—including human rights organizations, former diplomats, and former US officials—expressed misgivings. The *Washington Post* published two editorials critical of the commission. In the first, the editors declare that "Trump should focus more on defending human rights than redefining them." The editors' statement revolves around two themes: Pompeo's concern that the US lacks a "solid definition" of human rights and the administration's willingness to speak up about "human rights abuses only sporadically," "ignoring gross violations" such as the assassination of Jamal Khashoggi at the behest of Saudi Arabia's crown prince. The editors point out that a "solid definition" of human rights "already exists" in Pompeo's own Bureau of Democracy, Human Rights, and Labor, and suggests applying the State Department's human rights expertise and principles to abuses committed by authoritarians the Trump administration seemed to want to "butter up."[42]

Two months later, after Pompeo had defended the commission in the *Wall Street Journal*, the second editorial points out that Pompeo had not yet clarified the need for the commission and characterizes the Secretary's "goals and intentions" as "murk[y]."[43] In both essays, the editors cite concerns that the commission would be a vehicle for curtailing rights of women andLGBTQ people, and they call attention to a wide range of international human rights abuses that had been condoned by the Trump administration. Later, after the commission concluded its public meetings, Rob Berschinski and Andréa Worden echoed the *Washington Post*, pointing out a paucity of interest in gross human rights violations among commissioners that mirrored the administration's interests:

> The Commission's meetings were equally noteworthy for what they didn't include: namely, reference from the commissioners to the Trump administration's steady human rights backsliding at home, coziness with dictatorships and authoritarians abroad, and assault on multilateral institutions that protect human rights and advance U.S. interests.[44]

In addition to the many concerned voices from US civil society, fifty Democratic members of Congress signed a letter to the secretary of state that demanded additional information regarding the purpose of the commission. The letter notes two particular areas of concern, denoted first by a characterization that the commission constitutes an "end run" around law, experts, and procedures; and, second, by a statement of what the signatories assume the secretary intended to accomplish through the Commission:

> We are deeply concerned that your plan to establish a Commission on Unalienable Rights is an attempt to make an end run around career experts, statutorily established State Department structures, and widely accepted interpretations of human rights law to push a narrow, discriminatory agenda that decides whose rights are worth protecting and whose rights the Administration will ignore.[45]

Despite the concerns of the House Foreign Affairs Committee and Democratic members of Congress, the commission's work proceeded. Even if the commission's findings wouldn't have direct implications for US human rights foreign policy, the secretary's politicized defense of the commission's work vindicated the concerns that motivated the members' letter to Pompeo.

Soon after the commission's founding, human rights advocates began to call meetings to discuss possible implications of the commission's formation and operation. One example is a Human Rights Campaign forum convened while the 2019 ministerial was being held at the State Department. The forum included speakers from Human Rights Watch and Advocates for Youth. Like other LGBTQ activists who have weighed in on the commission, the activists at this meeting voiced a number of arguments and concerns, including that the commission was an effort to undermine the moral authority of the UDHR; that the commission's work ran the risk of condoning human rights violations by authoritarian regimes; that the commission's work would influence not only US support for international human rights but also the space for human rights discourse within the US; that the commission was intended to empower already politically powerful groups (such as, presumably, the US Christian right); that the commission signaled a reorientation of the State Department's human rights policy and assistance; and finally, that the commission was a subterfuge to vitiate US human rights commitments to girls, women, immigrants, and LGBT people.[46]

In accordance with its mandate, the commission began to hold public meetings in October 2019. The State Department hosted five monthly meetings before the Covid-19 pandemic forced the suspension of public-facing events in March 2020. Meetings were announced in the Federal Register, and prospective attendees had to register in advance to pass through State Department security. Sessions were structured with lectures by invited guests followed by a colloquy between the guests and commission members and, finally, a question-and-answer period with the audience. The invited guest speakers who delivered remarks before meetings were suspended in March were as follows: Michael W. McConnell (Stanford), Wilfred M. McClay (University of Oklahoma), Cass Sunstein (Harvard), Orlando Patterson (Harvard), Michael Abramowitz (Freedom House), Miles Yu (State Department and US Naval Academy), Kenneth Roth (Human Rights Watch), Diane Orentlicher (American University), Martha Minow (Harvard), and Thor Halvorssen (Human Rights Foundation). Journalists, researchers, and members of civil society organizations from across the political spectrum, progressive to conservative, were among the attendees who posed questions to invited guest speakers.

If the commission tended to be asymmetrically identified with conservative and religious views on human rights, those invited to address the commission represented a range of perspectives and philosophies. Human rights scholars and advocates who would reject a philosophy of pruning ostensibly superfluous human rights might be characterized politically as feminist, liberal, or progressive. Such scholars and advocates engaged the commission and its mandate in different ways. For example, a December 2019 speaker was Michael Abramowitz, president of Freedom House, a nongovernmental organization that defends human rights and promotes democracy. Freedom House is also an implementing partner of the State Department for the Global Equality Fund.

In his remarks, Abramowitz challenged the commission directly on the possible outcomes of their project and deliberations, noting the malign historical genealogy of "America First"; the concern of many critics that the commission would recommend abridging rights, especially those of women and LGBT people; and the authoritarian practice of labeling rights and democracy as Western impositions. Abramowitz lays out his vision of what a commission on human rights *should* do, including exposing both egregious violations of human rights throughout the world and the "growing influence and power of authoritarian states." He also expressly urges the commission "not to seek out a rationale for narrowing our definition of freedom."[47]

Another approach to the commission's mandate was modeled by Glendon's Harvard Law School colleague, the 300th Anniversary University Professor Martha Minow, who addressed the commission in February 2020. Instead of the direct challenge to the commission favored by Abramowitz, Minow crafted a nuanced academic document that reminds commission members of values, precedents, and connections between rights and rights claims that some human rights proponents might be reluctant to disavow.[48] Even if, as appears likely, the result of the commission's efforts was predetermined from the start, these statements from academia and civil society provided foundations for a US commitment to human rights in the post-Trump era. The intellectual tone of the discussion between the mostly orthodox, academically trained believers on the commission and those who disputed the need for such a commission contrasts strikingly with the tone of Trump's remarks when he addressed what Christian conservatives took to be his most laudable contribution as president: religious freedom.

The 68th Annual National Prayer Breakfast

What is now known as the National Prayer Breakfast, called the Presidential Prayer Breakfast at its inception, was conceived in 1953 by Abraham Vereide, an immigrant from Norway and the founder of Goodwill Industries. Vereide, a conservative and fundamentalist, imagined the breakfast—actually, a set of meetings and meals—as a context for a gathering of "strong, Christ-centered men" from government and business. The two most prominent original participants were President Dwight Eisenhower and Billy Graham.[49]

Most Americans don't know Vereide, and many Americans probably regard the annual event as a benign political ritual. As Jeff Sharlet explains,

Vereide founded not only the National Prayer Breakfast but also the Family, a "movement of elite fundamentalism bent not on salvation for all but on the cultivation of the powerful 'key men' chosen by God to direct the affairs of our nation." The Family, or "the Fellowship," still exists, and, from Sharlet's account, has a far better claim to be regarded as a "deep state" than does the administrative state disparaged by right-wing media. The National Prayer Breakfast is the Family's "only publicized gathering." Beyond its public face, the breakfast includes networking and private meetings among public officials and powerful private citizens, Americans as well as foreigners; and "behind-the-scenes acts of diplomacy."[50]

Trump didn't create the National Prayer Breakfast, and it's likely that he understood neither its origins nor its mission. But as he did with other platforms, institutions, and fortuitous opportunities, he used the annual event for his own purposes and aggrandizement. The sixty-eighth Prayer Breakfast was held at a significant moment for Trump's political prospects. The president had been impeached on December 18, 2019, and his trial in the Senate ended in acquittal on February 5, 2020, the day before he appeared before the prominent guests at the Washington Hilton. Trump seized the moment to raise a copy of that day's *Washington Post* with the banner headline, "Trump Acquitted."[51]

Mainstream news reporting juxtaposed the president's remarks with those of keynote speaker Arthur Brooks, who preceded him. Brooks, a conservative, called upon Americans of all political persuasions to reject what he framed as a "crisis of contempt" and dedicate ourselves to "national healing" of our disdain for those with whom we disagree.[52] When he took the podium, Trump playfully repudiated Brooks's remarks and then, more seriously, turned to the impeachment trial, praising Senate Republicans for acquitting him and indirectly vilifying Representative Nancy Pelosi and Senator Mitt Romney for invoking their faith during the proceedings.

Trump's choice of the Prayer Breakfast as a venue to castigate his political opponents was a perfect illustration of Brooks's diagnosis of our collective dilemma. Given less attention was the credit Trump took for reviving religious freedom in the US and the self-congratulatory connection he drew between religious freedom in the US and internationally. Here is the relevant passage:

> As we revive our economy, we are also renewing our national spirit. Today we proudly proclaim that faith is alive and well and thriving in America. And we're going to keep it that way. Nobody will have it changed (Applause). It won't happen. As long as I'm here, it will never, ever happen (Applause).

Something which wasn't done nearly enough—I could almost say wasn't done at all—we are standing up for persecuted Christians and religious minorities all around the world— (applause)—like nobody has ever done.

Last year, at the United Nations, I was honored to be the first President to host a meeting of religious freedom. It was based all on religious freedom. That was the first meeting of its kind ever held at the United Nations. There I called upon all nations to combat the terrible injustice of religious persecution. And people listened.

And countries that we give billions of dollars to, they listened because they had to listen (Laughter). It's amazing how that works, isn't it? (Laughter). That nobody ever played that game before (Laughter).[53]

In his remarks, Trump referred to the announcement on the previous day of the International Religious Freedom Alliance, a partnership, as the charter describes it, of "likeminded countries fully committed to advancing freedom of religion or belief around the world." Describing either the announcement or the alliance itself, Trump noted that "it was something. Really something."[54]

After the president's performance, Cal Thomas, syndicated columnist, Christian conservative, and former vice president of the Moral Majority, pointed out the callous and partisan nature of Trump's remarks. Although he had been closely involved with the breakfast since the 1970s, Thomas suggested in terms consistent with his previous criticisms of Christian right politics that it "might be time to suspend the National Prayer Breakfast."[55]

Commission on Unalienable Rights, Part 2

In March 2020, Democracy Forward, "a nonprofit legal organization that scrutinizes Executive Branch activity across policy areas," filed suit over the founding of the commission and its mandate on behalf of four human rights CSOs: Robert F. Kennedy Human Rights, CHANGE, the Council for Global Equality, and the Global Justice Center.[56] Named as defendants were Mike Pompeo, Peter Berkowitz (State Department director of policy planning and commission member), and the State Department. The lawsuit accuses the defendants of "outsourcing . . . foreign policy to a group of hand-picked academics with an essentially uniform perspective on the core issue the Commission was created to examine" in violation of the Federal Advisory Committee Act. More specifically, the suit alleges that most commission members

> hold well-documented views that privilege religious liberty above all other fundamental human rights, and treat with skepticism, or outright derision, rights claims by lesbian, gay, bisexual, transgender, queer and intersex ("LGBTQI") individuals, proponents of gender parity, and women and girls seeking access to sexual and reproductive health and rights.[57]

Christian right media depicted the suit as a product of "the organized homosexual movement . . . deeply entrenched in the State Department."[58] Neither the lawsuit nor the criticisms of the commission from members of Congress, former government officials, and human rights professionals interfered with its functioning or the promulgation of its final product.

A draft of the commission's report was made public on July 16, 2020, rolled out in a ceremony held at the National Constitution Center in Philadelphia and released for public comment. Cardinal Timothy Dolan, archbishop of New York, provided an invocation before Secretary Pompeo's remarks, and Pompeo then joined his former professor, chair Mary Ann Glendon, for a conversation about the commission's work. Much can be said of Pompeo's remarks, which cynically depicted an alternative reality in which the most urgent human rights challenge facing the US was "rioters pulling down . . . monuments to those who fought for our unalienable rights." Perhaps more disturbing was the fact that Pompeo, who as secretary of state is the nation's chief diplomat and has no authority over domestic politics, had nothing whatever to say about Trump administration foreign policy decisions and affinities with implications for human rights. These include support for authoritarian regimes in Russia, Hungary, the Philippines, and Brazil, among others; the president's refusal to support the embattled government of Ukraine against Russian aggression; the president's attacks on Western allies and alliances; and his tacit support for mass human rights violations against Uighurs by the Chinese government.[59]

Like a number of conservatives before him, Pompeo decried the "proliferation of rights" that underwrote the justification for the commission and touched off concern that the commission might serve as a cover for an anti-LGBTQ and anti-women's rights foreign policy. To differentiate legitimate, fundamental rights from illegitimate ones, Pompeo asked, "Does a new rights claim that's being presented represent a clear consensus across different traditions and across different cultures, as the Universal Declaration did, or is it merely a narrower partisan or ideological interest?"[60] Such a criterion could easily point subtextually to the human rights of LGBTQ people. However, as commission members know, there is no "clear consensus" on religious freedom in practice; if there were, religious persecution would be rare and would only be committed by nonstate actors. Governments frequently hail human rights they have no intention of upholding, making what seems like a clear consensus a hollow promise. This reality would suggest that Pompeo and the commission agree on the standard for finding a human right genuine and legitimate rather than a "partisan or ideological interest": the willingness of regimes to cynically embrace a human right they have no intention of protecting.[61]

The draft "Report of the Commission on Unalienable Rights" consists of a legal-philosophical-historical narrative of the development of American human rights and positive law. Most narratives of the expansion of human rights and democratic inclusion in the US chart the extension of citizenship to groups that were not originally included in the social contract, especially Indigenous people, enslaved people, and women of all other groups. The report likewise traces this path to greater democratic inclusion for these groups. Not included in the narrative of group-based discrimination and violence are gender and sexual minorities, many of whom have been prevented from enjoying a range of fundamental rights until quite recently, especially if they were open about their status or had their status revealed involuntarily.

Indeed, only in one section does the commission address the issue of LGBTQ rights directly, and there the authors ignore a range of contentious issues and injuries that have afflicted gender and sexual minorities in the US: violence (and impunity for those who commit violence), criminalization, labor discrimination (including in government service and the military), police harassment, discrimination in family policy, designation of mental illness, and discrimination in educational institutions. Instead of gesturing to these multiple grounds that have rendered LGBTQ people as "sexual strangers" to citizenship,[62] the report briefly mentions an issue that remains salient for Christian conservatives: same-sex marriage. Targeted advocacy for same-sex marriage is relatively recent, but LGBTQ people have struggled throughout American history to overcome these many other forms of violence and discrimination, and in recent decades the Christian right has consistently opposed those efforts. Besides same-sex marriage, the other "divisive social and political controvers[y]" the commission repudiates as a human right is abortion.

I don't have space in this study to thoroughly examine the commission's findings, but I'll address one telling point here. The authors allude disparagingly to "the view that human beings are entirely explainable in terms of the physical properties of their bodies" as having "grown in popularity."[63] Just because many Americans—Christians, religious independents, and adherents of other faiths—are skeptical of the conception of ensoulment endorsed by Christian conservatives doesn't mean those Americans believe that "human beings are entirely explainable in terms of the physical properties of their bodies." Such a peculiar reading calls into question the capacity of the commission's conservatives to comprehend conceptions of humanness that reject Christian conservative beliefs but include values, beliefs, emotions, aspirations, intimacy, suffering, and commitments, all of which transcend "the physical properties of [our] bodies."

As we would expect, the commission's report was immediately praised by the FRC and other Christian conservative organizations. In July 17's Washington Update subscriber email, Tony Perkins responded to Pompeo's speech, the commission's report, and Pompeo's outreach to Christian media, including Perkins himself, with "America Finds Its Mr. Rights." There, Perkins congratulates the secretary and the commission for vindicating the search for fundamental rights by "clear[ing] the 72 years' worth of weeds that ha[ve] cropped up" since the ratification of the UDHR. What specific weeds have cropped up since 1948?

> Too many people want to bury what the Founders' believed about our God-given, unalienable rights so that they can twist the definitions into something new. Like organizations on the far-Left, who've spent the last several years cloaking their social agendas in the language of "human rights" for the purposes of global activism.[64]

The term, "human rights," in ironic quotes, links to a December 6, 2011, *New York Times* article, reported from Geneva, Switzerland, that describes the Obama administration's SOGI foreign policy and Secretary Clinton's speech in support of LGBTI human rights.[65] Perkins doesn't mention LGBT rights or official US advocacy in the text, but he clarifies for readers that the primary concern of Christian conservative allies of Trump, Pompeo, and the commission with regard to foreign policy is US support for SOGI human rights. Or, to be more specific, Perkins clarifies that the most salient issue for Christian conservatives at the time he was writing in 2020 was *the*

Obama administration's support for SOGI human rights. The cynical political utility of Perkins's and FRC's condemnation of US support for SOGI could not be more obvious.

The FRC provides two other interpretations of the commission's work for subscribers. Instead of an article, "Mike Pompeo: In His Own Words," posted on July 21, is a brief notice that introduces audio from a July 16 call between Perkins and Pompeo.[66] The conference call, dubbed "Undeniable," consists of a "special conversation" on "how pastors are essential to the promotion and protection of human rights, individual liberty, and democracy all around the world."

After Perkins introduces Pompeo by briefly describing the founding of the "nonpartisan" commission, Pompeo repeats many of his arguments from his public address earlier that day in Philadelphia, including pejorative assertions about the racial injustice protests then taking place across the US and Pompeo's characterization of State Department and foreign service officials as needing additional clarity and education to carry out human rights work most had been performing for years before Pompeo was appointed to his position. At one point, Perkins interrupts the conversation to report the results of a straw poll of pastors on the call. In response to the question "Are you concerned that Americans are losing an understanding of their fundamental rights and their importance?," one hundred percent of pastors on the call answered in the affirmative. The straw poll highlights what seems to be the point of the conversation: reinforcing a particular Christian conservative conception of religious freedom as synonymous with "founding principles."[67]

A similar domestic political goal is evident in "Lost and Founders: America's Answers in the Past," posted on July 24. The expert FRC cites on the miseducation of children is Katharine Gorka. A former *Breitbart* writer and political appointee in the Trump administration before she landed at the Heritage Foundation, Gorka is married to Sebastian Gorka who—in addition to his writing for *Breitbart*, and affinities for far-right authoritarians and neo-Nazis—was dubbed by *Foreign Policy* as a "terrible scholar."[68] After Sebastian Gorka served in the White House as a deputy assistant to the president for the first seven months of the administration, he parlayed his pro-Trump, anti-Islamic views into a close association with the Christian right, becoming a popular speaker at events such as the Values Voter Summit. In "Lost and Founders," Katharine Gorka laments progressive "group think" in civics education and identifies contemporary Christian conservatives with the religious dissidents "who came from England" to what would become the United States "in the 1500s."[69]

Human rights CSOs, LGBTQ activists and organizations, and others expressed apprehension about the Commission on Unalienable Rights at its founding and throughout its operation, even while Christian conservative organizations celebrated its formation. Most critics assumed or feared that the commission's report would serve as a pretext for the administration to terminate US support for SOGI and undermine LGBTI civil rights. It's possible that, in addition to aspiring to repair a deficiency in US foreign policy, the commission was also intended as a vehicle for projecting Christian conservative ideology to Americans. Writing for the *Bulwark*, David J. Kramer concludes on the strength of Pompeo's defenses of the commission's report that "Mike Pompeo has given up being Secretary of State."[70] Given his pugnacious defense of the commission and its findings—which, after all, were never in doubt—it may be more accurate to say that Pompeo used the commission in part to audition before the Christian right for his next elective office.

The Christian conservative search for a leader who would be up to the task of disciplining government and fulfilling the interests of the Christian right culminated in Trump. There are few ways in which Trump was consistent and predictable as president. Perhaps his most stable preference was to surround himself with admirers, sycophants, and people who excelled at using him and the opportunities he provided to advance their own fortunes, ambitions, and ideology. Not all of these appointees and close associates identify and are identified as Christian conservatives, but many do and are. And some of those who so identify were in positions that either gave them leverage over human rights foreign policy or a platform from which to broadcast—or narrowcast—alerts to audiences outside government. It's true that foreign policy hasn't been the locus of most Christian right mobilization and activism. However, the Christian conservative movement has interests in US foreign policy, especially in the areas of SOGI, women's reproductive rights, and religious freedom.

The Christian right perceived Trump's first secretary of state as an adversary to the movement's values and policy preferences, but in due course it did see one of its favorite sons installed as secretary. In chapter 3, I examine Trump's two secretaries of state using their own words. I'm interested in how both candidates communicated their values and aspirations to key constituencies, especially State Department subordinates and, for Pompeo, Christian conservatives. And I'm interested in what these values and aspirations can tell us about how US commitments to human rights—including, but not exclusively, SOGI—can be rendered precarious.

Chapter 3

The Human Rights of Tillerson and Pompeo

Who Was Minding the SOGI Store?

Straight Talks

Like some other agencies of the US government, the Department of State was led by more than one secretary during Trump's tenure in office. Confirmed a little over a week after Trump's inauguration, Rex Tillerson left his position as CEO of ExxonMobil to lead the agency. Skepticism about Tillerson's commitment to human rights arose in his Senate confirmation hearing, where his business interests in Russia precipitated questions about how he would administer US foreign policy. Human Rights Watch summed up the concerns shared by human rights civil society organizations and some members of Congress: "Rex Tillerson's reluctance to acknowledge human rights abuses by Russia, Saudi Arabia and the Philippines raises serious questions about whether he can effectively serve as secretary of state."[1]

During his brief tenure as secretary, Tillerson had a difficult relationship with Trump, and the two disagreed on some foreign policy issues. Indeed, in 2017 a frustrated Tillerson vociferously corrected Trump at a meeting at the Pentagon and then called him a "fucking moron" in front of senior military officers. When reporters inquired, Tillerson refused to confirm or deny the claim.[2] Before this contretemps, however, Tillerson addressed State Department personnel from the stage of the agency's Dean Acheson Auditorium.[3] The speech gave Tillerson the opportunity to introduce himself formally and to lay out the administration's and his own vision for the agency, its work, and its future. As with other addresses by senior government officials, the "Remarks" can be interpreted in a variety of ways. It's always possible that a more complete perspective on a public address and its reception can be obtained by viewing its delivery, either in person or by video, in addition to reading the text. This is certainly true of Secretary Tillerson's speech. As an interpreter, I highlight what I regard as significant claims, metaphors, phrases, and concepts. Relatively rare in the genre of annotations of official speeches is my focus on a physical gesture.

To no one's surprise, in March 2018, the president fired Tillerson. Nominated to replace him was Mike Pompeo, Trump's director of the Central Intelligence Agency and former member of Congress from Kansas. In testimony before the Senate Foreign Relations Committee in April, Pompeo was questioned by Senator Cory Booker (D-NJ) about his views on same-sex sexuality and marriage, and the implications of those views for his leadership of the State Department. As the *Washington Post* reported, human rights activists were concerned about what Pompeo's attitudes on same-sex sexuality might portend for human rights advocacy and LGBT people abroad.[4]

On May 1, 2018, just days after he was confirmed as Trump's second secretary of state, Pompeo addressed State Department employees from a staircase landing in the South lobby of the C Street entrance to the main State Department building.[5] Pompeo delivered his brief remarks surrounded by senior State Department officials at a stand-up meeting and then waded into the crowd, shaking hands and posing for photos with employees. Approximately two weeks later, Pompeo delivered a lengthier speech to State Department officials in the Dean Acheson Auditorium, but those remarks were never posted to the State Department website.

In this chapter, I offer my readings of Tillerson's speech to State Department personnel and specifically Christian conservative references from four sets of remarks—speeches and an interview—by Pompeo. The first reference is from Pompeo's stand-up remarks to State Department personnel. The second is from a speech Pompeo delivered in September 2018, when he became the first sitting secretary of state to address the Values Voter Summit at the Omni Shoreham Hotel in Washington, DC. The third reference, which received extensive news coverage, is from an interview in early 2019 to the Christian Broadcasting Network during an official visit to Israel. Unlike Tillerson, Pompeo appeared in Christian conservative media on several occasions, speaking in an explicitly Christian, at times prophetic, register about Trump, the administration, and his own beliefs as a "Christian leader." The fourth set of remarks I analyze are from Pompeo's formal address, "Being a Christian Leader."[6]

I anticipate questions: Why pay particular attention to Tillerson's framing of US foreign policy and his message to State Department personnel when his tenure as secretary ended abruptly in March 2018? And why focus on remarks delivered both within the State Department and within the precincts of Christian conservative institutions? My response to the first question is that different forms of leadership of US government agencies in the Trump era mattered. That is, some people tapped to be leaders in the administration presented themselves, implicitly or explicitly, as "adults in the room" whose goal was to prevent harm to US policy, political norms, or institutions. Others were selected to disable government functions, protect the president from political or criminal liability, or root out what Trump and his cronies labeled "treason" hidden within the "deep state." Investigating whether or not a secretary's stated priorities were executed—and if they weren't, why—helps us understand the processes by which human rights policies are promulgated and implemented across administrations.

With regard to the second question, since Pompeo publicly identifies with the Christian conservative movement, it's useful to evaluate public statements for signs of the secretary's outreach to the movement and for the ingroup messages such statements convey. As it has been in the past, the Christian conservative movement remains the most persistent source of anti-LGBTQ and anti-SOGI attitudes and policy advocacy within the US. Thus, it may be that outreach to and identification with this movement is a useful source of information about a leader's goals and intentions. Here again, however, investigating the ways in which a secretary's commitments as they are expressed in a variety of venues and discourses comport with policy outcomes provides researchers with essential information.

Although both of Trump's secretaries of state stimulated concerns about their commitments to human rights in general and SOGI in particular, neither terminated the policies and programs that provide resources to people who suffer human rights violations based on sexual orientation and gender identity. In this chapter, I consider Tillerson through the lens of his interpretation of US "values" and human rights. And I consider Pompeo through the lens of membership in and affinity for the Christian conservatism that provides the principal opposition to LGBTQ/SOGI human rights.

Secretary Tillerson

A corporate CEO with no government experience before he was nominated, Rex Tillerson attained the position of America's top diplomat without a record of commitment to human rights. Tillerson's lack of experience worried human rights defenders, and those concerns increased when he offered a tepid defense of a US commitment to human rights in his confirmation hearings. On March 3, 2017, Secretary Tillerson failed both to attend the public release of the *2016 Country Reports on Human Rights Practices* and to hold a press conference in conjunction with that release. His failure to place a cabinet-level imprimatur on the reports was widely reported and criticized by Democrats and some Republicans.[7] The pattern of a lack of interest in human rights continued in June 2017, when the White House budget request to Congress for fiscal year 2018 revealed the administration's plan to reduce the State Department budget by approximately one third and the budget of the Bureau of Democracy, Human Rights, and Labor (DRL) by nearly one half. The budget request, which Tillerson defended, attracted bipartisan criticism and was ignored by Congress.[8]

Although Tillerson seems to have been willing to push back against many of the president's illegal or populist impulses, he was not a reliable proponent of a US commitment to human rights. Tillerson also had few allies within the agency for his quest to "right size" the State Department and conduct a corporate-style reorganization. Thus, Tillerson was viewed warily by State Department officials and the president. He was also distrusted by Christian right elites, who knew, for example, that as president of the Boy Scouts of America, Tillerson had led the organization to admit openly gay scouts. Tony Perkins responded to Tillerson's lack of anti-abortion and anti-LGBT bona fides by declaring that he might "be the greatest ally liberals have in the Cabinet for their abortion and LGBT agendas."[9] Christian conservatives applauded when he was replaced with the former member of Congress from Kansas and director of the CIA.

One sign of Tillerson's disdain for government institutions is obvious in the speech: in May 2017, he chided State Department employees for having failed to "transition [them]selves" to the over twenty-five-year-old "new reality" of the post–Cold War world. At that time, by his own admission Tillerson was still trying to learn enough about the operations of his department to initiate a reorganization and nominate appointees to fill vacant positions.

What's That on "Our" Shoulder?

The tone and language of Tillerson's "Remarks to U.S. Department of State Employees" is casual and conversational. He characterizes it for his audience as a "chat" rather than a formal speech. To facilitate my reading of Tillerson's lengthy remarks, I divide the speech into five segments with themes the secretary alludes to early in his comments. After Greetings (paragraphs 1–3), the first substantive segment, "America First" (paragraphs 4–8), outlines the big picture of "how you translate 'America first' into our foreign policy." Next is "Our Values" (paragraphs 9–13), which offers a brief primer on balancing US values against US policies and interests. From the perspective of human rights policies, commitments, and assistance, this portion of the speech is most fruitful for deciphering the Trump administration's and Secretary Tillerson's orientation toward human rights. Segment four, the longest portion of the speech, constitutes a "quick walk around the world" that includes relations with allies and challenges in global "hot spots." Finally, in "Deliver[ing] on Mission" (paragraphs 50–61), the secretary addresses the future of the State Department and its personnel. In that section, Tillerson uses the phrase "deliver[y] on mission" eight times, a repetition that underscores the salience for him of this term of business jargon.

Tillerson begins the speech by explaining what it means to put "America first" in foreign policy. Then, from the perspective of human rights policies, commitments, and assistance, the portion of Tillerson's speech that is most fruitful for deciphering the Trump administration and the secretary's orientation toward human rights is the brief tutorial (paragraphs nine to thirteen) on balancing US values against US policies and interests. Following "America First" as it does, the concentration on "our values" is significant for the way that Tillerson exhorts US diplomats and other officials to acknowledge the difference between "our values" and "our policies." Addressing values, he asserts that "we . . . advocate for and aspire to freedom, human dignity, and the treatment of people the world over. We do." Then Tillerson gestures to his shoulder as he instructs that, even if the US acts in accordance with its interests—or policies—instead of its values, "we will always have [our values] on our shoulder everywhere we go."[10]

It's hard to mistake Tillerson's use of a very old trope: an angel (symbolizing virtue, conscience, or the sacred), on one shoulder, contending and competing with a devil (symbolizing vice, temptation, or the profane), on the other. Perhaps the earliest reference to this trope in Western Christian thought is found in the allegorical work, *The Shepherd of Hermas*, believed to have been written in the second century AD. One "commandment" offered to Hermas instructs that "there are two angels with a man—one of righteousness and the other of iniquity" and offers guidance as to how to recognize these "two spirits . . . and how to distinguish the suggestions of the one from those of the other." The Christian can recognize these angels by their fruits, that is, by what path the angels encourage once they have "ascend[ed] into your heart." The "angel of righteousness is characterized by "righteousness, purity, chastity, contentment and . . . every righteous deed and glorious virtue." Marks of the "angel of iniquity," on the other hand, include "anger," "harshness," "overreaching," "pride," and "blustering," as well as "a longing after many transactions, and the richest delicacies, and drunken revels, and divers luxuries, and things improper, and by a hankering after women."[11]

In other words, the angels represent traditional Christian (im)morality, but they also represent self- or other-directed impulses and behavior. *The Shepherd* and other examples of the genre acknowledge that the capacity for virtue and vice are within each person—that the boundary between good and evil runs through the self and not, for example, between groups.[12] In that respect, the trope of shoulder angels must be translated from one level of analysis, the individual, to the level of the state to be employed, as Tillerson uses it, for the purpose of contrasting US values with US interests.

We might wonder whether Tillerson called on this Christian legacy of good and wicked angels on "our" shoulders in his speech deliberately, perhaps even to persuade Christians about his intentions for US foreign policy. I suspect not. It's more likely that Tillerson reached for the trope because of the ways in which it's been secularized, and even parodied, in popular culture. The trope has been common in American films for many decades, at times—as in the 1978 film, *Animal House*—imbued with graphic and potentially malign sexual humor.[13] The animated television feature *Family Guy* has deployed Peter Griffin's "shoulder" angels and devils when Peter confronts a moral dilemma.[14] Interestingly, in both *Animal House* and *Family Guy*, the shoulder devil manifests on the character's right shoulder, while the angel manifests on the character's left. This is a reversal of the historical identification of the right hand with virtue and the sacred, and the left hand with vice and the profane.[15] However, this apparent reversal may merely take into account the difference between actor/character and audience perspective. An actor's stage right is the audience's house left, and an actor's stage left is the audience's house right; thus, the viewer's perspective places the angels where they belong by virtue of long precedent.

In his speech, Tillerson facilitates his audience's grasp of the shoulder angel/devil trope by tapping his left (the viewer's right) shoulder with his left hand to locate "our values" and his right shoulder with his right hand to locate "our policies." Of course, another explanation is that Tillerson signals a transvaluation of values by identifying "our policies" with the sacred and "our values" with the profane. The text of the speech does nothing to dispel this possibility.

THE BUSINESS OF FOREIGN POLICY

Throughout his remarks, Tillerson relies on clichés to make points about US foreign policy and its reorientation under Trump. Some of these are just general cultural clichés, and others emerge from, or are related to, business management. General clichés include, in paragraphs 6 and 7 ("America First"), ruminations on "balance": the State Department having "kind of lost track of how we were doing," "things got a little bit out of balance." Again, "things have gotten out of balance," and "we've got to bring them back into balance." In particular, on trade, "things have gotten a little out of bounds . . . a little off balance," and the goal is "to bring that back into balance."

A more specific recurring trope involves variations on the phrase "deliver [or delivery] on mission" (variations of which appear in paragraphs 51 and 54–57). Tillerson's language here is business jargon that may be rendered as the exhortation to "deliver your mission" or "deliver on your mission." He seems to assume that the agency's staff will either recognize this business jargon or infer its meaning from the contexts in which he uses it. He also seems to be well aware of the cognitive effects of repetition in enhancing the persuasiveness of messaging.[16] Even so, it's worthwhile to recall that Tillerson is addressing officials who support human rights policies and programs, urging them to deliver on their mission. Mere months later, the White House forwarded to Congress a budget request for the next fiscal year that would have halved funds for international human rights programs.

WHO WE ARE VS. WHAT WE DO

In the speech, Tillerson contrasts the values we passively "have" that define who we are as a nation and the actions we engage in that are consistent with our interests. For example, noting that just because we don't condition foreign policy on other countries adopting our values

> doesn't mean that we leave those values on the sidelines. It doesn't mean that we don't advocate for and aspire to freedom, human dignity, and the treatment of people the world over. We do. And we will always have that on our shoulder everywhere we go [Tillerson touches his left hand to his left shoulder].

Another speech by a secretary of state provides a vivid contrast with Tillerson's doctrine that human rights violations shouldn't prevent the US from making deals and alliances: Secretary of State Hillary Clinton's "Remarks in Recognition of International Human Rights Day," delivered in Geneva on December 6, 2011. In her speech, Clinton presents a US posture of persuasion rather than coercion, but she is clear that the Obama administration was committed to upholding the fundamental human rights of LGBTI people. She also explicitly drew the distinction between holding beliefs that some people, such as gender and sexual minorities, should not enjoy the same rights and protections as others and being free to act on those beliefs with impunity.[17]

Taken as a whole, Tillerson's speech reveals a perspective that's unapologetically transactional and instrumental. Unfortunately for Tillerson, neither his framing of US interests against US values nor the administration's bid to reduce the budget of the Bureau of Democracy, Human Rights, and Labor by half was embraced by the State Department officials and members of Congress he was trying to persuade. For these reasons and others, many State Department personnel welcomed Tillerson's departure and the confirmation of Michael Pompeo to lead the agency.

Secretary Pompeo

Mike Pompeo's confirmation as secretary of state was met with enthusiasm by two groups. The first group was State Department officials who were demoralized by Tillerson's corporate approach and lack of interest in diplomacy and human rights. When he arrived at the agency, State Department officials perceived Pompeo as an anti-Tillerson. Although observers noted of his tenure that his advocacy was situational—dependent on Trump's idiosyncratic foreign policy alliances—Pompeo cast himself as a proponent of human rights. The second group that welcomed Pompeo's arrival was Christian conservatives.[18]

However, from the beginning of his tenure, LGBTI advocates identified Pompeo as a potential threat to US support for SOGI human rights and carefully scrutinized the agency for signs that SOGI policy was in a parlous state. In the next chapter, I address in more detail the symbolic gestures related to SOGI that the State Department continued to make under Pompeo and the substantive SOGI policies and practices that the agency continued to undertake.[19] But here I look carefully at the Christian conservative–directed messaging that Pompeo personally disseminated during his tenure as secretary.

From the beginning, Pompeo spoke directly to Christian conservatives even when he might not have appeared to be doing so to those outside the parameters of the movement. Of course, I assume, as most Christian conservatives do not, both that the meanings of scriptural phrases have evolved and adapted to changing circumstances over time, and that they've become fixed through repetition by elite opinion leaders and followers. By contrast, Christian conservatives tend to subscribe to the ideal of a literal reading of God's word. So persuasive is Christian conservatives' conviction that they have no choice but to follow the clear meaning of scripture on every issue that perhaps most who identify with the movement agree to regard the Bible as having only one meaning: the "literal" reading sanctioned by trusted moral entrepreneurs on the Christian right. The problem, as Randall Balmer points out, is that this "literalism" is "selective," identifying objects of outrage and activism by way of moral disapproval and political expediency rather than through a singular, authoritative reading of biblical texts.[20]

A feature of Christian conservative political pedagogy with followers is biblical flexibility. Moral entrepreneurs select proof texts and related arguments that function to rationalize particular policies, positions, critiques, and leaders that Christian right elites hold out to followers and characterize either positively or negatively. At times, the utility of these proof texts and arguments becomes visible as elites select new texts and rationales when political conditions change. With regard to my interpretation of these texts, I concede that it's not possible for any interpreter to ensure that particular deployments of biblical phrases have only one meaning for all possible recipients. However, I argue that as biblical phrases come to hold specific politicized meanings for Christian conservatives, their use by conservative policymakers and political appointees is deliberate, not accidental.

Because Trump wasn't personally adept at speaking to Christian followers directly using quotes, tropes, and lyrics from the archive of Christian—especially Protestant—worship, he had to rely on Christian right elites to do so on his behalf. By contrast, George W. Bush and those around him were fluent in this language. Consider an example of a debate over this kind of communicative process in the presidency of Bush, a leader who was known for his faith and public witness. In late 2004, Bush speechwriter Michael Gerson spoke to journalists from national media outlets during a Florida conference on religion and politics sponsored by the Pew Forum and the Ethics and Public Policy Center. Responding directly to charges that Gerson seeded Bush's speeches with "code words" meant to communicate exclusively with evangelical Christians, Gerson addressed the issue of biblical references in the speeches: "They're not code words; they're our culture. It's not a code word when I put a reference to T. S. Eliot's 'Four Quartets' in our Whitehall Speech; it's a literary reference. Just because some people don't get it doesn't mean it's a plot or a secret."[21] This comparison between literary and religious allusions might have been persuasive if those to whom literary allusions speak and those to whom Christian religious allusions speak were politically equivalent groups. However, as Gerson knew, they were not. To this day, there is no significant English major constituency in the Republican Party that would discern meaning from the deployment of figurative language in *The Waste Land*.

Contemporary Christian conservative appointees like Mike Pompeo are fluent in politicized Christian rhetoric even if Trump is not. Indeed, when it came to Trump, Christian conservative elites worked to project scriptural and prophetic meanings onto his acts and speech. They performed this function in a variety of ways, from identifying Trump with multiple biblical figures to constructing post hoc biblical justifications for Trump's improvisational rhetoric. Today, distinguishing himself from Trump's myriad Christian conservative apologists, Gerson is an eloquent critic of Trump and of the process by which Christian conservative elites have debased their faith by reading scriptural and prophetic meaning into his utterances.

In the following analysis, a key phrase in the initial remarks by which Pompeo introduced himself to his new subordinates at the State Department is "standing in the gap." From his September 2018 speech to the Values Voter Summit, there is Pompeo's allusion to hiding one's light under a bushel. From his interview in Jerusalem with the Christian Broadcasting Network, there is Pompeo's concurrence with the interviewer's assessment of Trump having been elevated by God to the presidency "for such a time as this." Although there is no one key phrase in Pompeo's "Being a Christian Leader" speech that communicates special political meaning to Christian conservatives, I find some items of interest there as well. In what follows, I take each of these public communications in turn, explicating what meanings Pompeo likely conveyed to his ideal audience of Christian right leaders, activists, and ordinary Christian conservatives.

STANDING IN THE GAP

The optics of the introductory speeches by Trump's two secretaries of state are quite different. After Pompeo concludes his brief remarks, we see the officials standing in close quarters with Pompeo on the "stage"—the

State Department South lobby's high staircase landing—continue to clap enthusiastically for several seconds after the applause of the group below has subsided. We see Pompeo bypass security officers at the foot of the staircase and walk through the crowd greeting attendees. Unlike Tillerson's more complete foreign policy exposition delivered to an audience of seated officials, Pompeo's brief "stand-up" remarks were mostly vague boilerplate. The text was quickly posted to the State Department website.[22]

What interested many readers of Pompeo's address to his State Department subordinates was the promise that under his leadership the agency would be "getting back [its] swagger." CNBC reported "loud applause from hundreds of staffers" at the line but cautions that "U.S. diplomats are taught . . . to be understated rather than overbearing, given U.S. economic and military might. 'I have not heard anyone say: This is awesome. Thumbs up. Fist bump,' one agency official said of Pompeo's swagger campaign. 'No.' "[23]

For a student of Christian conservative beliefs and politics, a more striking locution in Pompeo's remarks comes at the very beginning, when he thanks then Deputy Secretary John J. Sullivan, who has just introduced him, "for [his] service and *standing in the gap*." In context, it appears that Pompeo thanks Sullivan for serving as acting secretary during the period between Tillerson's departure and Pompeo's Senate confirmation. However, the reference to "standing in the gap" introduces excess meaning to what would otherwise be a pro forma expression of gratitude to Sullivan for temporarily leading the agency. The reference is from Ezekiel 22:30–31:

> And I sought for a man among them, that should make up the hedge, and stand in the gap before me for the land, that I should not destroy it: but I found none.
>
> Therefore have I poured out my indignation upon them; I have consumed with the fire of my wrath: their own way have I recompensed upon their heads, saith the Lord God. (KJV)

The speaker in Ezekiel 22 is God, who has searched for a man morally pure enough to intercede between a noxiously corrupt Jerusalem and God's judgment. As in other Old Testament stories, including the one that relates the vile sinfulness surrounding Abraham in Sodom, there are too few men virtuous enough to persuade God to stay his wrath.

Many contemporary US Christians associate the phrase, "stand[ing] in the gap," with intercession: praying for another or on behalf of another. Christians often offer to "stand in the gap" for others in times of personal need or announce that they are "standing in the gap" for a loved one who may be so reprobate as to fail to recognize that such intercession is necessary. However, Christian conservatives also frequently understand themselves as "standing in the gap" for a sinful nation that refuses God's laws and grace. Indeed, in ingroup discourse they often suggest that it is the role of biblical Christians to stand in the gap for America until with God's assistance they are able to bring the nation into submission and govern it by punishing forms of sinfulness and immorality, especially sexual sins.

Consider the Christian author Stormie Omartian, the author of a book franchise that highlights the phrase, protected by registered trademark "The Power of a Praying." The franchise includes 2002's *The Power of a Praying Nation*, a response to the attacks of September 11 that integrates cultural and political critique with personal and spiritual prescriptions for avoiding future catastrophic episodes of divine judgment on the United States. Omartian was one of many Christian conservatives who attested that September 11 was God's response to immorality in America: "The things we tolerate in our nation that break the heart of God."[24] In October 2017, Omartian posted a prayer to Facebook entitled "Standing in the Gap for Our Nation" that included this passage: "I lift up my nation to You, with all its sin and rebellion, and ask that You will have mercy upon us and help us not reap the full consequences of what we have sown. I stand in the gap to invoke Your power on our behalf."[25]

A current example of this deployment of the phrase is in the mission statement of the American Pastors Network (APN): "Standing in the Gap for Truth." The APN is a Christian conservative organization founded by Sam Rohrer, a former Republican member of the Pennsylvania House of Representatives. While the APN defines itself as a nonpartisan organization, APN's account of its mandate is readily recognizable as politically conservative and anti-LGBTQ. The organization describes itself as "a network of biblical and faith based pastors and church liaisons whose objective is to build a permanent infrastructure of like-minded pastors" with goals that include "affirm[ing] the authority of scripture" and "encouraging" informed biblical thinking about contemporary social issues.[26] The APN sponsors a podcast entitled "Stand in the Gap" that features discussions of faith and family as well as social and political issues. Appearing on the podcast in July 2019, former US representative Michele Bachmann declared Trump to be the "most biblical president ever," a description she repeated in Washington, DC, at the 2019 Values Voter Summit.[27]

The "gap" invoked in Ezekiel 22 is a location between an angry, venge-ful God and the people who have rejected him in favor of wickedness. It's possible that Pompeo's use of the phrase was reflexive—a product of long use in religious circumstances such as the Sunday school classes he often mentions teaching. It's possible that Pompeo alluded to Sullivan holding the post of secretary until Pompeo could assume the position and begin to transform the aims and culture of the State Department in a more moral or biblical direction. It's also possible that Pompeo used this charged phrase deliberately to signal to the Christian right a set of specific theopolitical intentions that he might or might not have expected to fulfil.

Our Light under a Bushel

After the announcement that Mike Pompeo would succeed Tillerson, the Christian right expressed satisfaction with the choice and excitement about the possibilities it portended in ingroup messaging and a press release.[28] In September 2018, Pompeo became the first sitting secretary of state to address the Values Voter Summit, the premier Christian conservative activist con-ference, in its thirteen-year history. The crowd of values voters, accustomed to being addressed by members of Congress, media personalities, governors, and other famous Christian conservatives, lavished Pompeo with applause.

Most of Pompeo's speech centered on "religious freedom as a God-given human right" and threats to religious freedom throughout the world. The summit was being held not long after the State Department sponsored the first international Ministerial to Advance Religious Freedom, hosted by Pompeo and Ambassador Sam Brownback, which brought together religious leaders and survivors of religious persecution. Summit attendees responded enthusiastically when Pompeo recounted Trump administration successes in repatriating imprisoned Christians from North Korea and Turkey. He also addressed the challenges to freedom of religious exercise confronting Muslims, Baha'is, and Zoroastrians in Iran.

Most of the phrasing of Pompeo's speech relied on public discourse, some drawn from Christian natural rights concepts, including "God-given rights" and religion as "the"—not a—"fundamental freedom."[29] However, Pompeo offered a biblical phrase to argue that Christians shouldn't conceal or fail to act in accordance with their faith, especially when many people in the world lack the freedom to exercise theirs: "I urge each of you to *never hide [that belief that we have] under a bushel.*" We first encounter the

exhortation to Christians not to hide their light under a bushel in Jesus's
Sermon on the Mount, recorded in the New Testament book of Matthew,
5:14–16:

> Ye are the light of the world. A city that is set on an hill cannot
> be hid.
>
> Neither do men light a candle, and put it under a bushel,
> but on a candlestick; and it giveth light unto all that are in
> the house.
>
> Light your light so shine before men, that they may see your
> good works, and glorify your Father which is in heaven. (KJV)

Other versions of the metaphor can be found in Mark 4:21–23 ("Is a candle
brought to be put under a bushel, or under a bed? And not to be set on
a candlestick?") and in Luke 8:16–18 ("No man, when he hath lighted a
candle, covereth it with a vessel, or putteth it under a bed; but setteth it
on a candlestick, that they which enter in may see the light").

The image of a "light" or "lamp" hidden under a bushel [basket]
has become a common secular metaphor for hiding one's talents. Indeed,
Merriam-Webster defines the phrase "hide your light under a bushel" as "to
not tell others about one's talents, successes, [and] ideas"[30] Children in many
Christian churches have learned the trope by singing Harry Dixon Loes'
nearly one-hundred-year-old song "This Little Light of Mine," in which the
singer promises to "let it shine, let it shine, oh let it shine."[31] Americans
who came of age in the 1960s and 1970s may also associate the trope of
hiding—or refusing to hide—one's light under a bushel with the gleeful
irreverence of Stephen Schwartz's Broadway musical *Godspell*—in particular,
with the first verse of "Light of the World."

The second verse of "Light of the World" invokes the biblical exhortation to be "the salt of the earth."[32] And, indeed, Christians associate the
divine charge not to hide their light under a bushel with the verses that
precede it in Matthew 5:11–13:

> Blessed are ye, when men shall revile you, and persecute you,
> and shall say all manner of evil against you falsely, for my sake.
>
> Rejoice, and be exceeding glad: for great is your reward in
> heaven: for so persecuted they the prophets which were before you.
>
> Ye are the salt of the earth: but if the salt have lost his
> savour, wherewith shall it be salted? It is thenceforth good for

nothing, but to be cast out, and to be trodden under foot of men. (KJV)

From these verses in Matthew, Christian conservatives derive the injunction to be salt and light, in personal relations as well as in politics: to influence the world in ways that God commands. The phrase is a common one among Christians of different traditions and denominations.

But the phrase has taken on a particular significance for Christian conservatives as shorthand for taking back American culture and government in ways that students of US religion and politics have associated with Christian Reconstructionism and dominionist theology. Although Reconstructionism and dominionism have received a great deal of attention from students of religion and politics in recent years, in 1989 Sara Diamond identified the doctrine of Reconstructionism as providing a "proto-theory behind Christian Right activism." Reconstructionism is a key foundation of dominion theology, which teaches that "Christians are Biblically mandated to 'occupy' all secular institutions," a view Diamond identifies as "the *central unifying ideology* for the Christian Right."[33] In her more comprehensive study of Reconstructionism, Julie Ingersoll offers ethnographic and archival evidence that attests to the ways in which Reconstructionism and dominionism have shaped the political and theological commitments of the mainstream Christian right. And these commitments can be traced through many Christian right political projects and organizations.[34]

Returning to the American Pastors Network, the organization lists its goals as "affirm[ing] the authority of scripture," "tak[ing] seriously Jesus' command to be 'salt and light' to the culture," and "encourag[ing] informed Biblical thinking about contemporary social issues." Addressing the social and political issues that necessitate the formation of a national network of pastors, the APN website explains:

> We know it comes as no surprise to you that today our society is struggling morally and spiritually. You've seen the constant battle—the family's fight for its very soul. The attack on our culture is underway and the truth is, when God's people repent of their sins and return to biblical obedience (II Chron. 7:13–14), God will hear our prayers and heal our land. . . . As you are well aware, in today's cultural climate, it is a daunting task to be [a] church leader, and to maintain the resources to assist families struggling against such issues as deteriorating traditional marriage,

pornography, rampant sexual permissiveness, the undermining of a biblical worldview in our public schools, abortion and other evils that seek to destroy the core teachings of our Christian faith.[35]

Among the many organizations, initiatives, and projects launched by and for Christian conservatives in recent years are many "prayer projects" that deliver political information and interpretation, and position believers to serve as "prayer warriors" for causes and public policies advocated by the Christian conservative movement.[36] One project that fulfills this function but goes beyond it to explicitly mobilize Christian conservative activism is the Salt and Light Council. The Salt and Light Council describes itself as a "Biblical citizenship ministry" that "train[s]" and "equip[s]" church members to "impact the culture in America for Christ and reverse the godless elements in media, education and government." Having as its "mission field" US culture and civil government, the council invites Christians to "rediscover . . . the joy and privilege of being a citizen of the United States—under God—and preserv[e], as salt does, our Judeo-Christian heritage." The organization endorses clerical hierarchy by insisting that trainees receive permission of their pastor for affiliating with the group.[37] Attendees of Christian conservative activist conferences are familiar with the Salt and Light Council as one of many Christian conservative organizations that offers information and recruits participants at booths in conference exhibit rooms.

Pompeo opened his speech to the values voters by referring to critics of his decision to address a partisan political event hosted by Christian conservatives or, in Pompeo's words, "some folks who didn't want me to come here today." Pompeo also tacitly endorsed the SOGI human rights vs. religious freedom social movement frame of Christian right discourse—that the Obama administration neglected universal religious freedom in favor of LGBTQ human rights—in terms the audience would have understood from long familiarity with Christian right discourse:

> *This* State Department, under President Trump, is fighting to make sure that American citizens and American interests come first in our foreign policy [applause]. At the very heart of our mission is the preservation of human dignity. And *this* administration understands an eternal truth: that each person has an essential worth simply because he or she is human and has been created by God.[38]

When he finished speaking, Pompeo received a standing ovation from the values voters. Taking the stage as Pompeo departed, Gil Mertz, assistant to Family Research Council president Tony Perkins and sardonic longtime event emcee, noted a double standard on the part of the Christian conservative movement's adversaries: while prominent Democrats address abortion and gay rights groups, they did not consider it appropriate for Pompeo to breach what those critics understand to be the separation of church and state to address a Christian conservative gathering.

For Such a Time as This

In March 2019, Pompeo attracted a great deal of media attention when, during a trip to Israel that coincided with the Jewish holiday of Purim, he offered an exclusive interview to journalists from Christian Broadcasting Network News, a branch of the network founded by televangelist Pat Roberts. During that interview, Pompeo was asked, "Could it be that President Trump right now has been sort of raised *for such a time as this*, just like Queen Esther, to help save the Jewish people from the Iranian menace?" In reply, Pompeo ventured that Trump might, indeed, have been raised up by God, like Esther, for such a time as this.[39] The interview clearly surprised American reporters and others outside the ambit of the Christian right. In its reporting, the *New York Times* took the high road with the title, "The Rapture and the Real World: Mike Pompeo Blends Belief and Policy," while the *Washington Post* took the path of headshaking humor with "Holy Moses, Mike Pompeo Thinks Trump Is Queen Esther."[40]

How did Trump become Esther? Many journalists and researchers have noted what they regard as the ironies inherent in the imperturbable support of Christian conservatives for Donald Trump. That support was not in place when Trump announced his candidacy for president in a race with several other prominent Christian conservative contenders. However, as support for Trump grew during the presidential campaign, some Christian right moral entrepreneurs and believers began to identify him with Esther, the progenitor of the Jewish festival of Purim whose story is related in the book that bears her name. In the story, the orphaned Esther becomes the wife of the Persian king Xerxes I, during a time when the diasporic Jews of Persia are threatened by a genocide planned by the king's close advisor. Queen Esther's cousin, her guardian, challenges her to plead her peoples' case to her husband, suggesting that perhaps she had been elevated to her position "for such a time as this" (Esther 4:14). At some risk to herself, she complies, revealing not only the plot but her own Jewish identity. The king's advisor is executed, and the Jewish people are saved.

Trump isn't the first Esther president. At times, Christian conservatives identified George W. Bush with Esther. Especially after the September 11 attacks, Christian conservatives frequently noted among themselves that Bush was "heaven sent" to deal with the nation's dilemmas and direct it back to God.[41] Just because Trump is Esther, however, doesn't mean he cannot also be other biblical kings, if not queens. Indeed, Trump has been identified with a number of biblical figures besides Esther, including Cyrus, Nebuchadnezzar, Samson, and David.[42] At times, Christian conservatives have also identified him with Jesus, and Trump has referred to himself as "the chosen one." Indeed, biblical rationales for the Trump presidency and denunciations of the moral wickedness of Americans who disapprove of Trump have produced the mobile and flexible identifications of Trump that students of the Christian right have collected since 2016.

In these identifications we see that biblical rationalizations may shift under changing political conditions or may remain in the movement's ideological inventory, available for use whenever they are most appropriate. The sociologist Mary Jackman characterizes ideas that are "the property of the group" and that "gain or lose currency according to their efficacy in meeting the political need of the moment" as "ideological baggage."[43] In the case of Pompeo's CBN News interview, the equation of Trump with Esther during Purim had already been made by Israeli prime minister Benjamin Netanyahu, a Trump ally whose political interest was served by depicting Trump in heroic and prophetic terms.

Being a Christian Leader

Finally, another controversy erupted in 2019 over Pompeo's decision to deliver a speech on "Being a Christian Leader" to a Christian conservative organization and then have that speech posted to the Department of State website.[44] The speech itself is mostly anodyne and, although Pompeo embeds Bible verses in the text to make his points, the verses he quotes haven't been politicized in ways that would constitute a hidden transcript for Christian conservative listeners.[45] The absence of such an ingroup political messaging doesn't, however, imply that nothing useful can be said of the "Christian Leader" speech, either as commentary on Pompeo's vision of leadership or on the SOGI human rights vs. religious freedom frame.

The speech is structured around Pompeo's recognition of the importance of, and adherence to, three *d*s of leadership: disposition, dialogue, and decisions (paragraph 8). Across multiple explications of the criteria he outlines, the leader who emerges in the speech bears little resemblance to Trump's secretary of state. Pompeo defines the first *d*, disposition, through a question: "How is it that one carries oneself in the world?" In addition to other traits that might distinguish a Christian leader, Pompeo's conception of "disposition" encompasses humility and truth-telling. No leader who aspires to demonstrate virtuous character traits will succeed all the time, and all leaders will fail at times to live up to their own standards. But Mike Pompeo's failures to live by his own standards seemed to become more frequent and calculated over time.

One of these was Pompeo's use of scripture to smear and retaliate against a journalist he saw as an adversary. In January 2020, NPR reporter Mary Louise Kelly reported that Pompeo berated her after an interview in which she had asked him about Trump and Ukraine. Pompeo accused Kelly of unprofessional conduct and lying about the fact that she intended to ask him about Ukraine, tweeting, "Whoever conceals hatred with lying lips and spreads slander is a fool" (Proverbs 10:18). The subsequent examination of emails between Kelly and Pompeo's office confirmed Kelly's position and exposed Pompeo as a truculent liar.[46]

The "Christian Leader" speech is revealing in other respects as well. Pompeo uses a crowd-pleasing analogy whose empty comparator invites listeners to fill in an insult toward Washington, DC, the federal government, the State Department, the media, or some other entity that Trump allies might liken to fifth graders:

> But back—Susan and I have been—had Christ at the center
> of our lives. Back in my church in Wichita I was a deacon.
> She and I taught fifth grade Sunday School, which was a great,
> great lesson for my time as Secretary of State. (Laughter and
> Applause.) (paragraph 12)

Pompeo's earnest exposition of his relationship to his subordinates certainly rings false after the information Americans learned about the secretary's treatment of Marie Yovanovitch, US ambassador to Ukraine from 2016 to 2019:

> The people who work for me know this, too: I have high standards for excellence. I hold them accountable and give them

authority. I hold myself to that high set of standards because there is so much riding on what we do to keep the American people safe that we can't accept anything less. (paragraph 20)

But when there is failure, when the people close to me misfire, I don't strip away their responsibilities. I don't cut them out of meetings. I keep them in the fold. I keep giving them important work. That's what Christ does for us; we have an obligation to do the same. (paragraph 21)

Yovanovitch was removed from her post in Kyiv in May 2019 at the behest of the president, because he perceived her as an obstacle to his plan to coerce Ukrainian president Zelensky to announce an official inquiry into Vice President Joe Biden. Current and former State Department officials tried to prevail upon Pompeo to defend Yovanovitch from Trump and his agents' mendacious campaign against her, and Democratic senators implored him to protect Ambassador Yovanovitch from "political retaliation" for discharging her responsibilities.[47] Pompeo declined to do so.

From the perspective of interest in the Trump State Department's orientation on SOGI human rights policy and practices, the most important passage of Pompeo's "Christian Leader" speech is his comparison between Trump and "previous administrations" on protecting religious freedom. Here Pompeo offers a somewhat softened version of the first prong of the SOGI human rights vs. religious freedom frame. Attributing the contrast with Trump on dedication to global religious freedom to "previous administrations," Pompeo nevertheless indirectly invokes the charge that Obama (Clinton, Democrats, liberals, and progressives) deliberately refused to undertake the urgent task of protecting religious freedom:

This administration has spoken to the truth in many ways that previous administrations haven't done. (Applause.) For example, on China's rule-breaking and authoritarianism; for example, on why the Islamic Republic of Iran is an aggressor, not a victim; for why, in fact, we know in our hearts that America is a force for good in the world. (Applause.) (paragraph 30)

Here, Pompeo accurately cites China and Iran as examples of countries that commit human rights violations while remaining silent about decisions he made to disregard human rights considerations in US foreign policy.

For example, Pompeo supported US arms sales to Saudi Arabia for its war in Yemen after Saudi agents assassinated Jamal Khashoggi in their country's consulate in Istanbul, Turkey. Doing Trump's bidding, Pompeo pursued an emergency declaration process that "bypass[ed] Congress" to complete the sale. He also bypassed officials in DRL who, in other administrations, would have consulted on the human rights implications of the transaction and who are familiar with the faulty human rights record—including on religious freedom—of the Saudi Kingdom.[48] When Trump fired State Department inspector general Steve Linick on Pompeo's recommendation in May 2020, Linick was investigating both the suspicious arms sale process and Pompeo's alleged misuse of government personnel to perform personal tasks.[49] Of course, much more could be said of Pompeo's decision to cast himself as a Christian leader and the disjunctions between the conception of leadership he described and the one he practiced.

Different Blokes for Different Folks

Policies and practices such as SOGI human rights assistance for LGBTQI people whose human rights are threatened may be executed or undermined in a variety of ways for different reasons. As we saw in policy areas such as reproductive rights and climate change in the Trump administration, leaders can matter, either upholding or undermining policies and practices. Elise Carlson Rainer points out that, as models of policy continuity would predict, SOGI human rights policies and programs have been characterized more by continuity than by disruption between the Obama and Trump administrations.[50] Because policies can be revoked or quietly undermined—including by defunding, personnel attrition, and the refusal to nominate officials to key posts—it is worthwhile to closely examine the contexts in which policy change or continuity occurs.

As secretaries, Tillerson and Pompeo demonstrated many differences in areas that might be relevant to SOGI human rights policies and practices. First, they had different visions of the role of the State Department in the administration. Second, the two secretaries used different rhetorical models of leadership. And, third, the divergent priorities of Tillerson and Pompeo present different ways in which a US commitment to SOGI could be diminished or undermined.

As secretary, Tillerson's corporate vision consisted of "right-sizing" the agency and elevating US interests over US values. The first half of this vision required a downsizing and reorganization of the State Department that was to be effected in part by slashing the 2018 State Department budget by one third from its Obama-era funding. The second half of this vision Tillerson expressed explicitly in his remarks to State Department personnel and indirectly through his support for halving the budget of DRL, which implements human rights policies and programs. Members of Congress, including some Republicans, pushed back forcefully against the administration's plan and used their appropriations power to increase the State Department budget and demand that human rights programs not be excised.[51]

Although Pompeo was perceived from the beginning of his tenure as the executor of Trump's foreign policy preferences, he was circumspect about outlining his own vision, with the exception of frequently touting "human dignity." However, something like a vision of the role of the agency emerged piecemeal through many decisions Pompeo made. A turning point for many State Department officials came during the period surrounding Trump's first impeachment, when the secretary refused to provide subpoenaed documents to Congress, pretended to be unaware of the content of Trump's corrupt phone call with Ukrainian president Volodymyr Zelensky, and declined to defend Ambassador Yovanovitch from attacks aimed at discrediting her and serving Trump's personal interests. Many Trump critics also saw in Pompeo's Commission on Unalienable Rights a commitment to defining "human dignity" in a way that was partisan and ideological.

Second, the secretaries deployed different models of leadership. In his introductory speech, Tillerson adopts the posture of ethos, the authority figure who uses his expertise and character to persuade his subordinates to adopt his perspective on the role of the US in the world and the State Department in the US government.[52] Positioning himself as an expert and an authority, Tillerson instructs State Department personnel about the meaning of keeping "America first," the difference between policy and values, and the necessity of catching up to the realities of a post-Cold War world. He admonishes State Department officials for regarding US foreign policy as, in part, a realm of values instead of consistently subordinating those values to narrow national interests. For Tillerson, values get in the way of business and must be cast aside, or at least perched out of the way on our shoulders where they can't do any harm.

By contrast, Pompeo generally persuaded by using emotional appeals and by identifying with his audiences rather than instructing them. In his initial stand-up talk to his new subordinates at State, he promises that under his leadership they'll get their "swagger back"; though a *Washington Post* editorial concluded that, in retrospect, Pompeo's swagger was "really about" "advancing Mr. Pompeo's personal political career."[53] When he addressed Christian conservatives, Pompeo relayed ways in which he and they shared a belief system, as well as how they all look to God and the bible for inspiration and answers in a complicated world. These choices were surely deliberate. They amount to the performance of a kind of leadership—leading by identifying with listeners and incorporating them into a homogenous "we." This perspective may be a more useful than merely comparing Pompeo's behavior to the account of Christian leadership that Pompeo outlined. By the time Tillerson departed, State Department officials had rejected his leadership and his claims to expertise.[54]

Finally, both Tillerson and Pompeo threatened to diminish the US government's capacity to support human rights. Tillerson denigrated American values in favor of American interests and attempted not only to slash the budget of the State Department as a whole but to focus cuts on DRL. Pompeo also tried to severely cut the State Department's budget. Indeed, after Pompeo succeeded Tillerson, Congress continued to appropriate funding for human rights programs and rebuke the administration for efforts to defund human rights. In 2018, the report that accompanied the Senate Appropriations Committee appropriations bill features an epigraph from John McCain's last book, *The Restless Wave*: "We live in a land made from ideals, not blood and soil. We are custodians of those ideals at home, and their champion abroad." It would be possible to read this citation as a pro forma homage to a dying colleague, but the text of the introduction doesn't support this reading. In response to the administration's efforts to slash the State Department's budget, the committee states that "greater security and stability cannot be achieved with cuts to the budget, which are a self-inflicted wound."[55]

However, Pompeo's principal contribution to undermining US support for human rights was his insistence that US foreign policy on human rights was compromised and incoherent. Pompeo signaled his agreement with the Christian right movement's fundamental values and policy goals. He selected Christian conservative media venues and deployed key biblical tropes that have specific politicized meanings to Christian conservatives. In addition, he rectified what he diagnosed as an alarming confusion about human rights in the ranks of US officials by convening a commission of religious conservatives to reconceptualize the domain of human rights. Not unreasonably, proponents of women's and LGBTQ rights feared this commission might function as a vehicle for disabling US support for SOGI human rights.[56]

When pressed, Christian conservatives generally concede that all political leaders—and not only those with whom they feel a particular affinity—are placed in their positions of authority by God. Indeed, they often cite Daniel

2, in which, brought before King Nebuchadnezzar to interpret the king's dream, Daniel testifies (in verses 20, 21, and 37):

> Blessed be the name of God for ever and ever: for wisdom and might are his:
>
> And he changeth the times and the seasons: he removeth kings, and setteth up kings: he giveth wisdom unto the wise, and knowledge to them that know understanding:
>
> Thou, O king, art a king of kings: for the God of heaven hath given thee a kingdom, power, and strength, and glory. (KJV)

However, typically Christian conservative elites and followers voluntarily offer this analysis only about presidents they understand as carrying out the will of God. So, for example, Pat Robertson said of George W. Bush during the 2004 presidential campaign that "God lifts him up," which Robertson plainly meant as a mandate for those of God's people who relied on Robertson's leadership to do likewise. Indeed, early in Bush's first term, movement eminence Gary Bauer speculated that Pat Robertson left his position of leadership in the Christian Coalition not because of backlash from his comments about the September 11 terror attacks, but because the position of Christian right leader had "already been filled" by George W. Bush.[57] Many prominent Christian conservatives vigorously supported Trump and warned that Americans who opposed him courted God's punishment.

As it has been since the inception of recent national and global movements for LGBTQI civil and human rights, the Christian conservative movement remains the most persistent foe of these LGBTQ/SOGI rights. When Obama was president and Hillary Clinton and, later, John Kerry, were secretaries of state, the Christian right sent consistent signals that it aspired to terminate US programs and policies that provide SOGI human rights assistance. Mike Pompeo has long been identified with anti-LGBTQ Christian conservativism, and he consistently reinforced his association with the doctrine and politics of the Christian right while in office. At the same time, unlike Tillerson, he was one of Trump's most loyal and reliable appointees. As Never-Trump foreign policy expert Max Boot pointed out:

> The most important qualifications for service in the senior ranks of the Trump administration are a total lack of self-awareness, utter shamelessness and a cynical contempt for the truth. Sec-

retary of State Mike Pompeo is thus the perfect person to serve
as President Trump's chief diplomat.[58]

Even with his loyalties to the Christian right and Trump, however, Pompeo
made no discernable effort to terminate SOGI diplomacy and public diplomacy or gut the Global Equality Fund, which provides the majority of
SOGI human rights assistance to grassroots movements and implementing
partners around the world.

In spite of the differences in their political views and dedication to
the president, there's no evidence that either Tillerson or Pompeo set to
work to extirpate US SOGI human rights diplomacy and assistance. There's
also little evidence that the secretaries highlighted US SOGI policy as an
example of Trump's commitment to LGBTI equality or US progressiveness,
as the theory of homonationalism would predict.[59] Not only Democrats but
even some Republicans in the Senate were concerned that Tillerson would
undo Obama administration support for SOGI and quietly took steps to
communicate their expectations for SOGI and other human rights policies
to the secretary. Congress continued to appropriate funds for SOGI human
rights when Pompeo led the agency. And while Pompeo often didn't support
career diplomats and officials in executing their responsibilities, he also didn't
fulfill the Reconstructionist yearning to begin staffing the State Department
with businessmen and missionaries.[60]

Besides their interest in diminishing the State Department, what do
Tillerson's and Pompeo's orientation toward their colleagues in the agency
have in common? Toward the end of his 2017 talk to State Department
personnel, Tillerson likened the project on which he and his subordinates
had embarked to a "voyage." In the section of the speech I've called "Deliver[ing] on Mission," Tillerson said:

> We're all on this boat, on this voyage—I'm not going to call it a
> cruise; it's not—may not be that much fun. (Laughter.) But we're
> on all this ship, on this voyage together. And so we're going to
> get on the ship and we're going to take this voyage, and when
> we get there, we're all going to get off the ship at wherever we
> arrive. But we're all going to get on and we're going to get off
> together. We don't intend to leave anybody out. (paragraph 57)

Of course, that voyage was cut short when Pompeo replaced Tillerson at
the helm.

In the summer of 2020, Pompeo testified before the Senate Foreign Relations Committee on the president's fiscal year 2021 budget request for the State Department. Queried by senators about the Commission on Unalienable Rights, which had recently submitted its report, Pompeo revived a complaint he had made before about the philosophic confusion on human rights he'd encountered when he took over the agency, complaining that DRL "didn't have a founding." I suspect that Pompeo deliberately substituted "founding," an ideological term that alludes to a sacralized national origin, for the word that would have made more sense in context: "grounding." In any case, Pompeo quickly concluded that DRL officials needed to be instructed by conservative academics in order to clear up their confusion about the human rights project. In line with this conclusion, Pompeo declared DRL's understanding of human rights "unmoored." The nautical metaphors may be telling: between Tillerson's allegory of State Department personnel being on a voyage (under his command) and Pompeo's suggestion that he was having to secure a ship that threatened to drift away, it's not farfetched to suggest that both Tillerson and Pompeo understood and represented the agency as being "at sea."

SOGI human rights assistance involves many actors and stakeholders besides presidents and their like-minded cabinet and other appointees. These include Congressional committees that appropriate funds and individual members who must run for public office; diplomats and US officials who design and execute human rights assistance programs (these officials often interact directly with local grassroots and international human rights defenders); and recipients of human rights assistance. All of these actors and stakeholders have their own perspectives, and all have some kind and degree of efficacy in processes by which human rights assistance is conceived, designed, solicited, administered, managed, utilized, assessed, and justified.

I've indicated throughout this book that the Trump administration didn't curtail US support for LGBTQI human rights, but the details matter. Clues about the direction of human rights policies and practices may be found in multiple sites. These include government documents and participant observation at events that bring together grassroots activists and US government officials. In the next chapter, I turn from the secretaries of state to other actors, statements, and practices that provide information about the state of US commitment to SOGI in the Trump administration. Collectively, these data provide evidence that the Trump administration continued to supply human rights diplomacy and assistance and, thus, support international LGBTI human rights. The data also point to dynamics that can occur beneath the surface of policy stability, including budget politics, changes in policy priorities, intra-agency conflict, personnel changes, oversight, quiet diplomacy, and cooperation between US officials and civil society organizations.

Chapter 4

On the Trail of SOGI in the Time of Trump

SOGI Supply

Under ordinary circumstances, much SOGI advocacy takes place offstage, among CSOs, government officials, and activists. However, because of the dismay among LGBTQ human rights defenders after Trump's election, some advocates kept a US commitment to SOGI human rights in the public eye in order to hold the administration to account and rally SOGI supporters. An example of this public advocacy was a Council for Global Equality (CGE) forum in June 2018: "U.S. Support for Global LGBT Equality."[1] The event, held in a meeting room of the US Capitol, featured two panels and a brief closing address. One panel of the forum, "Looking Back and Looking Forward: Rebuilding American Leadership in Advancing an LGBT-Inclusive Human Rights Vision," featured three former US ambassadors: Scott DeLesi, David Pressman, and Michael Guest, the former openly gay ambassador to Romania and a senior advisor at the Council for Global Equality. All three spoke to challenges and strategies of monitoring and institutionalizing US support for human rights values and SOGI. In brief closing remarks, Representative Dina Titus (D-NV) noted the Trump administration's "disdain" for many parts of the Obama administration's agenda, including among her examples the failure to appoint an LGBTI special envoy and administration support for religious exemptions to antidiscrimination laws.

Alluding to the Trump administration's "avalanche of news and . . . clouds of intrigue" that have stymied close attentiveness to individual decisions, journalists and researchers urged citizens to "watch what they do, not what they say" across a range of policy areas.[2] So what did the administration do on SOGI human rights? And what was the condition of the "supply" side of US SOGI human rights support and assistance at the end of Trump's presidency? A complete answer includes Congress as well as the White House and executive branch agencies. Some analysts have pointed out that, behind the scenes, even many Republican members of Congress tried to "t[ie] Trump's hands" and ensure policy continuity on a number of fronts.[3] When I spoke with State Department officials about SOGI policy and programs during the Obama administration, they pointed out broad, bipartisan support for SOGI human rights in Congress. The data contained in appropriations bills and reports produced during the Trump administration support these assertions.

In the spirit of the exhortation to "watch what they do," I examine a set of "data points" under three categories of tools by which foreign policy is conducted: public diplomacy, diplomacy, and foreign assistance. These items may mean little individually as clues to the administration's orientation toward and actions on SOGI human rights. However, collectively they can inform our understanding of similarities and differences that prevailed between the Obama and Trump administrations on SOGI human rights. Documenting these data points also enables us to perceive shifts in rhetoric, including rhetoric designed to be consumed by domestic US audiences, even as the policies and most practices related to SOGI human rights remained intact.

Public Diplomacy

Foreign Service officer and diplomat Hans N. Tuch defines public diplomacy as "a government's process of communicating with foreign publics in an attempt to bring about understanding for its nation's ideas and ideals, its institutions and culture, as well as its national goals and current policies." Unlike traditional diplomacy, which often requires confidentiality, public diplomacy is an "open process" that has "publicity [a]s its inherent purpose"[4] As countries seek to manage their image and reputation, much public diplomacy is expressive or symbolic rather than a formal representation of a government's position. Scholars have explored connections between public diplomacy and public relations, and many have identified overlaps between conceptual and practical frameworks of the two sets of practices.[5]

The category of SOGI public diplomacy encompasses official state-ments identified with the secretary of state, such as the agency's mission statement. It also encompasses events and statements such as embassy engagement and Pride celebrations. Here, I briefly examine four categories or discrete examples of strategic communication that provide insight into the Trump administration's orientation toward US support for human rights, especially SOGI human rights: (1) the State Department's revision of the agency's mission statement; (2) LGBTI embassy engagement; (3) recognition of LGBTI Pride and IDAHOT (International Day against Homophobia, Transphobia, and Biphobia) by the State Department; and (4) the putative Trump administration initiative to advocate for decriminalization of same-sex relations worldwide.

State Department Mission Statement

In August 2017, news outlets reported that the State Department was con-sidering revisions to the agency's mission statement. The State Department's mission statement typically doesn't emerge as a worrisome sign of changes to US foreign policy, but these possible revisions provoked concern across the political spectrum. Criticisms focused on two particular revisions then under deliberation that would have emphasized security and prosperity while deleting a US commitment to a "just" and "democratic" world.[6] Perhaps in response to these public critiques, the finalized mission statement pledged commitment to "a more secure, democratic, and prosperous world for the benefit of the American people and the international community."[7]

LGBTI Embassy Engagement

Embassy engagement has been one prong of official US government support for LGBTI human rights in recent years. Before 2012, US embassies were free to sponsor activities and engage with LGBTI people. After her 2011 speech in Geneva, Clinton instituted a requirement for all US embassies to engage in "innovative public diplomacy" to support the human rights of LGBTI people in the countries in which they served.[8] The result was a plethora of outreach, activities and—depending on the degree of safety associated with minority gender and sexual identities—public displays of affiliation with LGBTI people.[9] In response to concerns that the Trump administration might curtail SOGI embassy engagement, in early June 2017, the State Department confirmed that it had issued a guidance to US embassies providing permission for embassies to recognize LGBT Pride month.

However, in 2019 a controversy arose over the LGBT rainbow flag that pitted some LGBTQ activists and US embassies against the State Department. The Trump administration rescinded the blanket permission granted during the Obama administration for US embassies to fly the LGBTQ Pride flag below the US flag on official flagpoles.[10] Instead of receiving preapproval, embassies that wanted to fly the Pride flag had to seek permission individually, but when they did so, no such approvals were granted. In response to the policy change, a number of US embassies displayed the Pride flag elsewhere on embassy buildings or grounds, some flamboyantly.[11] In 2020, one US embassy that displayed a pride flag was Embassy Moscow, led by Ambassador John J. Sullivan, former deputy secretary of the Bureau of Democracy, Human Rights, and Labor (DRL) and master of ceremonies for Trump administration Pride @ State events. When Embassy Moscow hung the rainbow flag vertically on the embassy's façade, Vladimir Putin weighed in, suggesting that the flag signaled that embassy personnel were queer.[12]

Both the LGBTQ movement and the Christian right exploited the controversy over Pride flags in messaging with constituents. The Family Research Council (FRC) messaged their subscribers on June 10, 2019, with "Rogue Embassies: Along for the Pride?" Using the narrative of cultural imperialism—the Obama administration's imposition of LGBTQ rights on other countries—the FRC explained that "after eight years of rubbing their extreme agenda in other countries' faces, some ambassadors [were] having a hard time letting go." Here, the reference to ambassadors also implicitly implicated a deep state of civil service holdovers from the Obama administration without indicting the Trump administration for SOGI policies or practices occurring on Trump or Pompeo's watch. In 2021, the Biden administration reversed Trump's ban on Pride flags at US embassies.

PRIDE/IDAHOT EVENTS AND STATEMENTS

In June 2017, Secretary Tillerson issued a press statement on LGBTI Pride in which the State Department "affirm[ed] its solidarity with the human rights defenders and civil society organizations working around the world to uphold the fundamental freedoms of LGBTI persons to live with dignity and freedom." The statement concluded with the declaration that "the United States *remains* committed to human rights and fundamental freedoms for all persons. Dignity and equality for all persons are among our founding constitutional principles, and these principles continue to drive U.S. diplomacy."[13]

After Pompeo took over as secretary, foreign affairs agencies continued to mark Pride month with statements in support of LGBTI human rights. The statement released by the office of Mike Pompeo affirmed that "the United States joins people around the world in celebrating Lesbian, Gay, Bisexual, Transgender, and Intersex (LGBTI) Pride Month, and reaffirms its commitment to protecting and defending the human rights of all, including LGBTI persons. . . . The United States stands firmly with you as you exercise your human rights and fundamental freedoms. We wish you a safe and happy Pride Month."[14] The US Mission to the UN and the office of Ambassador Nikki Haley released a statement that included a similar affirmation of US commitment: "At the UN, we see the importance of defending freedoms of LGBTI persons from governments that violate their own people's human rights. The United States embraces personal freedom, rejects discrimination, and supports the global LGBTI community in standing up for their human rights."[15]

In June of 2018 and 2019, I attended Pride @ State, co-sponsored by glifaa, the LGBT State Department employee organization whose motto is "LGBT+ Pride in Foreign Affairs Agencies." The 2019 Pride event was also sponsored by the Native American Foreign Affairs Council (NAFAC). Pride @ State celebrates, as Deputy Secretary John J. Sullivan put it in 2019, "the diversity of our department's workforce." However, State Department Pride events can also provide a platform for expressions of concern about a range of issues affecting LGBTQI people, from the history of discrimination against LGBT people in federal employment to the human rights challenges that confront LGBTI people in the US and abroad.

The 2018 Pride @ State was held in the Burns Auditorium of the State Department's George C. Marshall Conference Center. In his opening remarks, Deputy Secretary Sullivan alluded to his LGBT son in the audience and extended "best wishes from the Secretary," whom we were told could not attend because of a scheduling conflict. In his keynote speech, Representative Mark Takano (D-CA) noted the stubborn existence of human rights challenges around the world, including perceptions in many places that LGBTI people constitute a "threatening other" who deserve disapprobation and harm. Takano focused on the US as well, noting the "narrow" decision in *Masterpiece Cakeshop v. Colorado Civil Rights Commission* and reminding attendees that civil rights "progress is not irreversible." Takano also urged Mike Pompeo to "do the right thing" and "finally appoint a successor to Randy

Berry and fill the position of special envoy." As for Pompeo, printed on the back page of the program for the 2018 Pride @ State was the "Statement by Secretary Pompeo" reaffirming the US "commitment to protecting and defending the human rights of all, including LGBTI persons."[16]

In 2019, the keynote speaker was Representative Sharice Davids (D-KS), who identifies as lesbian and Native American. Sullivan again provided opening remarks to attendees assembled in the Dean Acheson auditorium, whose top rows had been curtained off to demarcate a smaller space for the audience that had diminished since Pride events held during the Obama administration.[17] Sullivan attested to the commitment of the agency to "diversity, inclusion, and respect." In addition, invoking the language of the controversial 2017 State Department mission statement, Sullivan added the adjective, "inclusivity," to the list of US goals: security, democracy, and prosperity. The deputy secretary moved beyond general paeons to diversity, however, when he noted particular officials, some anonymous, whom he credited with promoting respect for LGBTI people in their respective foreign service spheres. Those acknowledged in their absence included former special envoy Randy Berry and Tom Gallagher, the State Department's first openly gay foreign service officer, as well as officials who have worked to recognize and address the challenges LGBTI people face in the countries in which the officials have served.

As in 2018, the secretary did not attend the event. The year 2019 saw a potentially more significant difference, however, when Pompeo's office declined to release a new LGBTI Pride month press statement. The statement bearing his imprimatur on the back of the 2019 program—expressing US support for LGBTI people being "free to enjoy their human rights and fundamental freedoms" without suffering "violence, arrest, harassment, and intimidation"—was recycled from 2018.[18] Because of the Covid-19 pandemic, no Pride celebration was held at the State Department in 2020.

INITIATIVE TO SUPPORT DECRIMINALIZATION WORLDWIDE

In early 2019, news organizations reported a Trump administration campaign to decriminalize same-sex sexuality worldwide. The vocal face of the campaign was Ambassador Ric Grenell. In announcing the campaign, the *Washington Blade* reported its launch in Berlin as an "international summit" that excluded most LGBT groups and included only a small set of activists handpicked by Grenell, who was identified as "leading the initiative."[19] By contrast, the *New York Times* insightfully represented the effort as a vanity project of the ambassador to Germany:

> Richard Grenell, [who was then] rumored to be a candidate as the next American ambassador to the United Nations, invited about a dozen gay and transgender activists from around Europe to a dinner at his Berlin residence Tuesday night where the effort was discussed.
>
> Guests from the Lithuanian Gay League posted a photo on its Twitter account showing two members posing with Mr. Grenell at the event, thanking him and calling on their country and other European Union members to support the effort, which the Lithuanian guests described as a "Global US campaign."[20]

Grenell emphasized the criminalization of same-sex sexuality in Iran, a focus that can be placed in a context of Trump and Grenell's denunciation of the Iranian regime and advocacy against the Iran nuclear deal (the Joint Comprehensive Plan of Action).[21]

The putative Trump administration campaign against decriminalization of same-sex sexuality appears to rest on three events. Chronologically, the first and third events were Trump speeches to the General Assembly of the UN in New York City in 2019 and a briefer refrain in his speech the following year. The most thorough exposition of these was the first, when Trump included the following passage in his remarks:

> As we defend American values, we affirm the right of all people to live in dignity. For this reason, my administration is working with other nations to stop criminalizing of homosexuality, and we stand in solidarity with LGBTQ people who live in countries that punish, jail, or execute individuals based upon sexual orientation.

Trump's speech was described variously by commentators as somber, nationalist, instrumental, and transactional. It also contained a particular kind of "bold challenge to coherence" that bears scrutiny.[22] On the one hand, Trump endorsed SOGI human rights in language similar to that employed by the Obama administration and religious freedom in language that recalled his administration's ministerials. On the other hand, the speech was framed by a conception of cultural relativism that can easily be identified both with

Trump's belligerent nationalism and with the Christian right's defense of cultural relativism against SOGI:

> Americans know that in a world where others seek conquest and domination, our nation must be strong in wealth, in might, and in spirit. That is why the United States vigorously defends the traditions and customs that have made us who we are.
>
> Like my beloved country, each nation represented in this hall has a cherished history, culture, and heritage that is worth defending and celebrating, and which gives us our singular potential and strength. . . .
>
> The future does not belong to globalists. The future belongs to patriots. The future belongs to sovereign and independent nations who protect their citizens, respect their neighbors, and honor the differences that make each country special and unique.[23]

It should go without saying that an American president cannot call for respect for the dignity and integrity of LGBTI people (or persecuted religious minorities) *and* simultaneously demand uncritical respect for each nation's traditions, customs, culture, and heritage. As Hillary Clinton pointed out in 2011, SOGI human rights and religious freedom are universal values that are often explicitly contested in the name of customs, tradition, culture, and heritage.[24]

Given the incoherence of the 2019 speech to the General Assembly on this particular point, it's likely that a person close to Trump inserted the paragraph declaring support for the ability of LGBTQ people "to live in dignity." In 2020, Trump repeated the claim in a truncated form in a list of what he characterized as his administration's human rights accomplishments: "America will always be a leader in human rights. My administration is advancing religious liberty, opportunity for women, the decriminalization of homosexuality, combatting human trafficking, and protecting unborn children."[25]

The second venue that can be identified with the decriminalization campaign occurred two months after Trump's 2019 UN speech. Grenell and Kelly Craft, the Republican Party donor and US ambassador to Canada who was tapped for the position of US ambassador to the United Nations that Grenell had hoped to fill, cohosted a panel at the UN on "Decriminalizing Homosexuality in Solidarity with LGBTQ People." The event surveyed the "current status of efforts to decriminalize homosexuality in at least 69 countries" and reiterated a US commitment "to the principle that all governments must respect the equality and human dignity of each person under their jurisdiction, regardless of sexual orientation."[26] Joining Craft and Grenell were a panel that included assistant secretary for DRL Robert Destro and two activists (one American and one from the Middle East) who had become personally identified with Grenell and his campaign.[27]

Grenell's next appointment, which he held simultaneously with his post as US ambassador to Germany, was as the administration's acting director of national intelligence (DNI). From that perch, Grenell suggested terminating intelligence sharing with countries that continue to criminalize same-sex sexuality.[28] When the Senate finally confirmed John Ratcliffe, the former member of Congress from Texas, to fill the position of DNI, Grenell resigned as ambassador to Germany and joined Carnegie Mellon University's Institute for Politics and Strategy as a senior fellow. With his resignation, the decriminalization campaign effectively ended.

The relevant context for Grenell's decriminalization campaign is the Obama administration's goal of decriminalizing same-sex relations announced as a component of its SOGI human rights policy in late 2011. In Obama's presidential memorandum on "International Initiatives to Advance the Human Rights of Lesbian, Gay, Bisexual, and Transgender Persons," addressed to foreign affairs agencies, the administration set out "combatting criminalization of LGBT status or conduct abroad" as a key task in the US mission to "promote the fundamental human rights of LGBT people everywhere." Indeed, the memorandum directed foreign affairs agencies to use "U.S. diplomacy and foreign assistance" to achieve several aims, the first of which was "combatting criminalization."[29] During the Obama administration, State Department and USAID officials sometimes spoke of the US favoring decriminalization as a matter of policy. However, they always indicated that decisions to oppose criminalization in particular countries must be made by grassroots activists. This was both because activists understood the social, legal, and political climate better than US officials, and because an untimely demand for decriminalization could backfire and harm LGBTI people.[30]

Grenell had an agenda for SOGI; he aspired to use US power and leverage to force governments to decriminalize same-sex sexuality. But he was unable to induce either the secretary of state or the White House to translate his idea into policy, and his insistence on a grandiose public profile made it impossible to pursue his objective through quiet diplomacy. If the decriminalization campaign had been a genuine government initiative to integrate a US demand for decriminalization of same-sex sexuality into

US foreign policy and to condition foreign assistance on decriminalization, the campaign would straddle the boundary between public diplomacy and diplomacy proper, incorporating elements of both. I place the decriminalization campaign under the category of public diplomacy alone to point out that it originated with Ric Grenell and wasn't institutionalized in any form that substantially revised the Obama administration's foreign policy. Julie Dorf, a senior advisor at the Council for Global Equality, described the purported campaign as "nothing more than a series of self-promoting Twitter photos."[31] Or, as *Mother Jones* summed it up, "There's nothing."[32]

Diplomacy

US diplomat George Kennan argued that the "classic function of diplomacy" is "to effect the communications between one's own government and other governments or individuals abroad, and to do this with maximum accuracy, imagination, tact and good sense."[33] In formal or traditional diplomacy, state actors conduct international relations through nonviolent means that include negotiation, communication, information-gathering, and reporting. In sharp departures from the foreign policy of other administrations, the Trump administration undermined US diplomats, withdrew the US from treaties and commitments, and persistently threatened to dissolve longstanding alliances. Jeremy Shapiro and Philip H. Gordon argue that the administration's punitive measures toward adversaries and allies alike constituted a de facto practice of "sadistic diplomacy."[34]

Seven items can help to construct a picture of SOGI diplomacy in the Trump administration: (1) the State Department's Country Reports on Human Rights Practices; (2) official State Department statements regarding LGBTI persecution; (3) the status of the post of special envoy for the human rights of LGBTI persons; (4) US membership in the United Nations Human Rights Council; (5) US sanctions imposed under the Magnitsky acts; (6) US membership in the Equal Rights Coalition (ERC); and (7) the Commission on Unalienable Rights. I briefly consider each of these data points before turning to foreign assistance, the third tool of foreign policy.

Country Reports on Human Rights Practices

During the Carter administration, Congress committed the US to taking human rights into account in foreign policy by directing the State Department to produce and submit reports on all United Nations member states in accordance with the Foreign Assistance Act of 1961 and the Trade Act of 1974.[35] Submitted every year since 1977, the country reports constitute an official record of human rights conditions and publicize those conditions. However, the country reports also have more specific effects. These include enhancing the information about human rights conditions that policymakers and diplomats use to formulate policy, and complicating the ability of presidents and legislators to make foreign policy decisions without taking human rights into account.[36]

The format of the country reports changes over time as DRL updates categories of information that embassies will collect and report to the State Department. The most significant revision with regard to SOGI is the instruction embassies received to report on conditions for LGBTI people during Obama's first term in office. The new category, "Societal Abuses, Discrimination, and Acts of Violence Based on Sexual Orientation and Gender Identity," appeared for the first time in the 2009 country reports, published in early 2010.

Tillerson was widely criticized for skipping the rollout of the 2016 country reports in the spring of 2017, a decision that aroused concerns about the administration's commitment to human rights. In early 2018, other kinds of concern about the reports emerged when news media reported that State Department officials preparing the 2017 annual reports had been directed to "pare back" sections of the reports on women's access to contraception and abortion; "societal views of family planning"; and "racial, ethnic, and sexual discrimination," including reporting on human rights violations against LGBT people.[37] By the time the 2017 country reports were released in April 2018, Tillerson had been fired. Acting Secretary John J. Sullivan presented the reports at a press conference. In his introductory remarks, Sullivan pointed to a change in the format of the reports and, perhaps in response to vociferous criticism of Tillerson's apparent lack of interest in human rights, Sullivan noted several categories of reporting, including on LGBTI:

> This year, we have sharpened the focus of the report to be more responsive to statutory reporting requirements and more focused on government action or inaction with regard to the promotion and protection of human rights. For example, each executive summary includes a paragraph to note the most egregious abuses that occurred in a particular country, including those against

women, LGBTI persons, persons with disabilities, indigenous persons, and members of religious minorities.[38]

In June 2018, the report that accompanied the Senate Appropriations Committee bill for fiscal year 2019 includes the following directive in the "Democracy Fund" (HRDF) section:

> Discrimination Against LGBTI Persons.—The Committee directs the Department of State to include in its annual country human rights reports descriptions of official government discrimination of lesbian, gay, bisexual, transgender, and intersex [LGBTI] persons and consider such discrimination in assistance decisions, and urges the Department and USAID to continue to allocate funding for the Global Equality Fund and the LGBTI Portfolio within USAID's Human Rights Division.[39]

The 2019 country reports continued to employ a category that focuses on human rights violations against gender and sexual minorities.[40] Their roll-out in the spring of 2020 included press interviews with Secretary Pompeo, Assistant Secretary for DRL Robert Destro, and Deputy Assistant Secretary Scott Busby. In that venue, we would expect officials to address the history of the reports and their value for furthering the US commitment to improving human rights. Busby, who functioned as acting special envoy for the human rights of LGBTI persons during the Trump administration, also mentioned SOGI human rights. Asked by a journalist specifically about human rights progress in Vietnam, Busby noted some progress on respecting the rights of disabled and LGBTI persons and some improvement on religious freedom.[41]

RESPONSES TO LGBT PERSECUTION

Official US responses to the persecution of marginalized groups may take the form of statements or sanctions. In July 2017, the State Department issued a statement expressing disapprobation about reports of gay men and men who have sex with men being tortured, murdered, and confined in secret prisons in the Russian Republic of Chechnya. Despite condemning the violence, Tillerson told the House Foreign Affairs Committee he had not raised the issue of antigay violence with the Russian foreign minister or other Russian officials.[42] The State Department under Tillerson also issued statements "express[ing] concern" about state-sanctioned violence directed against gay men in Egypt and Azerbaijan.[43] By contrast, when Uganda passed the Anti-Homosexuality Bill, which was later rescinded on a technicality, the Obama administration took a number of actions. These included banning Ugandan officials involved in human rights abuses against LGBTQI people from the US and redirecting funds originally intended for government programs to civil society.[44]

An early response of Pompeo's State Department to human rights violations against LGBTQI people abroad was a press release, "On the International Day against Homophobia, Transphobia, and Biphobia," released May 17, 2018. Stating that "the United States stands for the protection of fundamental freedoms and universal human rights," the statement confirms US opposition to "criminalization, violence and serious acts of discrimination such as in housing, employment and government services, directed against LGBTI persons."[45] Particularly notable in this statement is the reference to US opposition to the criminalization of LGBTI identity or behavior. Ambassador Grenell didn't launch his campaign to embed a demand for decriminalization in US foreign policy until early 2019, so Pompeo's statement reflects the general opposition to criminalization that was already understood to have been incorporated into US foreign policy by Obama's presidential memorandum on the human rights of LGBT persons.

Expressions of US concern and disapproval are not only promulgated by the office of the secretary, however, but are sometimes issued by diplomats within the agency. A 2019 incident in Zambia provides an example of this kind of diplomatic statement. Under color of a British colonial-era law against same-sex sexuality, a Zambian court had sentenced two men to fifteen years in prison for having sex together. The US ambassador to Zambia, Daniel Foote, condemned the conviction and sentence, and his disapproval incited threats from some Zambian citizens and stern rebukes from Zambian public officials. Foote responded with a lengthy statement that the editors of *Foreign Policy* characterized as "unusually direct for an ambassador."[46]

In his statement, Foote acknowledged the evolution of the US on slavery and other human rights–related "historical misdeeds"; described his role as an Ambassador as representing the "interests, values, and ideals of the United States"; praised ordinary Zambians, whom he characterized in part as victims of a corrupt, authoritarian government; conceded that Zambians have a right to their laws; spoke to Christian values, ostensibly one of the justifications of the prosecution; responded to Zambia's foreign minister's challenge to Foote's familiarity with the Zambian constitution; and pointedly

contrasted high per capita US aid to Zambia, especially in the areas of HIV/
AIDS and other health issues, food insecurity, and electrification with dis-
respect toward US representatives and perspectives on human rights by the
Zambian government.[47] The Zambian government complained to the State
Department about what they understood as Foote's interference in Zambian
internal affairs, demanding his recall. Foote was subsequently recalled, an
outcome CNN noted was "rare, especially when an ambassador is arguing
for American values abroad."[48]

LGBTI Special Envoy

In early 2015, members of Congress called for the creation of the position
of special envoy for the human rights of LGBTI persons, and Secretary of
State John Kerry appointed Foreign Service officer Randy Berry as the first
special envoy. The post of special envoy is a senior staff position in DRL,
reporting to the assistant secretary. During his tenure in the position, Berry
engaged in SOGI diplomacy abroad and coordinated SOGI human rights
programs and initiatives with officials in DRL. In late 2016, Berry was
appointed as deputy assistant secretary of state for South and Central Asia
in DRL in addition to his post as special envoy.

When I interviewed Berry in December 2016, with less than one
month to go before Trump's inauguration, he talked about the value for
advancing SOGI human rights of being able to meet not only with LGBTQ
activists but also with leaders of governments for conversations about the
human rights of gender and sexual minorities. He also cautioned that US
advocacy of SOGI human rights is more credible when "we don't whitewash
our own history" on LGBTQ issues.[49] Berry indicated that he was willing
to serve as special envoy under the new administration. In September 2018,
the Senate voted to confirm him to serve as the US ambassador to Nepal.

After Trump took office, members of Congress took an interest in
protecting the Global Equality Fund (GEF) and the position of LGBTI
special envoy. In its budget bill for fiscal year 2018, the Senate Appropriations Committee included the following stipulation aimed at preventing
the closing or relocating of offices and the elimination of positions: "None
of the funds appropriated by this Act, prior Acts making appropriations for
the Department of State, foreign operations, and related programs, or any
other Act may be used to downsize, downgrade, consolidate, close, move, or
relocate to another United States Government agency—[the following, items
A through T, including] (C) the Bureau of Democracy, Human Rights, and

Labor, Department of State [and] (R) the Special Envoy for the Human Rights of LGBTI Persons, Department of State."[50]

In a context of congressional concerns about the administration's efforts to downsize State and, especially, DRL, Tillerson sent a letter to Senator Bob Corker, chairman of the Senate Committee on Foreign Relations. Tillerson justifies cutting some special envoy/representative positions to further the reorganization and downsizing he made a centerpiece of his leadership of the agency. However, he promises to retain the position of special envoy for the human rights of LGBTI persons and continue to staff the position at the level of deputy assistant secretary.[51] Nor did congressional concern about the State Department's commitments to human rights in general and LGBTI human rights in particular end when Tillerson was fired. In the report that accompanied its 2019 appropriations bill, the Senate Appropriations Committee also directed the State Department to continue to fund the position of special envoy for the human rights of LGBTI persons.[52]

After Berry stepped down, LGBTI activists, members of Congress, members of the US human rights community, and others made public pleas to the secretaries of state to appoint a new special envoy. Throughout the course of the Trump administration, deputy assistant secretary Scott Busby served as acting special envoy, assuring international communities that the US continued to be "concerned about the safety and security of LGBTI persons and their advocates, including in crisis zones."[53] Taking into account how slowly the Trump administration nominated people to positions of leadership, how many people served in acting capacities, and the likelihood that the post was controversial with some Trump allies, it's not surprising that no LGBTI special envoy was appointed. In June 2021, the Biden administration appointed Jessica Stern, executive director of Out-Right Action International, to become the new special envoy to advance the human rights of LGBTQI+ persons.

HUMAN RIGHTS COUNCIL

On September 29, 2017, the US attracted a domestic and international outcry for voting "no" on a United Nations Human Rights Council resolution that condemned the application of the death penalty to punish apostasy, blasphemy, adultery, and consensual same-sex relations. In the face of vociferous criticism, US ambassador Nikki Haley defended the vote as a reasonable response to the resolution's condemnation of capital punishment. Indeed, the resolution raises numerous problems with the death penalty, including, "*strongly deploring* the fact that the use of the death penalty leads to violations of the human rights of the persons facing the death penalty and of other affected persons" and

> *deploring* the fact that, frequently, poor and economically vulnerable persons and foreign nationals are disproportionately subjected to the death penalty, that laws carrying the death penalty are used against persons exercising their rights to freedom of expression, thought, conscience, religion, and peaceful assembly and association, and that persons belonging to religious or ethnic minorities are disproportionately represented among those sentenced to the death penalty.[54]

The US was one of thirteen nations voting against the resolution. The other twelve were: Bangladesh, Botswana (which decriminalized same-sex sexual relations in 2019), Burundi, China, Egypt, Ethiopia, India, Iraq, Japan, Qatar, Saudi Arabia, and the United Arab Emirates.

The Trump administration's relationship with the international community by way of multilateral organizations was contentious, as evidenced by indicators like the failure of Haley's campaign to persuade any other Security Council member to support a resolution introduced by the US to blame Hamas for inciting violence that led to Israeli soldiers shooting Palestinians near the border with Gaza.[55] More consequential than individual votes in the council, however, was the Trump administration's decision to withdraw the US from membership in the UN Human Rights Council.[56]

Among the many other positions taken by the Human Rights Council has been its affirmation of LGBTI human rights. In 2011, the council passed Resolution 17/19 and commissioned a study on SOGI human rights violations subsequently published as "Discriminatory Laws and Practices and Acts of Violence against Individuals Based on Their Sexual Orientation and Gender Identity."[57] Between 2011 and 2016, the council took a number of steps to support SOGI human rights, including designating professor of law Vitit Muntarbhorn, a cochair of the experts group that produced the Yogyakarta Principles on the Application of International Human Rights Law in Relation to Sexual Orientation and Gender Identity in 2006, as the first UN independent expert on sexual orientation and gender identity. After Muntarbhorn resigned because of poor health in late 2017, in January 2018, Costa Rican attorney and human rights advocate Victor Madrigal-Borloz was appointed as independent expert. Like other unilateral acts of the Trump administration in foreign affairs, the withdrawal of the US from the Human Rights Council diminished US influence in international human rights venues. In early 2021, the Biden administration rejoined the Human Rights Council.

Sanctions under the Magnitsky Act

In 2012, Congress passed and Obama signed the Russia and Moldova Jackson-Vanik Repeal and Sergei Magnitsky Rule of Law Accountability Act, colloquially known as the Magnitsky Act. The law was intended to punish Russian officials alleged to be connected to the death of attorney Sergei Magnitsky in Russian detention. Magnitsky had investigated official Russian corruption and expropriation of public funds at the behest of William Browder, an American businessman who had done business in Russia and who lobbied Congress to pass a law to punish corrupt Russian officials. The law placed these officials on a list, refused them entry to the US, and confiscated their assets in US banks. Russian president Vladimir Putin retaliated with a law prohibiting Americans from adopting Russian children, an act that provided the pretext for a Russian lawyer's meeting with Donald Trump, Jr., Jared Kushner, and Paul Manafort at Trump Tower during the presidential campaign. In 2016, a second law, the Global Magnitsky Human Rights Accountability Act, extended the sanctions aimed at government officials responsible for human rights abuses to countries other than Russia.

What connects the Magnitsky Act with SOGI human rights? After the imprisonment and torture of gay men in the Russian Republic of Chechnya in 2017, the State Department denounced the abuses, and State and Treasury invoked the Magnitsky Act against law enforcement official Ayub Kataev, who oversaw the men's imprisonment and torture, and Ramzan Kadyrov, head of the Chechen Republic.[58] In July 2020, the State Department announced that Kadyrov had been publicly designated under section 7031(c) of the Department of State, Foreign Operations, and Related Programs Appropriations Act of 2019 for "horrific reports of abuses against LGBTI persons, human rights defenders, members of the independent media, and other citizens." The public designation enhanced sanctions on Kadyrov by barring his wife and two of his children from entry to the US.[59]

Equal Rights Coalition

Since 2010, a series of international conferences for LGBTI human rights have been organized by CSOs and government representatives to address the policy side of SOGI human rights, and the responsiveness of national policies and officials to SOGI human rights needs and claims. After meetings in Stockholm (2010), Berlin (2013), and Washington, DC (2014), the fourth international conference for LGBTQI advocacy was the "Global LGBTI Human Rights Conference: Nonviolence, Nondiscrimination, and Social Inclusion," held in July 2016 in Montevideo, Uruguay. A goal of the Montevideo conference was to continue the process initiated at the 2014 State Department (Washington, DC) conference of broadening the meeting's focus from SOGI human rights donors to international diplomacy and the foreign policies of states.[60]

The Montevideo conference hosted the launch of a new partnership under the leadership of Uruguay and the Netherlands: the Equal Rights Coalition (ERC). Made up of 39 nations and many CSOs, the coalition's principles affirm the applicability of the Universal Declaration of Human Rights to LGBTI people and pledge to "coordinate their diplomatic efforts, share information and work together at the international level" for SOGI human rights. The initial coalition fact sheet emphasizes its function as a diplomatic rather than a funding partnership; membership in the ERC does not require a financial contribution to SOGI human rights advocacy. However, membership is predicated on agreement that providers of human rights assistance will consult with civil society and be accountable to SOGI advocates and CSOs.[61]

Unlike the Global Equality Fund, the ERC isn't led or administered by the US, so the partnership wouldn't be endangered by official US animus toward SOGI human rights or international agreements. However, the US could have withdrawn from the partnership as it has from other international multilateral agreements, and it didn't do so under Trump. In 2017, Canada and Chile assumed a two-year term of ERC leadership and declared that the partnership would be oriented toward advances in "international and regional diplomacy," "LGBTI inclusion in the 2030 Agenda for Sustainable Development," "coordination of donor funding," and "national laws, policies and practices."[62]

In August 2018, the ERC held a meeting in Vancouver, British Columbia: "Leaving No One Behind: The Equal Rights Coalition Global Conference on LGBTI Human Rights and Inclusive Development." The conference was planned to take place the day after Vancouver's Pride march during which Prime Minister Justin Trudeau made a "surprise appearance."[63] US participation in the Vancouver conference included Deputy Secretary John J. Sullivan who, in video remarks, praised the ERC for making "significant strides" in responding to SOGI human rights violations. Sullivan pledged that the US would continue to be a "steadfast partner" "as [the] coalition works to uphold human rights and fundamental freedoms" and would "striv[e] to do better by sharing our own challenges, particularly in addressing bias-motivated violence targeting the LGBTI community." Acting as LGBTI special envoy, Scott Busby was among the officials from DRL and USAID attending the meeting in person.[64]

In 2019, the UK and Argentina took over as cochairs and announced an ERC conference that was to be held in London in May 2020. Policy objectives to be pursued by international government officials and representatives from civil society included "progress on decriminalization, reducing violence and discrimination, and promoting LGBT inclusion in areas such as health and education."[65] The conference had to be postponed because of the coronavirus pandemic. However, the ERC issued a diplomatic statement in May "on Covid 19 and the human rights of LGBTI Persons" that called attention to the enhanced vulnerability of many LGBTI people to the global pandemic:

> Although the virus may seem to strike indiscriminately, its spread and consequences along with measures taken to combat the pandemic affect specific groups differently depending on existing inequalities and exclusion mechanisms in societies and power structures, leaving the most marginalized even more vulnerable. Lesbian, gay, bisexual, transgender and intersex (LGBTI) persons are amongst the most marginalized and excluded because of historic and ongoing stigma, discrimination, criminalization and violence against them, and they are and will continue to be among those most at risk during this crisis.

Signatories called on governments "to ensure that their measures to combat the COVID-19 pandemic consider the specific impact on LGBTI persons" and "to ensure humanitarian relief efforts and funds include a response to the specific needs of marginalized communities, such as LGBTI persons." Of the government members of the Equal Rights Coalition, the US was the only one that didn't endorse the statement.[66]

COMMISSION ON UNALIENABLE RIGHTS

The commission issued its draft report in July 2020, and critics found many grounds for being disappointed in the report. It was even graded by international politics professor Daniel W. Drezner, who gave it a C+ in an evaluation published in the *Washington Post*.[67] After a two-week comment period, the commission finalized its report in August, choosing to make only small changes, because members had already been exposed to a wide range of critiques beginning with the announcement of the commission's formation. The final report was translated into seven languages: Farsi and the six official languages of the United Nations—Arabic, Chinese, French, German, Russian, and Spanish.[68]

On September 23, a little over a month after the commission's report was finalized, two events were coordinated: the US Mission to the UN released a brief statement calling on UN member states to recommit themselves to the human rights protections inscribed in the Universal Declaration of Human Rights (UDHR); and Pompeo addressed the UN General Assembly virtually about the commission's report. Signed by 57 governments, the Joint Statement on the Universal Declaration of Human Rights, is an anodyne statement of support for the "fundamental freedoms and rights" inscribed in the UDHR. However, to understand the impetus for such a statement, it's necessary to place it in the context of Pompeo's diplomacy on behalf of the Commission on Unalienable Rights. Indeed, the Western European governments that refused to sign onto the statement despite their robust support for human rights and the UDHR were clearly considering this context.[69]

Although brief, the speech is replete with information about the administration and Pompeo's perspective on human rights that would be likely to raise concerns among US allies. In the address, Pompeo echoes claims he'd already made about the human rights work of the State Department being in disarray. With a global audience, this time he indicts colleagues around the world by averring that "the international human rights project is in crisis." In the text of the speech, there are three main claims, helpfully bulleted, that US allies would likely read as cynical tenets of Trump administration human rights doctrine:

- Authoritarian governments—from China, to Iran, to Venezuela—are depriving our fellow human beings of their basic rights.

- Meanwhile, many multinational organizations have lost their way, focusing on partisan policy preferences while failing to defend fundamental rights.

- And even many well-intentioned people assert new and novels
  [*sic*] rights that often conflict.[70]

As many critics of the commission pointed out beginning in 2019, the only
regimes the commission and the secretary were willing to censure were those
the president regarded as enemies, not those of dictators Trump flattered
and emulated. Many criticisms might reasonably be made of multilateral
organizations, but, emanating from an administration that repeatedly sab-
otaged international cooperation, the second bullet point is transparently
mendacious. As for the third, there's nothing "novels" about extending
fundamental rights to members of groups from whom those rights have
been deliberately withheld.

The internal inconsistency of Pompeo's effort to insert the Commission on Unalienable Rights into American diplomacy can be located in the
following set of assertions, which evince an incoherence similar to Trump's
2019 remarks to the General Assembly:

> To uphold universal human rights, we should look to the framers
> of the UDHR, who identified a clear set of principles that apply
> to all people, everywhere, at all times. They stood unwaveringly
> in defense of the dignity of every human being. . . .
>
> We hope the Commission's recently published Report will
> serve as an inspiration to other nations and peoples.
>
> They should turn to their traditions and rededicate them-
> selves to their moral, philosophical, and religious resources to
> affirm the rights inherent in all persons—the rights at the core
> of the UDHR.[71]

Here, Pompeo argues that (1) the UDHR is the only resource the international community needs to acknowledge and protect the dignity and
human rights of all people; (2) the report of the Commission on Unalienable Rights finds these same ideas and resources—"wide and deep support
for unalienable rights"—in the American founding; and (3) these same
ideas and resources are similarly available in all other traditions and human
communities: "Abrahamic faiths, Confucianism, Hinduism, and other religious,
philosophical, and political traditions." If all of these assertions are valid, as
Pompeo insists they are, I can only imagine one reason why Pompeo might
consider "the international human rights project" to be "in crisis": this is because
cosmopolitan elites who have used multinational organizations and international

agreements created since 1948 to defend human rights insist on challenging practices ostensibly based on traditions, customs, culture, and heritage that have been used to justify harm against marginalized groups. Fortunately for the international human rights project, America's European allies saw through this charade and declined to participate.

Particularly in his aggressive defenses of the commission, Pompeo justified the need for "fresh"—which is to say, eighteenth century—thinking about human rights, but he also accomplished other ends. He denounced the agency over which he presided. In spite of his attempts to incorporate the report into US foreign policy in the last months of the Trump administration, the product enabled him to align himself with nationalist, populist, and Christian right Trump constituencies. The insignificance of the commission for foreign policy suggests that, although there may have been some expectation that it would influence international discourse, the unalienable rights project was also aimed squarely at boosting Pompeo's political prospects.

Foreign Assistance

Finally, I turn to the final tool of foreign policy, which is foreign aid or assistance. In 2009, the State Department characterized the goal of foreign assistance as aid intended to "help build and sustain democratic, well-governed states that respond to the needs of their people, reduce widespread poverty, and conduct themselves responsibly in the international system."[72] Redefining the goals of foreign assistance in 2020, the State Department emphasized "defend[ing] U.S. national security," "assert[ing] U.S. leadership and influence," "generating demand for U.S. goods and services abroad," and "ensur[ing] effectiveness and accountability to the U.S. taxpayer by optimizing military assistance."[73] The US government's primary vehicle for SOGI foreign assistance is the Global Equality Fund.

Global Equality Fund

As we know, the Trump administration withdrew the US from a number of high-profile international agreements, including the Paris climate accord (Paris Agreement) and the Iran nuclear deal, as well as less prominent agreements.[74] One less-publicized international partnership to which the US is party is the Global Equality Fund (GEF), the most significant global source for SOGI human rights funding and assistance.[75] Hillary Clinton announced the formation of the GEF in her Geneva speech in December 2011. The Bureau of Democracy, Human Rights, and Labor manages the GEF, enrolls partners, and administers "gift" funds from GEF members.

The GEF is an umbrella fund with seventeen country partners (including the US) that supports three kinds of assistance programs. The three categories of assistance are emergency support (Dignity for All), long-term technical assistance and organizational capacity building, and small grants disbursed by US embassies. With its three distinct categories of assistance and many partners and grantees around the world, the GEF is the best known of the SOGI human rights programs and initiatives of the US government.[76] Many grassroots LGBTQI activists outside the US are familiar with the GEF, and those who aren't often learn about the fund at meetings organized by grassroots LGBTI groups such as ASOGIHRO, which I discuss in the next chapter.

During the Trump administration, the GEF operated more quietly than it did during the Obama administration. Throughout Trump's term in office, the Senate Appropriations Committee, perhaps as a precaution, directed the State Department to continue to fund the GEF. The GEF continued to function and to solicit applications for grants related to the goals and purposes of the program.[77] One way to monitor the operation of parts of the GEF is through grants.gov, the federal government's free, official website that permits people to search and apply for appropriate grants. Of course, the anti-LGBT right can also glean information about federal government priorities and assistance from grants.gov.[78]

The GEF isn't unique in its funding structure. Created under Secretary Clinton, a similar assistance program is Lifeline: Embattled Civil Society Organizations Assistance Fund. Lifeline relies on an international group of partner countries to provide emergency assistance to human rights, including LGBTI, civil society organizations. Lifeline funds are disbursed through a consortium of CSOs led by Freedom House, a US-based "independent watchdog organization dedicated to the expansion of freedom around the world."[79] Although some GEF funding is allocated through responses to solicitations on grants.gov, other GEF funding is not. For example, in addition to serving as a partner of the State Department for Lifeline assistance, Freedom House and its partners also disburse funding for the rapid-response emergency subprogram of the GEF, Dignity for All, directly to LGBTQ organizations, human rights defenders, and vulnerable LGBTQ people. Dignity, which is based on Lifeline, funds such forms of emergency assistance as security training, medical or legal assistance, trial monitoring, prison visits, and temporary relocation of threatened activists or organizations.[80]

In the 2016 donor preconference session at the ILGA World conference in Bangkok, "Forecasting a Trump Development Agenda," the US official invited to serve on the panel and address possible changes to SOGI human rights assistance conveyed to the audience of concerned funders and activists some information relevant to the question of the fate of the GEF in the Trump administration. The official noted that some grants, such as Dignity for All, are multiyear in length, meaning that approval for grant activities would not be necessary for four years. If US funds were withheld, for example, under direction from the secretary of state or the assistant secretary for DRL, the official noted that contributions from other GEF partners could be used to fund the program. Finally, in response to a question about the possible relocation of GEF administration to another member nation if the program were threatened with termination, the official responded that GEF administration could pass to another member state if such a resolution became necessary to preserve the fund. However, under such conditions, a member state would need to have the political will as well as the administrative resources to assume leadership of the program.[81]

While researching *Because We Are Human*, I learned that GEF partners—that is, representatives of GEF country and organization members—generally met twice a year, once in the US and once outside the US. At meetings held during the Obama administration, representatives analyzed program results, processed feedback from activists and grantees, analyzed gaps in needs, determined priorities, and designed grants and solicitations for future programs. Although such meetings are neither advertised nor open to the public, GEF meetings continued to be held during the Trump administration. In 2017, GEF partner representatives met at least once, in Warsaw in early November.[82] Meeting at the same time in Warsaw, November 1–4, was ILGA Europe, and it's likely that GEF representatives met on the margins of the ILGA conference.

Evidence of the continuing operation of the GEF under the Trump administration came in May 2018, when Canada joined the sixteen countries that had become GEF members during Obama's second term in office to become the newest member of the fund and the only new country member during the Trump administration. In October, GEF representatives gathered in Berlin for an international meeting hosted by the German Federal Foreign Office.[83] US GEF representatives in attendance in Berlin were Keisha Adams,

Kerry Ashforth, Patricia Davis, and Jessica Huber; Mindy Michaels, director of emergency assistance programs for Freedom House, a GEF implementing partner, also attended.[84]

Because I'm a researcher, I was not invited to attend the full meeting of GEF representatives, grantees, and implementing partners. However, I attended one session on "Global LGBTI Rights Awareness and Outreach" and a reception hosted by the Canadian embassy for GEF representatives, activists, and other stakeholders. At the GEF reception, the Canadian ambassador to Germany, Stéphane Dion, welcomed GEF representatives to the embassy and praised their work on LGBTI human rights. During the Obama administration, the US embassy would typically host a reception for GEF representatives when meetings were held outside the US. We should recall that in 2018, the US ambassador to Germany was Ric Grenell. Although months after the GEF meeting he would launch a campaign for decriminalization from the US embassy in Berlin, Grenell declined both to host the GEF delegates at the US embassy and to attend the reception at the Canadian embassy. Grenell's own campaign to make decriminalization a condition for foreign aid wasn't coordinated with DRL, and during the campaign Grenell didn't indicate support for the GEF.

In October 2019, the Norwegian Ministry of Foreign Affairs hosted a GEF meeting in Oslo.[85] In March 2020, GEF implementing partners and donors assembled for the first GEF implementer's conference in South Africa. By the spring, most US officials were no longer traveling abroad because of the Covid-19 pandemic. However, though the end of the Trump administration, the GEF continued to solicit applications for funding of LGBTI programs, posting notices of funding opportunities (NOFOs). For example, near the end of Trump's term in office, DRL published a funding opportunity announcement

> for projects that provide lesbian, gay, bisexual, transgender, and intersex (LGBTI) communities with the tools to empower local movements and communities, prevent, mitigate, and recover from violence, discrimination, stigma, and human rights abuses, promote full social inclusion, or address critical issues of justice in the East Asia and Pacific region, with a particular focus on Burma, Cambodia, Laos, Malaysia, Mongolia, the Philippines, Singapore, Thailand, and/or Vietnam.[86]

When the Trump administration ended in January 2021, the GEF was funded and operational. Very quickly after Biden's inauguration, a new, more informational, webpage on the GEF debuted with a banner quote from Secretary of State Antony Blinken that cited the GEF's purpose: "catalyz[ing] positive change" on LGBTQI+ rights.[87]

And Yet SOGI Persists

It's possible to draw many conclusions from these instances of public diplomacy, diplomacy, and foreign assistance in the time of Trump. On the one hand, there is ample evidence to support a conclusion that the Trump administration was indifferent and transactional toward most claims and violations of human rights, including SOGI. A signal exception to this pattern was human rights claims of people persecuted for their religious faith. The Trump administration discounted and disdained human rights in a variety of circumstances, including when the president, his advisors, or other allies believed there was some economic or political benefit to be gained; when they wanted to reinforce the president's and the administration's status as a nationalist force that put "America first"; when they perceived some benefit to rejecting the values of cultural liberals, globalist cosmopolitans, or European allies; or when they wanted to distract Americans from other events or scandals.

Some variation in symbolic acts and rhetoric did occur between the Obama and Trump administrations, and Trump's secretaries of state made fewer official diplomatic efforts to protest violations against LGBTI people. Congressional concern about the Trump administration's orientation toward human rights was obvious in internal government deliberations and communiques that focused on policies, personnel, and appropriations. Throughout the Trump administration, Congress continued to support and appropriate funding for human rights programs. And some Senate Republicans pushed back quietly against the White House's desultory and transactional orientation toward human rights. They didn't single out SOGI assistance for support, but they did clarify their intent that SOGI shouldn't be extirpated from US foreign policy. In part, elected officials may have shared the pragmatic perspective of General James Mattis, who noted to members of Congress in 2013 that "if you don't fund the State Department fully, then I need to buy more ammunition ultimately."[88]

Even with all the chaos and sustained efforts to disable government functions, there was more continuity than discontinuity between SOGI human rights policies and practices of the Obama administration and those of the

Trump administration.[89] At the end of this book I draw some conclusions about the roots of this resilience in the context of an administration that defied so many norms, laws, subpoenas, regulations, and legal advisories.

In the next chapter, I rely on participant observation to investigate my final question: Even if Congress continued to appropriate funds for LGBTI human rights diplomacy and assistance, and DRL continued to administer funds from GEF partners, did LGBTI activists and organizations continue to work with State Department officials and accept assistance from the US government under the Trump administration? To answer the question, I returned to Africa to observe a second meeting of the SOGI human rights group to which I have given the pseudonym, African Sexual Orientation and Gender Identity Human Rights Organization, or ASOGIHRO (pronounced "a SOGI hero"). I didn't attend the meetings in Africa in 2015 and 2019 to report on or analyze grassroots LGBTQI activism. Instead, my goal was to observe the intersections and interaction of US government officials and the US human rights assistance they purveyed, and LGBTQI activists.

Even though there may be some overlap, the evidence that indicates the "supply" side of US SOGI human rights assistance has been sustained is different than the evidence for the existence of a "demand" side for such assistance. For example, if US officials and institutions have continued to pledge US support for SOGI human rights, and the policies and funds promulgated to effect such assistance remained intact, we have evidence that SOGI human rights support and assistance continued. However, it's still possible that grassroots LGBTQI human rights activists who work in situations of great human rights jeopardy distrusted the US government under Trump, refused to partner with US officials, and essentially left US human rights assistance on the table. Was there "demand" for US advocacy on behalf of SOGI human rights and for US SOGI human rights assistance during Trump's term in office? Let's see.

Chapter 5

The US Abroad on SOGI Human Rights in the Time of Trump

SOGI Demand

US SOGI human rights advocacy takes place in a variety of settings. These include multilateral meetings and conferences held around the world, quiet diplomacy that consists of interactions between US officials and representatives of regimes and civil society, and meetings between US officials and grassroots activists in venues organized by donors or grassroots groups. In my earliest attempt to assess donor and activist responses to the election of Donald Trump, I attended the 2016 International Lesbian, Gay, Bisexual, Trans, and Intersex Association (ILGA) World conference, held in late November in Bangkok, Thailand. The conference was held at a pivotal moment; earlier in November, Trump had defeated Hillary Clinton in an upset not foreseen by prognosticators.

Because Trump had not yet taken office, SOGI communities could only guess how the outcome might affect human rights. In Thailand, hundreds of activists met for networking and sessions on a diverse array of topics, including queer refugees; LGBTI-related data; activist video production; religious hate speech; pinkwashing and Palestinan liberation; LGBTI poverty; grantmaking; international health; media representations; activist performance art; strategic litigation; domestic violence; youth activism; LGBT sex workers; lesbian, bisexual, and queer women's organizing; trans parenting; and others. The conference also hosted meetings of regional caucuses and preconferences on (or for) health, transgender, bisexual, women, intersex, UN advocacy, and interfaith.

Meeting on the sidelines of ILGA, donor group representatives and some activists gathered for a donor preconference to which two US officials were invited. Anxiety about the possible reversal of US support for SOGI human rights was evident before the preconference began, when a session entitled "Forecasting a Trump Development Agenda" was added to the schedule after Trump's victory. In his introductory presentation, the panel's moderator, Matthew Hart, director of the Global Philanthropy Project, introduced a pie chart of SOGI human rights contributions published by Funders for LGBTQ Issues and Astraea's Global Philanthropy Project (GPP). The *2013–2014 Global Resources Report: Government and Philanthropic Support for Lesbian, Gay, Bisexual, Transgender, and Intersex Communities*, already dated on delivery, was the "first comprehensive report of its kind on all foundation and government funding for LGBTI issues." The report lists US dollar figures for US government contributions in 2013–14 and for pooled Global Equality Fund (GEF) funding from member countries as well as other donors. And it breaks down recipients of LGBTI human rights funding by region, an approach that doesn't identify recipient groups or even countries where outside funding for LGBTQI groups and individuals would be culturally or legally proscribed.[1]

The moderator walked the audience of donors, activists, and US government implementing partners through a series of pie charts with SOGI human rights assistance disaggregated by global region, and the US and aggregate GEF contribution to these total amounts highlighted. The moderator acknowledged that activists could not be certain that US financial and other contributions to SOGI human rights advocacy would disappear under a Trump administration. His goal was to highlight the US government role in SOGI advocacy because of the uncertainty that had beset SOGI advocates and their networks in the wake of the US election.

In late 2016, the panelists and activists in attendance at the ILGA World conference could only speculate about possible changes to US policy and their ramifications. By 2017, it was clear to some researchers and members of the international human rights community that the presidential election had, indeed, influenced environments for LGBTQ activism. In "The Trump Effect: Elections at Home and Abroad Dampen Liberia's Gay-Rights Revival," Robbie Corey-Boulet argues that Trump's election "alarmed" LGBTQ activists in Liberia because leaders of Liberian LGBTQ organizations—the one that existed in 2012 as well as others that have emerged in the years since 2012—"all view the U.S., and U.S.-based organizations, as critical sources of funding" and look to the US embassy for "low profile" support and advocacy. Corey-Boulet argues that it is precisely because the U.S. has been so central to the growth of Liberia's LGBT movement that last year's election of President Donald Trump alarmed Liberian activists, who feared an immediate drop in material and moral support. . . . The consequences of diminishing outside pressure to uphold these rights could be devastating in a nation that has already demonstrated a willingness to single out its LGBT citizens for abuse.[2]

In addition to "Trump-related anxiety," in 2016 prominent Liberian political figures were scapegoating LGBTQ people and identifying themselves with "traditional values" for political gain. Michael Bosia and Meredith Weiss identify such uses of LGBTQ people as threats to the nation and exemplars of Western decadence as instances of the global phenomenon of political homophobia.[3]

In chapter 4, I noted the concerns about the continuity in the Trump administration of a commitment to SOGI that emerged at the 2018 Council for Global Equality (CGE) forum, "U.S. Support for Global LGBT Equality." The activist panel at that forum was "The View from Abroad: A Conversation with On-the-Ground LGBT Advocates," with activists from Latin America (the moderator), the Caribbean, and Kenya. The three panelists engaged in a wide-ranging conversation about the value of US support for SOGI and what they, as LGBTQI activists, wanted the US to do with regard to SOGI. When the moderator asked fellow panelists how the US government had provided useful assistance for SOGI in the past, the activists gave several responses: as grassroots activists, they had "worked directly with the State Department" on programs such as PEPFAR; they had worked closely with US embassies, which had been "eagerly ready to support" activists; and they noted the value of Country Reports on Human Rights Practices for publicizing human rights violations and helping to hold governments accountable for them.

The LGBTI activists tendered a range of explanations for what was perceived among LGBTI people abroad as the "retreat" of the Trump administration from LGBTI advocacy. In her comments, the Caribbean activist pointed out that some differences between the Obama and Trump administrations were differences of personality and ideology, such as the differences in perspectives of former US ambassador to the UN Samantha Power and then-ambassador Nikki Haley. Invoking structural considerations, the Kenyan activist argued that a US failure to integrate SOGI human rights into its foreign policy would empower anti-LGBTI leaders and movements in countries where LGBTQI people are at risk. He noted that after Trump took office, the European Union and Canada increased their visibility in SOGI advocacy. But both the moderator and the Caribbean activist acknowledged that US disengagement on SOGI encouraged Christian conservatives in the US and Canada to intensify their anti-SOGI advocacy in places like the Caribbean and Latin America. On the perceived "retreat" of the Trump administration from SOGI, the Kenyan asked rhetorically, "Is this a concern for us?" and answered, "It is a concern."

In this chapter, first, I respond to the question of international demand for US foreign assistance by comparing two "cases": a 2015 meeting of African LGBTQI activists and the 2019 meeting, both organized by the same organization. When I attended the 2019 meeting, I didn't know how US officials and US foreign assistance would be received. Would activists from across the continent regard US officials as emissaries of a despised government whose president had already referred to majority-African countries as "shithole countries"? Would they talk with US officials about their experiences of discrimination and violence and discuss financial and other exigencies? Here is my reporting on these and other issues. My second goal in the chapter is to alert Western scholars to complexities that occur at the intersection of grassroots LGBTQI activism and US foreign assistance. Even those of us who are staunch proponents of LGBTI peoples' human rights may misapprehend some of what takes place at this intersection by assuming that we have complete information or by projecting our own political assumptions onto LGBTI people or activists outside the US.

ASOGIHRO

In 2014, I met a leader of a grassroots African LGBTQI human rights organization in Washington, DC. In 2015, I attended a conference organized by this group. Because of the precautions organizers took to protect the identities of activists at both conferences I attended, I refer to this organization using a pseudonym: the African Sexual Orientation and Gender Identity Human Rights Organization, or ASOGIHRO (pronounced "a SOGI hero"). ASOGIHRO is an indigenous LGBTI advocacy organization that functions as an umbrella group to support civil society activism on sexuality, sexual health, and SOGI human rights in Africa. ASOGIHRO is a grantor that provides resources to sexual minority groups, and it is a grantee of the US government as well as of other human rights and social justice funders.

My primary motivation for attending the ASOGIHRO conference was to observe firsthand a conference planned and executed by grassroots African human rights advocates to advance the cause of SOGI human rights that incorporated US government representatives and US assistance. By the time I attended the ASOGIHRO meeting, I had learned that US officials who work to support SOGI human rights and other members of a broad community of human rights partners go to venues hosted by grassroots LGBTQ human rights advocates and host those advocates in meetings in partner countries. Grassroots activists use such meetings to inform donors about the needs and challenges they and their movements face, and they collaborate with donors to design and target assistance.

I hoped to accomplish two tasks by attending the conference and collecting data about the group and its partnerships with a range of donors that includes the US State Department. The first task was to gain firsthand knowledge of how the US government engages in SOGI human rights advocacy with grassroots LGBTI groups. The second was to use my own observations and information I collected from the 2015 meeting to confirm or disconfirm information about US government SOGI human rights advocacy provided by State Department officials, government documents, and other sources. Attending the ASOGIHRO conference gave me an opportunity to observe how activists and US officials interact in a setting organized by a grassroots LGBTI organization and how US human rights assistance is received by grassroots activists. I included the 2015 ASOGIHRO conference as a case study in *Because We Are Human*, and, in 2019, I attended the meeting to repeat the case study in the "time of Trump."

2015

The ASOGIHRO meeting was organized by African activists, and donors— including five US government attendees—were invited guests of the organization. Participants understood that there might be danger associated with the meeting and its purpose. Before the conference began, organizers directed attendees not to disclose the purpose of their travel once they entered the country. Organizers gave attendees times and locations where buses would pick them up in a nearby city to carry them to the undisclosed conference site. At the conference, I collected literature from the wide variety of organizations whose representatives attended the meeting, and I spoke informally with activists and funders. I didn't observe every event at the conference.

Although I was present for some meetings that took place in public spaces, I didn't participate in private meetings between funders and human rights defenders. However, I did observe all plenary sessions and as many concurrent sessions as I could. I didn't attend the donor preconference in 2015, so my observations begin with the conference proper.

A plenary session held on the first day of the conference was: "We Don't Know All the Answers (But We Have a Few Explanations)." The title referred to a comment the US official on the panel had made at a previous SOGI conference, when she introduced herself by saying, "I'm from the United States, and we don't know all the answers." The purpose of the "We Don't Know All the Answers" session was to provide an opportunity for funders to explain to human rights activists and representatives of LGBTI organizations what specific conditions apply to funding from their organizations, to respond to questions about funding opportunities and constraints, and to suggest ways in which differently situated grantmakers—such as those whose representatives were in attendance at the conference—could assist local LGBTI organizations.

The discussion at this panel was rich and occasionally challenging; activists and panelists discussed a specific constraint on US government assistance: policies that prevent US funding of sex worker rights activism or sex work decriminalization. As State Department officials would explain again in 2019, the official on the 2015 panel explained that the constraint doesn't bar funding for assistance to sex workers as long as that assistance is not related to sex workers' rights or decriminalization of sex work. When some activists who attended the session reproved the US official over the sex worker rights/decriminalization constraint, the official noted that assistance funded by tax revenue is subject to statutory requirements and that the prohibition affected all US government assistance. She also emphasized, as US officials would in 2019, that sex workers are not barred from receiving US assistance for purposes related to, for example, health and human rights protections. And she encouraged sex worker advocates to apply for US funding for those purposes.

In her remarks in the "We Don't Know All the Answers" session, the US official set forth goals for cooperation between US government representatives and grassroots LGBTQI activists: to listen to activists about their needs and issues; to travel to meet activists in locations around the world; to bring activists to meetings in donor countries (including the US); to deploy knowledgeable personnel to work closely with activists to meet their needs;

to protect the safety and security of grantees and beneficiaries of human rights interventions; and to work with grantee activists and organizations to adequately report what they accomplish with the assistance they receive. Two questions addressed to the US official focused on the operational needs of organizations. The first criticized a typical model of assistance as geared to prioritizing and funding high-profile deliverables rather than meeting the fixed and ongoing costs of advocacy organizations. The official responded that State Department human rights programs funded through the GEF can, in fact, be used to pay fixed, "core," costs such as rent, personnel, and equipment, so that human rights groups are able to function effectively over time. The second operational question concerned the difficulties activists often have with the reporting and administrative demands of managing grants from international funders. The official's response outlined the practice by which the State Department funds a grant to a larger organization as an implementing partner, and the implementing partner then subgrants to the smaller group and agrees to take on the task of administering the grant. This practice provides a cooperative path to funding small LGBTI human rights organizations while shifting administrative tasks to groups with more infrastructure and expertise in grant administration.

A key piece of information about US government resources and assistance dedicated to SOGI human rights was revealed in the "We Don't Know All the Answers" plenary session: under the US government's marking policy, implementing partners and grantees must "mark," or brand, all products of US government assistance at public meetings, on organizations' websites, and on all other materials that might be produced from that assistance.[4] However, the Bureau of Democracy, Human Rights, and Labor (DRL) has received an exemption to this branding requirement because of the sensitive nature of many of its human rights programs and because association with the US could place many human rights defenders at risk. This exemption is explained in grant agreements that grantees and implementing partners sign when they receive funds. The exemption means that grantees are free to reveal their cooperation with the US, but they are not required to publicize an assistance relationship with the US government that may leave them open to charges of colluding with the US.

The second day of the conference included "Activist-Donor Speed Dating," organized in two sets of four concurrent sessions. Each one of the first set of sessions concentrated on a region of Africa: North, South, East, and West. Representatives from the State Department, USAID, and other funding organizations spread out and formed a funder panel for each session. These regional sessions were followed by a brief break, after which a new set of topical sessions convened. The conference program promised activists "open engagement" with funders in the speed dating sessions and, indeed, the discussion was lively and informative in the sessions I attended.

The topical session of "Activist-Donor Speed Dating" I attended focused on sexual health, and the US government panelist for that session was a second DRL official. This official offered the session attendees a quick yet detailed overview of the three types of assistance that make up the Global Equality Fund and represent opportunities for funding and assistance for SOGI human rights advocacy. He offered examples from funded projects that would be relevant to sexual health advocacy. One activist in this session asked how difficult or bureaucratic the process of applying for GEF funding is, and the official explained that the grant process had recently been revised and streamlined to be more proposer-friendly than previous processes. He noted that at the formal proposal stage, potential grantees could receive further guidance from State Department personnel to complete the proposal, and that DRL might encourage activists from smaller organizations to partner with more experienced LGBTI organizations, some of whose members were in attendance at the meeting.

SOGI human rights advocates attended the ASOGIHRO 2015 meeting from across the continent. Taken as a whole, the conference incorporated presentations and discussions on a variety of topics germane to the concerns of LGBTI people in different legal, social, and cultural positions in African nations, including the benefits and limitations of litigation; navigating conflict in and among LGBTI human rights organizations; the role of young people in the movement; promoting transgender rights and awareness; migration, asylum-seeking, and refugees; the role of art in the movement; addressing public health concerns of LGBTI people (including but not limited to HIV/AIDS); international advocacy; employment and entrepreneurship for LGBTI people discriminated against in labor markets; building movement sustainability; and LGBTI people and religion. Many funders also attended these sessions throughout the course of the meeting, no doubt learning more about the pressures, challenges, programs, and successes of LGBTI movements on the continent.

A final note about 2015: when I attended the 2015 ASOGIHRO meeting, I was curious about how African LGBTI activists would regard representatives of the US government. I believed for example, that many activists might resent the attendance of US officials or reject US human rights assistance on grounds of US or Western imperialism on the continent. Bearing in mind that I couldn't observe every session or interaction between the activists and their US government guests, I was surprised when I didn't hear or encounter disapproval of the presence of US officials. In the "We Don't Know All the Answers" session, sex worker activists did challenge the stricture on the US funding sex worker rights/decriminalization that the US official reported; that is, rather than rejecting US assistance, they challenged the fairness and legitimacy of such a stricture. In that same session, the audience spontaneously applauded two lines: the first applause line was the US official's plea to the assembled activists to "help me help you" by working with DRL officials to report not only immediate "outputs" associated with assistance but also longer-term "outcomes" that could justify aid and contribute to internal State Department accountability for continued assistance.[5] The activists in the audience also applauded when the US official noted that President Obama was committed—and had committed his administration—to LGBTI human rights.[6]

When I returned from the meeting in Africa, I wrote a chapter for Marla Brettschneider, Susan Burgess, and Christine Keating's edited volume *LGBTQ Politics: A Critical Reader.*[7] My chapter in that volume, "Top Down, Bottom Up, or Meeting in the Middle? A SOGI Human Rights Case Study," addresses a concern of many scholars of sexuality studies: that contemporary LGBTQ politics have been captured and (re)directed by powerful interests to the detriment of LGBTQ people. It is certainly true that social movements of disfavored and stigmatized people do suffer this fate. However, in my chapter and later, in *Because We Are Human*, I offer some evidence that in the case of US government assistance to SOGI human rights, it has been more accurate to say that grassroots LGBTQ/SOGI human rights advocates and US government officials have "met in the middle."[8]

By this I mean that during the Obama administration, SOGI advocates and organizations used a variety of mechanisms to inform US and other donors of the specific needs and challenges they face, solicit particular forms of assistance, and provide feedback to US officials about the efficacy of the human rights assistance they received. In their turn, human rights officials in DRL worked with activists to determine ways for activists to meet their needs and simultaneously remain in compliance with US federal regulations. Given the many concerns about how SOGI human rights might fare under Trump, I attended the ASOGIHRO meeting for a second time to see what might have changed about US assistance or LGBTI activists' responses to US officials.

2019

Setting and Logistics

Like the 2015 conference, this meeting was held in an undisclosed location to which attendees were bussed from prearranged sites in a nearby city. In the run-up to the meeting, donors and activists were instructed to acquire tourist visas to enter the country and not to disclose information about the meeting or its purpose to government officials or on social media. Warnings about tagging participants in photos and posting to social media were delivered by conference organizers throughout the meeting. There were a few format and logistical changes between 2015 and 2019. First, before we reached the meeting venue, all attendees had received a copy of the conference's code of conduct, which prohibited harassing conduct and set ground rules for photography. Attendees were solicited for their decisions about whether they could be photographed or preferred not to be: a green conference lanyard meant "yes," and a red lanyard meant "no." Keeping in mind the importance of respecting activists' safety, I took no photos of conference participants. Second, attendance at the meeting had expanded. Whereas a tent was required to hold attendees who would not fit in the venue's meeting rooms for plenary sessions in 2015, in 2019 a much larger tent needed to be pitched to accommodate the several hundred activists who traveled from many African nations to attend the meeting.[9]

The 2019 conference offered three preconferences: intersex, transgender, and donor. I attended the donor preconference, which included representatives of human rights and other donor organizations. And I obtained permission from an organizer to attend one session of the transgender preconference that focused on the funding of transgender human rights projects. The US government contingent, reduced from five US officials who represented the State Department and USAID in 2015, consisted of two State Department officials. As in 2015, no other country sent government officials, although in at least one case a European philanthropic organization that works closely with its country's foreign policy ministry represented that nation.

In addition to meeting with activists one-on-one and in small groups, the two State Department officials, Patricia Davis and Jessica Huber, spoke on a total of five panels. These were a concurrent session during the donor preconference on "Social Enterprise: LGBTIs, the SDGs [Sustainable Development Goals], and Economic Freedom through Interdependence" (Huber), a concurrent session of the transgender preconference on the funding landscape for trans issues (Davis), a session on the first day of the conference organized to help activists "Meet the Donors" (Davis), and two concurrent donor "speed dating" sessions during the conference proper (Huber and Davis).

As in 2015, during the conference proper, organizers arranged a set of donor speed dating sessions to introduce activists and donors in a small group setting that would facilitate questions and conversations about assistance. After the conference began, all attendees were solicited by email to register on a secure website to attend the session in each round of speed dating that best corresponded to their needs or the needs of their organization. The speed dating sessions were organized in two rounds of concurrent sessions as they had been in 2015, but the subject categories were different: the first set targeted different identity populations rather than, as in 2015, geographic regions, and the second set was organized around advocacy needs.

The populations in the first set of sessions were LBQ "womxn" organizing, sex work organizing, organizing for trans and gender nonconfirming people, and intersex organizing. The US officials split up and presented in sessions on funding LBQ women organizing and funding trans and gender nonconfirming people. Because this first set of donor speed dating sessions was concurrent, I opted for the session focused on LBQ women that included Jessica Huber. A second set of donor "speed dating" sessions was organized around advocacy needs, including general/core support; advocacy, litigation, and access to justice; HIV and sexual health programming and advocacy; and safety, security, and protection from violence.

A wide variety of other themed sessions attested to the needs and interests of activists, including sessions on information-driven organizing, art therapy and performing arts, litigation strategies, resilience, health and disability, religious fundamentalism, age activism, digital safety, refugee and migrant issues, empowerment economics, and storytelling. In addition to the speed dating session on funding related to protection from violence, three other sessions focused on violence against LGBTI people in Africa, including a session on violence associated with criminalization, one on strategies to mitigate violence, and one focused on safety from violence in francophone Africa. Taking into account the broad range of issues confronting LGBTI movements and activists on the continent, it's significant that four sessions—more than for any other issue—were dedicated to the subject of violence against LGBTI people.

Themes, Philosophy, and Analysis

As I observed conference sessions and listened to conversations among attendees, I was struck by the themes that emerged from multiple presentations and exchanges among organizers, activists, and funders. Some of these themes were familiar to me from other SOGI human rights meetings I have observed in a variety of venues, including the importance of listening and responding to activists about their needs and priorities, and the imperative of considering and protecting the security of activists in all human rights assistance. As I discussed in *Because We Are Human*, the theme of listening to, and to the extent possible being guided by, the needs of activists on the ground was prevalent and consistent in my interviews and conversations with State Department and USAID officials during the Obama administration, all of whom cited it in some form as a first principle of government human rights advocacy and assistance. Likewise, in meetings with activists and conversations about SOGI advocacy, US officials expressed concerns about the safety and security of LGBTI activists whose defenses of civil and human rights, and coordination with Western governments, could imperil them. Even as US officials enact practices to protect the security of activists from exposures of information or evidence of cooperation with the US, security practices can conflict with demands for government transparency. Unfortunately, the tension between the values of security and transparency probably cannot be neatly resolved.[10]

However, some themes I identified at the 2019 ASOGIHRO meeting were new to me in SOGI venues or seemed more widely embraced and enunciated than I had seen them be in previous meetings I've attended. These include the value of feminist principles in LGBTI movements and feminist approaches to grantmaking; the value of intersectionality, both as a political concept and a funding strategy; and the necessity for funders and movements to consider well-being and "livability" as goals of human rights assistance and advocacy. These three themes were features of the common language of actors in the meeting, and they were called upon fluently by activists and funders.

First, throughout the meeting, activists and donors alike described their goals, strategies, or practices as feminist. Many invoked feminism as providing guidelines for human rights advocacy and grantmaking, or pledged to conform to feminist principles in their funding and activism. The more explicitly feminist cast of the 2019 meeting as compared with the 2015 meeting may be attributable to the fact that, while a majority of 2015 attendees were men, a majority in 2019 were women. Of course, feminism is not just for women, but, as an empirical matter, women are more likely to be familiar with and adopt feminist political thought and goals. Indeed, we know that when underrepresented groups attain higher numbers and visibility in movements and organizations, decision-making and leadership styles reflect that diversity of personnel.[11]

When leaders of ASOGIHRO addressed the funders in the opening plenary of the donor preconference, they explicitly identified ASOGIHRO as a feminist organization. These activist-leaders cited the African Feminist Charter (AFC) as a source for their ideals and operating principles. First published in 2007, the charter, also known as the Charter of Feminist Principles for African Feminists, was codified at a 2006 pan-African feminist meeting in Accra, Ghana. The AFC is a manifesto of African feminism as a liberation struggle, an adumbration of feminist individual and institutional ethics, and a set of guidelines for women's movement leadership.[12]

Speakers at ASOGIHRO didn't offer a complete philosophy of feminism as it applies to LGBTI movements, and of course the AFC articulates a general philosophy but doesn't apply it specifically to LGBTI movements. However, in the contexts of their remarks, activists and funders did articulate particular feminist commitments, and these commitments were consistent with the AFC. They could also be identified in a booklet that was widely distributed at the conference: Astraea Lesbian Foundation for Justice, *Feminist Funding Principles*. Astraea is a grantor of African LGBTI human rights activism, in general, and of ASOGIHRO, in particular. The feminist principles are these:

1. Fund those most impacted by gendered oppression.

2. Fund at the intersection of women's rights and LGBTQI liberation movements.

3. Apply an intersectional lens to break down funding silos.

4. Provide flexible and sustained core funding to activists.

5. Fund efforts to make social and cultural change, alongside and as part of legal and policy changes.

6. Support cross-issue and cross-regional movement building.

7. Go beyond grantmaking: accompany activists with capacity building and leadership support.

8. Invest in holistic security and healing justice.

9. Support work at the crossroads of feminist activism, digital rights, and internet freedom.

10. Partner with women's and other activist-led funds to ensure that funding reaches the grassroots.[13]

In the context of the ASOGIHRO conoference, I don't interpret the convergence of the activists and funders on feminist principles such as those presented in the Astraea booklet as a sign that LGBTI activists (and funders) have been pressured by Astraea to understand and embrace a particular conception of feminism. Instead, I think it makes sense to see the principles as having been constructed from and through the experience of international and grassroots activists cooperating on projects relating to SOGI human rights. This perspective is supported by other international-grassroots projects such as *Intersecting Movements Resisting Authoritarianisms: Feminist and Progressive Analysis and Tactics*, funded by the Women's Rights Programs at Open Society Foundations.[14] Feminist principles of advocacy and grantmaking also constitute an overarching category in which the other key themes I heard repeatedly—intersectionality and livability—can be situated.

The second theme I encountered more frequently than usual was intersectionality, which is enumerated in Astraea principle 3 and in the African Feminist Charter: "We recognize that we do not have a homogenous identity as feminists—we acknowledge and celebrate our diversities and our shared commitment to a transformatory agenda for African societies and African women in particular. This is what gives us our common feminist identity."[15] In addition to discussion about the internal diversity of LGBTI communities and the significance of that diversity, ASOGIHRO hosted many conversations about the intersectionality of movements and intersectional approaches to funding. US officials talked about expanding intersectional programming by, for example, designing grant solicitations to simultaneously address the needs of marginalized groups such as, for example, disabled and LGBTI persons. DRL has issued solicitations for projects that address intersections between religious freedom and the rights of LGBTI people.

The third theme I heard invoked in a way that was unusual in my experience is livability, which for activists and funders signifies a holistic approach to funding movements that integrates concern with the mental and material well-being of members of disfavored groups with advocacy, and rejects "siloed" approaches to human rights and social enterprise/ economic development. The principle of livability is integrated into the African Feminist Charter as a matter of "individual ethics" (defined as "the support, nurture, and care of other African feminists, along with the care for our own wellbeing")[16] and addressed in Astraea principle 8. Throughout the ASOGIHRO conference, it was clear that assuring livability for gender and sexual minorities who are often deprived of employment was a goal of LGBTI movements in Africa. Funders and activists alike discussed strategies for increasing core support and well-being for gender and sexual minorities. The GEF doesn't provide funding to support livability for LGBTI people; however, unlike many donors, the GEF can fund staff costs for grassroots organizations. The GEF can also provide funds to organizations that in turn focus on livability issues for LGBTI people. And DRL officials facilitate conversations between funders with the goal of enhancing livability for LGBTI activists/people.

I will add a fourth theme that is prominent in human rights literature but that I haven't encountered as a prominent subject of discussion in activist spaces. It's often framed as a question: Are human rights universal, or is the claim that human rights are universal an imposition of the values of the Global North on peoples, cultures, or legal frameworks of the Global South? The academic literature on this question alone is daunting and includes a wealth of thoughtful works that yield diverse and incisive commentaries on the question of human rights universality. I believe that because the theme has been the subject of so much ethical and theoretical scrutiny among Western academics, it's useful to consider whether or how it's invoked in SOGI activist contexts. Here's the thing: in the SOGI events I've attended since 2013, I've never heard a single LGBTI activist renounce the universality of human rights in its application to sexual orientation and gender identity. By this I mean that activists consistently strategize about rhetorical frames, priorities, alliances with civil society groups, and which constraints in their countries or global regions should be the object of their resources and attention. And they advise international allies, including US officials, to follow their lead in targeting particular laws, elite rhetorics, political tactics, cultural prohibitions, or social practices.

But in my experience, the conversations in contexts structured by grassroots activists and contexts that include grassroots activists as well as other activists and funders are *strategic*. That is, the conversations don't disclose a concern that rights and freedoms to live as LGBTI without discrimination or violence are Western ideas or impositions. Instead, they assert that grassroots activists should always set movement agendas and priorities. The most succinct statement I've heard on the theme of human rights universality was offered by an African LGBTI human rights activist at the 2019 ASOGIHRO conference. She prefaced her remarks about the needs of LGBTI people by saying, "We all know that human rights are universal."

Turning from activists to US officials, the messages offered by the two US officials at the 2019 ASOGIHRO conference were consistent with each other and frequently overlapped. Both officials explained that, unlike the other funding organizations whose representatives attended the meeting, the State Department isn't a philanthropic organization and, thus, must be accountable to US law and taxpayers. One implication of this difference between the US government and other funders is that US officials may counsel activists affiliated with smaller groups to seek funding and other assistance from GEF implementing partner CSOs and foundations. Structuring funding relationships in this way allows smaller organizations to access assistance and receive the benefit of having grants administered by larger, more experienced organizations. US officials offered their assistance to activists in new or small activist groups to determine how and where such groups might seek funding, and they promised that GEF implementing partners could work closely with each other to meet activists' needs.

A final note on ASOGIHRO 2019: as I observed in *Because We Are Human*, an important feature of meetings that bring together activists and US human rights officials is the formation and renewal of relationships that manifest in such sites. At the 2015 and 2019 ASOGIHRO conferences, much of the work of sharing information about the challenges confronting activists, discussing movements' immediate exigencies as well as longer-term prospects, and planning collaboration that both meets the needs of activists and the capacities of funders was accomplished in small group meetings. As a researcher, I didn't participate actively in these meetings, but I was present for many that took place in public spaces and spoke with both funders and activists at meals, receptions, and in casual moments at both the 2015 and 2019 meetings.

In these personal conversations, some negotiation takes place between the parties that constitutes activists and funders "meeting in the middle"— working out the terms by which a human rights assistance relationship is possible for both sides and beneficial to an individual, a group, or the movement. I may have been naive when I began researching SOGI human rights assistance, but in 2015 I was surprised by another feature of many of the conversations between activists and US officials, even—perhaps especially—those who had never met before: activists explaining their experiences of violence and discrimination to US officials and other human rights advocates. In addition to the parties communicating about advocacy projects and the mechanics of human rights assistance, there is a personal dimension to these conversations that it's easy to elide or overlook in academic analysis. From these experiences, I've formed a conception of the ASOGIHRO and other meetings as comprised of communities of activists and funders that intersect in complex relationships that, in addition to involving exchanges of information, and processes of deliberation and negotiation, involve trust. In other words, I believe it's not wrong or naive to speculate that engagement over human rights violations and assistance often requires—or even, over time, generates—bonds of trust between donors and human rights advocates.

Having been engaged in investigating these matters for a number of years, I argue that it's also necessary to consider the possibility that many US officials who work in the area of human rights assistance, including those who enter government service with personal backgrounds in human rights activism, do so because they care deeply about working closely with members of disfavored groups to address situations of human rights jeopardy and trying to mitigate harm. That is, we can assume that human rights assistance relationships merely reflect the strategic moves of self-interested parties hoping to garner benefits from their interaction. Or we can consider the possibility that, like many academics whose objects of study and activism reflect their civil and human rights–regarding values, some US officials may be motivated by similar aims and values.

Of course, we cannot take for granted an assumption that US officials who design and execute human rights policies and programs are motivated by interests in empowering human rights organizations, activists, and vulnerable individuals. Indeed, interrogating the motivation of state actors may be a crucial part of analyses of US human rights policies and practices. But neither should we take for granted the principle that such actors execute covert, invariably nefarious nationalist or neoliberal designs under the guise of rendering assistance to marginalized people. Unfortunately, this is precisely the assumption—and when the assumption, inevitably the conclusion—about human rights policies and practices adumbrated by a significant set of scholars with radical political commitments who work in progressive humanist disciplines and subfields of the US academy. Such assumptions don't just remain in the academy. Rather, they can have implications for how Western academics engage with grassroots LGBTI activists and how academics theorize and report the products of their research.

Good Enough Queers

In *Because We Are Human*, I quoted a number of progressive critics of US government advocacy for and human rights assistance to LGBTQ people, especially progressive critics trained in humanities disciplines whose politics inform their research agendas and conclusions. I criticized the lack of empiricism of many of these critiques, but I concede that one impediment to research on SOGI human rights policies and practices is how difficult information is to obtain. Human rights donors are likely to be careful about disclosing information that can expose and endanger activists who receive it. In places where violations are most common and perpetrators operate with most impunity, human rights defenders may be careful to craft narratives about their advocacy and resources that won't backfire and harm their movements.

How do I know this? I know because on many occasions academic colleagues have given me the names of LGBTQ organizations they have worked with or studied as examples of grassroots organizations that achieve remarkable results while eschewing the resources of foreign governments or other international donors. My colleagues are convinced that these groups would never countenance entanglements with the US government. In most of these conversations, I knew that the organizations my colleagues offered as evidence that US support for LGBTQI movements was superfluous or worse were, in fact, grantees of the US and recipients of assistance from the GEF. I had obtained this information sitting in international meetings operating under the Chatham House Rule: the proviso that attendees not disclose information about other speakers or attendees, or attribute quotes or information garnered in the meeting to speakers without permission when addressing anyone outside the meeting.

It's possible that LGBTQI/SOGI advocates and human rights groups that operate in parlous conditions around the world may refuse funds and assistance from the US, other nations, or international organizations, either on principle or because of conditions that might be attached to such assistance. However, it's not as easy to discern that groups reject assistance as we might think. At times, grassroots SOGI human rights advocates and groups believe it's in their interest to profess—to fellow citizens as well as to researchers—that they do not receive such assistance. Indeed, with the human rights exemption to its marking policy, the State Department provides the mechanism for such professions of autonomy from US government assistance.

One LGBTI organization that makes use of the human rights exemption to the State Department's marking policy is ASOGIHRO. Although the group is a grantee of the US government, no information about its relationship with the US appears on materials produced by the organization. If Western academics were to study the organization outside the context of its pan-African conference, it might appear to be a grassroots LGBTI organization that does not accept US or GEF funding. Such a possibility should remind us that the information we gather may reflect judgments made by grassroots LGBTI organizations about their own interests.

Clearly, a disjunction exists between information grassroots LGBTQI activists sometimes share with Western academics and the information they share with each other, transnational activist networks, and donors in meetings called by donor countries, international human rights organizations, and those very grassroots advocacy organizations. The conclusion I draw from this disjunction is that grassroots activists in situations of peril make determinations about their interests with regard to a range of outside actors that include their own governments, fellow citizens, and citizens (including scholars) of other nations.

Besides calculating and exercising self-interest in conditions of human rights vulnerability, there are other possible explanation for some grassroots indigenous LGBTI groups telling Western academics that they receive no human rights assistance from the US when they do receive such assistance. First, some activists may not be aware of the entities that fund their work. And, second, other funding entities may judge that activists' security interests are best served by not disclosing to them the sources that fund their work. With regard to the first reason, many grassroots organizations are small or lack the resources to manage grants, and they may receive assistance through international or regional implementing partners. Often, multiple intermediaries stand between a funder such as the US and grassroots organizations, especially nascent groups. Speaking on a panel at the 2019 ASOGIHRO meeting, a representative of one African LGBTI advocacy group explained it this way: his organization receives funds from many sources, including the State Department, and pools those funds in "a magic box" from which the organization can provide "what the movement needs." Thus, we should not be surprised if some grassroots LGBTI organizations report to Western researchers that they are not—indeed, would never permit themselves to be—compromised by an assistance relationship with the US government when the US is providing assistance on which they rely.

The second reason why activists may not be aware of the original source of funding they receive is that the proximate entities from which they receive resources may not disclose that funding has come from the US government. For example, regional partners may judge that activists in grave danger of being arrested, detained, or tortured are better off not knowing information about the sources funding their work that they might be forced to disclose under duress. This scenario occurs not only in the case of threatened LGBTI activists but in a wide range of other cases of imperiled human rights defenders.

In her International Human Rights Day speech in Geneva that focused on SOGI human rights, Hillary Clinton addressed LGBT people outside the US directly, telling them that they had "millions of friends" in the US. This might seem like a hyperbolic claim. But even if they don't place the well-being of LGBTQI people at the top of their issues of concern, millions of US citizens do support LGBTQ civil and SOGI human rights. In addition, a smaller number in academic and activist communities likely hold even more intense preferences in favor of flourishing and self-determination for LGBTQI people than their fellow citizens even if they disagree among themselves over how or whether people and institutions in the Global North should respond to human rights threats and violations against gender and sexual minorities.

Academics may also be influenced by our own perceptions and biases about what we believe makes LGBTI advocates "good enough queers."[17] In her analysis of British race and sexuality politics of the 1960s to the 1990s, the political theorist Anna Marie Smith constructs and contrasts ideal-type figures that reflect the views about nonnormative sexuality of British New Right conservatives during the period. The "good homosexual," "keeps her expression of difference strictly behind closed doors." The alternative for these British conservatives—and many others, including US Christian conservatives—is the "dangerous queer," "a publicly flaunting *element* which strives to reproduce itself by seducing the innocent young." As Smith sums up these two configurations of identity:

> The good subject is *closeted* in every sense of the term, hidden and contained within closed frontiers, while the subversive element *comes out of the closet*, shows itself in its own self-staged spectacle and refuses to be contained.[18]

Generally speaking, progressive academics would be extremely critical of any attempt to valorize a moral standard that gender and sexual minorities would have to meet in order to qualify as good citizens. But my question is this: If Christian conservatives prefer closeted "good homosexuals," which of these ideal types do progressive or radical Western academics prefer? My concern is that progressive academics can enact our own idealizing representations. In the case of LGBTI people who campaign for their human rights, "good (dangerous) queers" are queers who reflect the values and politics that progressive academics respect. And whatever good queers may do, they don't partner with the US government. Such a conviction, and the stigma that might follow from violating it, can help explain why grassroots activists often don't report assistance relations with the US government to Western academics. But I would argue that "our"—academic and progressive—convictions about what makes queers "good" have consequences. Among those consequences is a willingness to dismiss as hypocritical and imperialistic assistance that grassroots activists rely on for projects as diverse as challenging discriminatory laws, monitoring and reporting human rights violations, helping activists flee from violence, and securing space in which to work.

What of the LGBTI people who organize and engage in activism in places where gender and sexual minorities are vulnerable to abuse, risking their lives or livelihoods to push back against denials of their human rights? Many progressives in the US might assume that disfavored LGBTI people and activists throughout the world would want as little to do with the US government under Trump as we did. It may make sense to assume that a US government headed by a reprobate authoritarian leader is a poisoned tree and that the fruits of such a tree are inevitably also toxic and anathema. Indeed, many progressives held this view of US government diplomacy and assistance even before Trump became president.

But to embrace this proposition is to project onto these activists our own politics and preferences. From my forays into sites where US officials collaborate with grassroots LGBTI activists, I know that empiricism about these engagements can be an antidote to certain progressive convictions. Just as they did before Trump became president, LGBTI activists worked with US officials after Trump—with his bellicose racism and ignorance of US government—entered the White House. Were grassroots activists in these spaces open about how they regarded the US president? Yes, they were. But their perspicacious grasp of Trump's antidemocratic behavior and lack of interest in human rights didn't prevent them from engaging with US officials in robust and productive ways that served their movements' interests. I'll share one brief story to illustrate this theme. At the 2019 ASOGIHRO meeting, a leader of a prominent African LGBTI organization introduced one of the US officials as someone who "works for Trump." The official began her remarks by correcting the statement, noting that as a US government official she "serve[d] the constitution of the United States" and did not, therefore, work for Trump. After this brief exchange, the participants shared a productive and informative discussion about the needs of activists and funders' capacities to meet those needs.

One goal of this chapter was to inform readers about the continuity of "demand" for human rights assistance, before and during Trump. That continuity might surprise some proponents of LGBTI human rights who assume that grassroots activists abroad would identify the US only with Trump, nationalism, right-wing populism, imperialism, and neoliberal capitalism. I also set out to suggest that there are a variety of reasons why Western scholars of LGBTI movements may not have complete information about sources of funding that enable activists to rent office space, buy computers, hire staff, document human rights abuses, leave the country when threatened, carry out programs, and fight for rights in social, legal, and political venues. Such information may not be easy to obtain, either because it's not in the interest of activists to disclose it or because some activists don't know it. But there's a warning here as well: confirmation bias can affect and afflict scholarship in ways we might not recognize. It's possible for progressive values to create mirrors that reflect our own image back to us when we believe we're seeing others and the world.

To solve the mystery of why neither the Trump administration nor the Christian right made any serious effort to disrupt or terminate SOGI foreign policy, it's been necessary to examine many pieces of evidence. These have included extensive Christian right messaging about the threat to international religious freedom posed by LGBTI human rights; the Trump administration's consistent outreach to the movement, its elites, and its voters; the aspirations and values of Trump's two secretaries of state; the Trump administration's antipathy to international agreements and alliances paired with its friendliness to right-wing authoritarian parties and regimes; congressional support for SOGI foreign policy; and the receptiveness of grassroots LGBTQI activists abroad to partner with US officials to advance SOGI human rights. In the conclusion, I return to Trump and the Christian right, identifying actions they could have taken to extirpate US support for SOGI and providing some explanations for why, to paraphrase Sherlock Holmes, those dogs didn't bark.

Conclusion

More Thoughts Than Prayers

On Not Even Trying

When I was researching *Because We Are Human*, I assumed that if the Christian right were in the position to extirpate SOGI human rights support and assistance from US foreign policy, they would do so. I was wrong. Now that something like that experiment has been run, it's clear that many politically influential Christian right elites didn't try to discontinue SOGI support, even to "save" international religious freedom. The survival of US support for SOGI human rights through the Trump administration requires explanation, and I'll provide a possible explanation and other relevant reflections in these final pages.

How do I know the most powerful Christian conservative elites didn't do their best to end US support for SOGI? We can trace the moves these elites could have made to attack SOGI if they'd been so inclined. Christian conservative movement elites could have used ingroup Christian right and mainstream media forums to advertise the continuity of SOGI human rights programs, policies, and practices in the Trump era, and to advocate against them. Christian right elites might well have advocated differently in ingroup versus mainstream forums, pointing, for example, to the immorality being enabled by the deep state and the continuing efforts of Obama partisans to effect a coup against Trump in ingroup messaging and, for example, the cost to taxpayers in mainstream messaging.

They would have produced reports on the continuing problem of US advocacy for SOGI human rights and networked with other organizations to publicize the problem. They would have organized letter-writing campaigns and highlighted the need to defund SOGI human rights in speeches and appearances in news media. They would have lobbied members of Congress and organized constituent trips to discuss the outrage of US support for SOGI on Capitol Hill. Instead, these elites were virtually silent on SOGI as it was being executed under the Trump administration and under Pompeo's stewardship of the State Department. When they did refer to SOGI during the Trump administration, they pointedly highlighted *past Obama adminis-tration policies and practices, not the fact that these had been sustained under Trump and Pompeo.*

A concerted effort by elected officials or political appointees inside the federal government to undermine SOGI foreign policy could have taken a number of forms. First, Trump could have spoken out against SOGI policy in tweets, rallies, or interviews with congenial reporters, applying his "deep state" calumny to State Department human rights officials. He could have directed either of his secretaries of state to terminate US support and com-plained publicly if they didn't obey. Second, the Senate, which remained in Republican hands throughout the Trump administration, could have struck against SOGI support by choosing not to appropriate funds or even declar-ing that no funds appropriated by Congress could be used for diplomacy or programs related to SOGI human rights. The latter action might have generated an LGBTI "gag order" of the kind that has long been instituted over abortion by the Mexico City Policy whenever a Republican president occupies the White House.

Third, within the State Department, the secretary could have terminated SOGI diplomacy and statements of concern about violations of LGBTI peoples' rights. And he could have solicited information from staff about the funds being awarded for SOGI programs and redirected the funds to programs related to international religious freedom. The State Department could have withdrawn the US from the Equal Rights Coalition, renounced US leadership of the Global Equality Fund (GEF), and terminated US administration of GEF programs. Such an action would withdraw US contributions to international SOGI human rights advocacy, but it would also leave GEF partners around the world without US administration of the fund, possibly compromising its existence. Defunding SOGI programs and redirecting a significant portion of GEF funds would have been possible because, during the Trump administration, the congressional appropriations bills didn't contain "hard earmarks" that directed the State Department to fund the GEF. Instead, "soft earmarks" directing the agency to fund the

GEF were contained in the reports that accompanied the State, Foreign Operations, and Related Programs appropriations bills. Such soft earmarks indicate congressional intent but don't enjoin the agency to follow Congress's instructions.

Christian right elites have sworn that US support for SOGI human rights is detrimental to international religious freedom, presenting the frame as common sense, not spin or disinformation. Believers who are the ideal consumers of this rhetoric would assume that Christian conservative elites who comprehend the danger to religious freedom associated with US support for SOGI human rights would act decisively to end the threat if they had leverage to do so. However, in spite of the dire portents for the destruction of religious freedom circulated for many years by Christian conservative elites, when they were in a position to act against the cultural imperialism of US advocacy for SOGI, they didn't. What we need is an explanation that accounts for the known data:

- the Christian conservative movement opposes both LGBT civil and SOGI human rights;

- the movement vigorously contested the Obama administration's announcement of support for SOGI human rights abroad and its subsequent policies and practices;

- the movement consistently put forward a social movement frame that cast SOGI human rights as causing an erosion of religious freedom abroad (with implications for American believers);

- the movement championed Donald Trump and his purported commitment to religious freedom;

- as I show in chapters 1 and 2, people in the upper echelons of the movement fabricated key elements of the SOGI human rights vs. religious freedom frame they disseminated (these elites knew their claims weren't accurate, and it seems safe to say that this discourse constitutes movement disinformation); and

- Christian right elites knew that the SOGI human rights policies promulgated in the Obama administration remained in force in the Trump administration.

An explanation that I believe is most consistent with the data requires that we make distinctions among Christian right elites. First-string Christian right elites—in this group I'd include Sam Brownback, Tony Perkins, and Mike Pompeo—are insiders who understand how government works. First stringers may have held the following kinds of positions: elective office in the federal government (Brownback and Pompeo) or state government (Brownback and Perkins); cabinet-level positions that require Senate confirmation (Pompeo); and positions that provide access to leaders and high-ranking officials of other governments (Brownback, Perkins, and Pompeo). Their work has acquainted them with the operations of the executive and legislative branches of governments and how to use the levers of power to accomplish their desired objectives. They are also intimately familiar with the anxieties of ordinary Christian conservatives and stoke these anxieties to achieve their ends. These elite insiders develop and disseminate disinformation that's geared to achieving political goals they value, including strengthening the Christian right movement and their own positions as elites who both lead Christian conservatives and rely on them as a constituency. And they work closely together.

Just as they internalize changing interpretations of scripture, Christian conservative believer-followers internalize and are socialized by the political scripts that circulate in the movement. Yet there is more complexity in this process than a simple binary between leaders and followers. The story of US SOGI policy under Trump reveals a bifurcation of elites. Like first-string elites, naive second-string elites may be well educated, have experience in political campaigns or movements, or achieve some level of authority in government as, for example, political appointees. However, second stringers don't set the movement's agenda or direct the production of its propaganda, and most of the benefit of the mobilization of the movement's believers doesn't accrue to them. Unlike elites at the top of the movement, these naive second-string elites may be not only believers but "true believers" in the messaging produced under the imprimatur of a movement.[1]

In the case of the Christian right's fealty to Trump, second-string elites may believe the "deep state" is an actual plot, not a convenient fiction by means of which those who wield it achieve other goals. They may believe that the Obama administration did, in fact, threaten governments that refused to allow same-sex marriage; that US support for SOGI human rights actually does displace support for religious freedom; or that the deep state deceptively contravened Trump's foreign policy goals by hiding SOGI policies and funding from them. I regard Assistant Secretary Robert Destro as such a second-string Christian conservative elite. In spite of their purported conviction that SOGI human rights constitute a threat to international religious freedom, first-string elites—Trump appointees and Christian conservatives to whom the administration granted access and influence—didn't act to extirpate SOGI human rights from US foreign policy. It's likely that some second stringers would have acted, directly or indirectly, but failed to understand enough about how government rules and institutions work to exercise the authority they had over SOGI. It's also possible that second stringers didn't act against SOGI because they were waiting for leadership on the policy from their bosses and movement idols: the first stringers.

Of course, the fact that US support for SOGI wasn't deliberately undermined doesn't mean that it's impossible or extremely unlikely that a future right-wing populist, nationalist administration won't extinguish SOGI human rights support or even substitute enmity toward LGBTI people as one foundation of its domestic and foreign policy. As Yascha Mounk has pointed out, the Trump administration didn't excel in expertise and consistency, and US institutions might be damaged more effectively by a more competent administration led by a "smarter and more strategic populist."[2]

Where does Donald Trump himself fit into this analysis of US policy toward SOGI human rights? I believed during Trump's campaign for president, and I believe today, that Trump is indifferent to, rather than personally prejudiced against, LGBTQ people. In this, I agree with Scott Lively, who concluded in 2016 that a Trump administration could undermine LGBTQ communities even though Trump himself wasn't an anti-LGBT culture warrior.[3] Another way to frame this conclusion is that although there are prominent members of the administration who demonstrated animus toward LGBT people, the administration's anti-LGBTQ actions were, for the most part, episodic and transactional.

This is not to say that Trump is *pro*-LGBTQ. Instead, I believe that Trump is, and always has been, indifferent to gender and sexual minorities, especially when they are white and male. This perspective comports better with information in the public domain about his personal relationships and bullying public rhetoric than the conclusion that he holds a special animus against gender and sexual minorities. Trump did engage in sporadic, malicious anti-LGBTQ acts and tweets as president. But he didn't strategically use his bully pulpit, as so many right-wing authoritarian leaders do, for example, to blame LGBTQ people for social ills, expose our identities on the public stage, and encourage violence against us.[4] Nor did he consistently speak of LGBTQ people with contempt and abjure personal relationships with us

This is faint praise, but it's essential information for drawing conclusions about prejudice and animus.

It's not that Trump doesn't hold strong prejudices. Indeed, he's driven by misogyny and prejudice against people of color both when those biases serve his interests and when they don't. He seems incapable of even pretending he's not animated by a belief that women and men of color, and white women are his inferiors. The differences in the way he speaks to and about members of these groups and people who don't belong to these groups have been robustly documented.[5] As many political commentators have pointed out, Trump's tendency to refer to African Americans, especially women, who cross him as people of low intelligence reinscribes longstanding racist American tropes of Black intellectual inferiority.[6] Rather than rehearsing the lists of comments and tweets compiled elsewhere, I defer to comedian Amber Ruffin, who wrote for the television show *Late Night with Seth Myers*. In videos, Ruffin offers a set of policy and other decisions Trump and his administration made and concludes from them that "this man is a total racist" and then offers another set to support the proposition that "this man is a total sexist."[7]

Because of domestic policy positions Trump embraced, such as barring transgender people from military service and defending the right of Christian conservatives to discriminate against LGBT people in the economic marketplace based on religious faith, many political observers would disagree with my conclusion that Trump isn't motivated by a particular animus toward LGBTQ people. Why make this distinction? Or, in other words, why bother to distinguish between Trump's contemptable treatment of, on the one hand, women and men of color and white women and, on the other hand, LGBTQ people *based on their status as gender and sexual minorities*? One reason is that this configuration of prejudice is significant and may help us interpret his presidency through lenses of character defects, patterns of enmity, and the policy impulses related to these defects and patterns.

Some mental health professionals have suggested that Trump may be a narcissist, even a malignant narcissist, and this hypothesis would explain much.[8] So does psychologist Bob Altemeyer's suggestion that Trump activated right-wing authoritarian (RWA) followers who exhibit high levels of submission to authority, high levels of aggression on behalf of the authorities to whom they submit, and high levels of conventionalism.[9] Such an analysis is consistent with the conclusions scholars have reached about the appeal of Trump as a strongman or the "American Caesar."[10]

However, there's another possible explanation for Trump's relative indifference toward gender identity and sexuality, especially for someone who represents himself as a conservative leader. This explanation is that it's likely he meets the criteria for high social dominance orientation (SDO), a measure of attitudes toward intergroup relations introduced by psychologists Jim Sidanius and Felicia Pratto. Sidanius and Pratto define SDO "as the degree to which individuals desire and support group-based hierarchy and the domination of 'inferior' groups by 'superior' groups."[11] Before he published *Authoritarian Nightmare: Trump and His Followers* with John Dean,[12] Altemeyer had summed up the studies of high RWA and SDO actors in the humorous style of a retired academic who no longer had to submit to editing. High RWA and SDO identify "a different clump of prejudiced persons—sort of like 'You round up the folks in the white sheets over there, and I'll get the pious bigots over here.' "[13] As this characterization suggests, unlike high RWAs, high SDO individuals are more likely to pretend to be religious than to actually be religious. And high SDOs exhibit less prejudice toward same-sex attracted people than they do toward racial minorities, in part because they're more indifferent to sin than RWAs and in part because they're more inclined toward prejudice based on longstanding social beliefs about inferiority based on sex and "arbitrary-set" racial classifications.[14]

Starting with the transition, Donald Trump's administration was consistent in pursuing xenophobic policies against immigrants, opposing women's reproductive rights, and dismantling policies to combat climate change. Trump was also consistent in attacking and undermining US allies, befriending antidemocratic leaders abroad, and reversing multilateral cooperation in the international arena. Of the policy domains that define Trump's record in office, many are directly related to Trump's personal prejudices: opposing immigration for people of color, including asylum for people fleeing human rights jeopardy; enacting a ban on immigration by Muslims; insisting on building a "beautiful" wall on the southern border with Mexico; supporting a reversal of women's reproductive rights; and, later, reflexively supporting police in the face of a national movement to hold law enforcement officers accountable for killing and injuring unarmed African Americans. Many other acts were either consistent with admiration for antidemocratic leaders, or they were directly or indirectly related to Trump's personal legal, political, and economic interests. Feminists have long maintained that the personal is political. Unfortunately, as president, Donald Trump put this motto into practice.

On Knowing Your Audience

In *Sin, Sex, and Democracy*, I set myself the task of discerning the differences between an early antigay Christian conservative discourse and its more mature bifurcation into ingroup and public rhetorics. One question students and others have occasionally asked me about the Christian right since the early 2000s is what the elites whose differentiated rhetorics I've investigated *really* believe about disfavored groups like gender and sexual minorities. In reply, I've sometimes paraphrased an observation from the film *Annie Hall*, noting that I don't know the answer to that question because I can't see into the soul of the boy next to me.[15] I've studied Christian right moral entrepreneurs for many years, and it's only now, after five years of investigating the alliance between Trump and Christian conservative elites, that I'm confident I can respond to that question in a way that meets standards of academic rigor: many of those who decry the corrosive effect of tolerance and support for the human rights of gender and sexual minorities don't believe the disinformation they developed to shape the perceptions of Christian conservative believers. That is, they don't believe that SOGI human rights—including US support for those rights—are a profound threat to religious freedom abroad.

But even if the Christian right elites I've named didn't believe they needed to terminate US support for SOGI human rights in order to advance the cause of religious freedom around the world, why didn't they do so to demonstrate resolve to their followers? Contemporary Christian conservatives can't return from battle holding aloft the head of the defeated Goliath, but they surely could have impaired SOGI foreign policy and then turned the news to their benefit. Here too, my investigations provide clues. In *Sin, Sex, and Democracy*, I documented examples of Christian right leaders protecting mainstream reputations and political opportunities by effectively tutoring their followers in how to use democratic rhetoric to talk to outsiders and by moderating their own public rhetoric on LGBTQ issues. For example, Jerry Falwell and Pat Robertson agreed, on Robertson's *700 Club* TV show, that God allowed the September 11 attack to proceed in part as punishment for America's sexual sins. After progressive monitors advertised the televangelists' comments, Falwell and Robertson defended themselves in terms as suited to mainstream audiences as was possible given the views they'd disclosed and the uproar that had ensued.[16]

When I first listened to Ambassador Sam Brownback's 2019 interview with *New York Times* reporter Wajahat Ali, I heard Brownback talk about LGBTI rights in a style suited to public democratic discourse, not the ingroup rhetoric of anti-LGBTQ culture war. Consider Brownback's primer on the positive correlation between religious freedom and LGBT rights—"One of the interesting things to point out globally, though, is that the countries that are the best on religious freedom also tend to be the best on LGBT rights"—and his mild rebuke of Obama on SOGI. If we didn't know Brownback's anti-LGBTQ history, we might perceive him as a political figure with a concern for religious freedom and no particular suspicion that recognition of gender and sexual minority rights crowds out rights for religious minorities.[17]

I think this is the point of such a public presentation: to normalize Christian right elites for mainstream colleagues and audiences while those same elites use ingroup platforms and media to propagate anti-LGBTQ messaging. And such mainstreaming works; I discovered that a State Department human rights official who interacted with Brownback during his tenure as ambassador at large for international religious freedom was surprised to learn of his long history of anti-LGBTQ rhetoric and found that history hard to square with the demeanor and concern for human rights he presented to his colleagues at State.

So where is the US Christian right on SOGI and religious freedom in 2021? Trump's term ended in January 2021, but I include one last source from six months after he left office: the 2021 International Religious Freedom Summit, a meeting sponsored by the International Religious Freedom (IRF) Secretariat, the Family Research Council, and other faith organizations. Held from July 13 to 15 at the Omni Shoreham Hotel—the site of FRC's annual Values Voter Summits—the meeting was advertised as a "first-of-its-kind event [that] will bring attention to the plight of persecuted religious groups around the world and empower attendees to make a difference."

On Not Saying the Quiet Part Out Loud

In the days leading up to the meeting, FRC emails declared it time for believers "to join the global movement to advance religious freedom."[18] Linking Biden to one prong of the SOGI human rights vs. religious freedom frame, the FRC proclaimed that the "growing global movement" for religious freedom "must be kept alive even under the Biden administration, which is not as enthusiastic about the issue as previous administrations."[19] Lest anyone mistake the charge being levied against Biden, the title of the article is "Promoting Religious Freedom Even When the Government Doesn't."

Neither the IRF Secretariat nor the IRF Roundtable with which it's associated has received much attention from scholars of religion and politics. On the IRF Roundtable website, the project is described as

> an informal group of individuals from non-governmental organizations who gather regularly to discuss IRF issues on a non-attribution basis. It is simply a safe space where participants gather, speak freely in sharing ideas and information, and propose joint advocacy actions to address specific IRF issues and problems. In response to various participant-led initiatives regarding the protection and promotion of freedom of religion, conscience, and belief in the U.S. and abroad, all participants have the opportunity to self-select into coalitions of the willing.
>
> The Roundtable meets every three months in the U.S. Capitol and average attendance has grown to 60–75 participants from civil society and goverment [sic]. . . . The goal of the Roundtable is to reverse the rising tide of restrictions on religious freedom that has been spreading across the world.[20]

The IRF Roundtable has been cochaired by Greg Mitchell and Chris Seiple, whose father, Robert Seiple, served as the State Department's first ambassador at large for international religious freedom.[21] Mitchell and Seiple are listed as coexecutives of the IRF Secretariat.[22] At the IRF Summit, Mitchell explained to the audience that although the roundtable (and individual roundtables convened in the US and abroad) date from the Obama administration, the IRF Secretariat is a recent innovation, incorporated as a vehicle to raise funds to expand and institutionalize roundtable work in the US and abroad.[23]

Focusing on Mitchell and the IRF Roundtable/Secretariat also enhances our understanding of the interlocking directorate of Christian conservative leaders and organizations whose activities are salient to LGBTQ and SOGI rights. In 2012, Mitchell published an article in the journal *Review of Faith and International Affairs*, the journal of the Center for Faith and International Affairs of the Institute for Global Engagement—the institute founded and lead by the Seiples. The article outlines both a philosophy of cooperation and coordination across faith traditions and a multipronged lobbying approach aimed at integrating religious freedom into US government operations and policy.[24] In many respects, the agenda and political strategy Mitchell outlines compares with the work of the Council for Global Equality, an advocacy organization that monitors the international landscape for SOGI human rights and advocates for the integration of SOGI human rights in US foreign policy.

Before the IRF Secretariat joined with the FRC and other faith organizations to host an inaugural summit, the roundtable and secretariat were central players in the virtual 2020 Ministerial to Advance Religious Freedom. Although it was held under the auspices of the Polish foreign ministry, the ministerial represented a collaboration between the Polish and US governments. What the FRC touted as a "first-of-its-kind" summit was obviously intended as a substitute for the Trump administration ministerials, which the State Department hosted in 2018 and 2019.[25] Indeed, several prominent figures who were affiliated with ministerial events—or, in the case of Katrina Lantos Swett, with the Commission on Unalienable Rights—appeared at the IRF Summit. They included: summit cochairs Swett and Sam Brownback, Daniel Nadel, Nancy Pelosi, Tony Perkins, Mike Pompeo, and Frank Wolf. Pam Pryor, a political appointee in the State Department during the Trump administration, was senior advisor for the summit. Pelosi and Secretary of State Antony Blinken provided video remarks pledging US support for religious freedom as a "universal" (Pelosi), bipartisan goal and value.[26]

Two themes from the summit are salient for examining the Christian right's use of SOGI human rights as a counterpoint to international religious freedom during the Obama and Trump administrations. The first theme is from former Secretary of State Mike Pompeo's speech to summit participants (Wednesday, July 14), especially his remarks on the controversial Commission on Unalienable Rights. The second theme emerged in a set of comments from three summit participants (July 14 and 15) about a policy matter in Guatemala. These brief discussions of the Guatemala policy reveal that although the IRF Roundtable and Secretariat were presented as nonpartisan projects focused exclusively on securing religious freedom, many who lead and affiliate with the groups understand these projects as vehicles for promoting US-style culture war goals.[27]

In his keynote speech, Pompeo confirmed that the Commission on Unalienable Rights was conceived and staffed to serve the same mission as the Trump administration's ministerials: establishing that "there is no right more fundamental to a society than the free practice of religion." For Pompeo, this means promoting religious freedom as a human right that both trumps other human rights and is a necessary condition for the exercise of what orthodox believers understand as legitimate human rights. Implicitly acknowledging the Trump administration's position, in his remarks, Secretary of State Blinken described religious freedom as "co-equal with other human rights." Likewise, David Saperstein, who served as ambassador at large for international religious freedom during the Obama administration, argued forcefully that there are many inalienable rights, that no single human right trumps the others, and that human rights "reinforc[e] each other."

Critics of the Commission on Unalienable Rights believed from the beginning that the outcome was a foregone conclusion. But in his defenses and justifications of the commission, Pompeo has suggested that the hand-picked members of the committee were engaged in a genuine inquiry with momentous consequences for US foreign policy. By contrast, at the summit, Pompeo linked the commission with the minsterials and boasted about using the commission to establish the priority of religious freedom: "It's why we worked on [religious freedom] so hard. . . . It's why I created the Unalienable Rights Commission: to re-ground our foreign policy—how we talked about human rights at the Department of State."[28] Even with this concession about the foreordained output of the commission's work, I would still argue that the commission was from its inception primarily a vehicle for Pompeo to boost his influence with the Christian right.

The second theme I emphasize from the IRF summit is the one specific policy touted by speakers that wasn't directly related to securing religious freedom: a Life and Family Protection bill in Guatemala (Bill 5272) that, according to Human Rights Watch, would "expand the criminalization of abortion," permit discrimination on the basis of SOGI, and ban same-sex marriage.[29] The impetus for the bill, first introduced in 2018, was a ruling by the Inter-American Court of Human Rights (IACHR) after Costa Rica requested clarification of transgender and same-sex marriage rights under the American Convention on Human Rights.[30] Because Guatemala is a signatory of the American Convention, opponents of the ruling—including religious conservatives—rallied to formulate a law that would repudiate it and legitimize discrimination against gender and sexual minorities.

The first laudatory reference to the Life and Family bill came from Guatemalan pastor Carlos "Cash" Luna in a speech from the stage. Luna is the pastor of Casa de Dios church in Guatemala City and the chair of the IRF Roundtable in Latin America. A video of Guatemalan President Alejandro Giammattei followed Luna's speech. Since Giammattei took office in 2020, human rights organizations have documented attacks on human rights defenders, excessive force by police, attacks on journalists, and restrictions on information about the Covid 19 pandemic in Guatemala.[31] Addressing the IRF Summit, Giammattei vehemently defended the Life and Family Protection bill, casting opposition as a sign of a "globalist agenda" that includes opposing religious freedom and destabilizing Guatemalan democracy.[32] The summit audience responded to Giammattei's remarks with enthusiastic applause. Finally, the Life and Family Protection bill came up in a breakout session dedicated to "The Role of Religious Freedom Roundtables, the IRF Summit, and IRF Secretariat in the Future of the Global Movement." When one speaker mentioned the bill, Mitchell noted it enthusiastically as an example of what's possible "when the faith community pulls together."

Thus, although the summit was bipartisan, a few speakers nonetheless signaled solidarity with right-wing culture war aims of international allies. This stance is consistent with the many forms of cobelligerence among orthodox religious believers that researchers continue to document. As the Life and Family Protection bill suggests, cobelligerent cooperation against LGBTQ and SOGI rights is also likely an unspoken dimension of the updated concept of "covenantal pluralism" echoed by several speakers. However, aside from the paeons of summit participants to the Guatemala bill—the specifics of which were never detailed—there were no denunciations of SOGI human rights as a—or the—particular threat to international religious freedom.

Given the ubiquity of Christian right rhetoric about the harm to religious freedom perpetrated by support for SOGI human rights, the absence of explicit references to LGBTI/SOGI is remarkable. Instead of blaming SOGI human rights for jeopardizing and diminishing religious freedom, IRF Summit presenters cataloged social and political conditions that are correlated with religious persecution and denials of religious freedom in many countries, including authoritarianism, legal restrictions on conversion, blasphemy and apostasy laws, ethnic (or religious) cleansing, genocide, conflict, and impunity for discriminating or directing violence against disfavored religious minorities. Recall that in 2017, the US voted "no" on a United Nations Human Rights Council Resolution that condemned the application of the death penalty to punish apostasy, blasphemy, adultery, and consensual same-sex relations.

US Christian right elites have framed LGBT/SOGI rights as the primary danger to religious belief and practice, in the US and throughout the world. Yet in a formally bipartisan venue, news of this threat virtually disappeared. Even without proclaiming the threat posed to religious faith and practice posed by recognition of the rights of LGBTI people, however, orthodox, conservative believers obviously continue to use international, ecumenical coalitions to restrict the rights of women and LGBTI people.

Given what political scientists know about the continuation of public policies from one administration to the next, we would expect for most policies and practices executed by US officials in foreign affairs agencies, including those associated with SOGI, not to be terminated by a new administration.[33] However, in the end, the explanation for why SOGI human rights advocacy and assistance survived isn't only that we can expect most government programs to be sustained across administrations. Trump administration foreign policy consisted of protecting pro-Trump authoritarian leaders, disrupting alliances with democratic allies, declaiming "America First" nationalism, and conspicuously declaring devotion to the cause of international religious freedom. With regard to religious freedom—what Trump officials often referred to as the "cornerstone" of Trump foreign policy—since Obama's second term in office, the Christian right had attested that the greatest threat was LGBT human rights. Especially minatory was the specter of a US commitment to SOGI. Thus, the die appeared to be cast: if Christian conservatives were to save international religious freedom from a US government determined to sabotage it, US support for SOGI would have to go.

In an administration that was more than motivated to break things, none of the figures who had long advocated against domestic LGBTQ civil rights and SOGI human rights abroad publicized or obstructed SOGI human rights policy or defunded programs. After all the protestations about the dangers of SOGI human rights advocacy for international freedom of religion, the Christian conservative first-string elites were more indifferent to SOGI than I would have believed and more calculating about their political interests than even I would have guessed. Whether they set out to do it or not, the narrow and strategic self-interest of Trump and Christian right elites saved US support for the human rights of LGBTI people abroad.

Appendix A

Remarks to US Department of State Employees[1]

Rex W. Tillerson, Secretary of State
US State Department
Dean Acheson Auditorium, Washington, DC

May 3, 2017

Greetings

SECRETARY TILLERSON: Good morning. (Applause.) Thank you. Thank you.

Are we on? Can you all hear me back there in the back? Can you hear me now? (Laughter.) Can you hear me now?

AUDIENCE: Yes.

SECRETARY TILLERSON:

[1] All right. I told them I have to walk around. My wife has always said if you tied my hands down to my side, I would be a complete mute. (Laughter.) So I'm not great at podiums. I do know how to read a speech, but I thought today we'd just have a chat.

[2] So I've been here about three months now, we've been working alongside one another, and so I thought it'd be worthwhile to just share a few of my

perspectives with you on where I think we are and some things that are coming that I know are of interest to you.

[3] But before I do that, I would be remiss if I did not thank all of those who have stepped into acting roles during these past three months to help me, and starting with acting Deputy Secretary Tom Shannon, who's just been stellar. (Applause.) But I also want to acknowledge the large number of people who are—stepped into under secretary, assistant secretary roles, director roles, and a number of chief of missions around the world as well. Your willingness to step up and not just fill that role, but to take responsibility for the role and to lead the organization through some pretty challenging first 90 days—it's not like we haven't had some things to work on. And so I want to express my appreciation to all of you for helping me and helping my team as we came on board. And I've just been really gratified at the work that everyone's undertaken in that regard.

"America First"

[4] So I thought we'd talk about a couple of things. I want to share my perspective as to how does this administration's policies of "America first" fit into our foreign policy and foreign affairs. And so I want to touch on that. And then I'll take a quick walk around the world. Most of you have some familiarity of what's going on around the world, but I thought just regionally I'd hit each one of them very quickly, to share with you my perspective on kind of where I feel we are, and then in some areas where we've not yet had time to devote the attention to we would like, and I don't want that to be in any way considered that we don't think those are important. It's kind of a—what's the hottest fire that we've got to deal with?

[5] So I want to talk about that a little bit, and then spend some time at the end talking about where we're going in the future of the department, USAID, and, as you know, we just kicked off this listening exercise.

[6] So let's talk first about my view of how you translate "America first" into our foreign policy. And I think I approach it really that it's America first for national security and economic prosperity, and that doesn't mean it comes at the expense of others. Our partnerships and our alliances are critical to our success in both of those areas. But as we have progressed over the last 20

years—and some of you could tie it back to the post–Cold War era as the world has changed, some of you can tie it back to the evolution of China since the post-Nixon era and China's rise as an economic power, and now as a growing military power—that as we participated in those changes, we were promoting relations, we were promoting economic activity, we were promoting trade with a lot of these emerging economies, and we just kind of lost track of how we were doing. And as a result, things got a little bit out of balance. And I think that's—as you hear the President talk about it, that's what he really speaks about, is: Look, things have gotten out of balance, and these are really important relationships to us and they're really important alliances, but we've got to bring them back into balance.

[7] So whether it's our asking of NATO members to really meet their obligations, even though those were notional obligations, we understand—and aspirational obligation, we think it's important that those become concrete. And when we deal with our trading partners—that things have gotten a little out of bounds here, they've gotten a little off balance—we've got to bring that back into balance because it's not serving the interests of the American people well.

[8] So it doesn't have to come at the expense of others, but it does have to come at an engagement with others. And so as we're building our policies around those notions, that's what we want to support. But at the end of it, it is strengthening our national security and promoting economic prosperity for the American people, and we do that, again, with a lot of partners.

"Our Values"

[9] Now, I think it's important to also remember that guiding all of our foreign policy actions are our fundamental values: our values around freedom, human dignity, the way people are treated. Those are our values. Those are not our policies; they're values. And the reason it's important, I think, to keep that well understood is policies can change. They do change. They should change. Policies change to adapt to the—our values never change. They're constant throughout all of this [left hand out to indicate setting something aside].

[10] And so I think the real challenge many of us have as we think about constructing our policies and carrying out our policies is: How do we

represent our values? And in some circumstances, if you condition our national security efforts on someone adopting our values, we probably can't achieve our national security goals or our national security interests. If we condition too heavily that others must adopt this value that we've come to over a long history of our own, it really creates obstacles to our ability to advance our national security interests, our economic interests. It doesn't mean that we leave those values on the sidelines. It doesn't mean that we don't advocate for and aspire to freedom, human dignity, and the treatment of people the world over. We do. And we will always have that on our shoulder everywhere we go [left hand to left shoulder].

[11] But I think it is—I think it's really important that all of us understand the difference between policy and values, and in some circumstances, we should and do condition our policy engagements on people adopting certain actions as to how they treat people. They should. We should demand that. But that doesn't mean that's the case in every situation. And so we really have to understand, in each country or each region of the world that we're dealing with, what are our national security interests, what are our economic prosperity interests, and then as we can advocate and advance our values, we should—but the policies can do this; the values never change.

[12] And so I would ask you to just—to the extent you could think about that a little bit, I think it's useful, because I know this is probably, for me, it's one of the most difficult areas as I've thought about how to formulate policy to advance all of these things simultaneously. It's a real challenge. And I hear from government leaders all over the world: You just can't demand that of us, we can't move that quickly, we can't adapt that quickly, okay? So it's how do we advance our national security and economic interests on this hand [right], our values are constant over here [left].

[13] So I give you that as kind of an overarching view of how I think about the President's approach of "America first." We must secure the nation. We must protect our people. We must protect our borders. We must protect our ability to be that voice of our values now and forevermore. And we can only do that with economic prosperity. So it's foreign policy projected with a strong ability to enforce the protection of our freedoms with a strong military. And all of you that have been at this a long time understand the value of speaking with a posture of strength—not a threatening posture, but a posture of strength. People know we can back it up.

"Around the World"

[14] So with that in mind, let me just quickly walk around the world and give you my assessment of where we are in some of the early stages of policy that's underway and some that's yet to be developed.

[15] So as all of you clearly understand, when we came in to the State Department, the administration came in, was sworn in, immediately confronted with a serious situation in North Korea. Now, the prior administration, as all of you know, President Obama told President Trump this was going to be your greatest threat that you're going to have to manage, and he was right.

[16] So it was—it's right on the doorstep. And so it got immediate attention. It was the first policy area that we began to develop in terms of what is our overarching strategic approach and how do we want to execute against that. In evaluating that, what was important to us and to me to understand was, first, where are our allies? And so engaging with our allies and ensuring that our allies and we see the situation the same—our allies in South Korea, our allies in Japan.

[17] And then, secondly, it was to engage with the other regional powers as to how do they see it. And so it was useful and helpful to have the Chinese and now the Russians articulate clearly that their policy is unchanged; they—their policy is a denuclearized Korean Peninsula. And of course we did our part many years ago. We took all the nuclear weapons out of South Korea. So now we have a shared objective, and that's very useful, from which you then build out your policy approaches and your strategies.

[18] So many people are saying, well, gee, this is just the same thing we've tried over and over—we're going to put pressure on the regime in Pyongyang, they're not going to do anything, and then in the end we'll all cave. Well, the difference, I think, in our approach this time is we're going to test this assumption, and when the—when folks came in to review the situation with me, the assumption was that China has limited influence on the regime in Pyongyang, or they have a limited willingness to assert their influence. And so I told the President we've got to test that, and we're going to test it by leaning hard into them, and this is a good place to start our engagement with China.

[19] And so that's what we've been doing, is leaning hard into China to test their willingness to use their influence, their engagement with the regime in North Korea. All of it backed up by very strong resolve on our part to have a denuclearized peninsula with a commitment to our security alliances on the peninsula and in the region to our important allies Japan and South Korea.

[20] So it's a pressure campaign that has a knob on it. I'd say we're at about dial setting 5 or 6 right now, with a strong call of countries all over the world to fully implement the UN Security Council resolutions regarding sanctions, because no one has ever fully implemented those. So we're going to lean into people to fully implement them. We've told them we're watching what you're doing. When we see you not implementing, we see companies or we see individuals that are violating these sanctions, we're going to contact you and we're going to ask you to take care of it. If you can't take care of it or you simply don't want to take care of it for your own internal political reasons, we will. We'll sanction them through third-country sanctions.

[21] So we are being very open and transparent about our intentions, and we're asking our partners around the world to please take actions on your own. We want you to control how that happens. We're not trying to control it for you, but we have an expectation of what you will do. So we're putting that pressure on. We are preparing additional sanctions, if it turns out North Korea's actions warrant additional sanctions. We're hopeful that the regime in North Korea will think about this and come to a conclusion that there's another way to the future. We know they have—they're—they aspire to nuclear weapons because it's the regime's belief it's the only way they can secure their future.

[22] We are clear—we've been clear to them this is not about regime change, this is not about regime collapse, this is not about an accelerated reunification of the peninsula, this is not about us looking for an excuse to come north of the 38th Parallel. So we're trying to be very, very clear and resolute in our message to them that your future security and economic prosperity can only be achieved through your following your commitments to denuclearize.

[23] So this is where we are. We're at—I would say we're at about the 20 to 25 percent stage of this strategy. Thus far, our assessment is it is going

like we had hoped for in terms of the response we're getting from others, but we've got a lot of work left to do to keep that pressure on. And so that's what the folks that are in the bureaus and out in the missions are doing to help us right now, is to continue this steady, resolute message and continue to talk out here to the North Koreans, but not here, yet, about what our intentions are and what we want. We are ready and prepared to engage in talks when conditions are right. But as you've heard me say, we are not going to negotiate our way to the negotiating table. That is what Pyongyang has done for the last 20 years, is cause us to have to negotiate to get them to sit down. We'll sit down when they're ready to sit down under the right terms. So that's North Korea.

[24] And then if I pivoted over to China, because it really took us directly to our China foreign policy, we really had to assess China's situation, as I said, from the Nixon era up to where we find things today, and we saw a bit of an inflection point with the Sochi—with the Beijing Olympics. Those were enormously successful for China. They kind of put China on the map, and China really began to feel its oats about that time, and rightfully. They have achieved a lot. They moved 500 million Chinese people out of poverty into middle class status. They've still got a billion more they need to move.

[25] So China has its own challenges, and we want to work with them and be mindful of what they're dealing with in the context of our relationship. And our relationship has to be one of understanding that we have security interests throughout northeast Asia and security interests throughout the Pacific, and we need to work with them on how those are addressed. So that gets to the island building in the South China Sea, the militarization of those islands, and obviously, we have huge trading issues to talk with them about.

[26] So we are using the entree of the visit in Mar-a-Lago, which was heavy on some issues with North Korea but also heavy on a broader range of issues. And what we've asked the Chinese to do is we're—we want to take a fresh look at where's this relationship going to be 50 years from now, because I think we have an opportunity to define that. And so I know there have been a lot of dialogue areas that have been underway for the last several years with China. We have asked China to narrow the dialogue areas and elevate the participants to the decision-making level.

[27] So we outlined four major dialogue areas with China, and we've asked them to bring people who report directly to the decision-maker, which is President Xi. So for the first time, we are seeking and we—so far it appears we will get people at the politburo level and at much higher levels of the government within China to participate in these dialogues so we can reframe what we want the relationship to be and begin to deal with some of the problems and issues that have just been sitting out there kind of stuck in neutral for a while. So it is a—it's a much narrower—as we make progress, those things will result in working groups where we can get after solving these things.

[28] So we're going to have the first meeting of the Diplomatic and Security Dialogue, which is chaired by myself and Secretary Mattis, with our counterparts here in Washington in June, and we've put it up as a kind of top priority. The second one is economic and trade, which is chaired by Treasury Secretary Mnuchin and Commerce Secretary Ross, and it's well underway also.

[29] So that's kind of the new approach we're taking with China, is elevate, let's kind of revisit this relationship, and what is it going to be over the next half century. I think it's a tremendous opportunity we have to define that, and there seems to be a great interest on the part of the Chinese leadership to do that as well. They feel we're at a point of inflection also. So that's China.

[30] Obviously, throughout Asia we've got a lot of work [to] do with ASEAN nations and re-solidifying our leadership with ASEAN on a number of security issues but also trade issues and the South China Sea, strengthen relations with Australia and New Zealand—really important partners with us on a number of counterterrorism fronts. And so throughout the region those engagements are underway. And the President has committed to make the trip to Vietnam and to the Philippines for those meetings this fall, and I think that's going to be very important that he is going, and we'll be going in advance, obviously, to prepare for all of that.

[31] So if we walk around to the next hot spot that we worked on, pretty quickly it was the Middle East around the campaign to defeat ISIS and instability that that's created in, obviously, Syria, Iraq, the issues in Afghan-

istan. And as those of you who work that region well know, you can just kind of draw the concentric circles out all the way into North Africa, parts of Africa, all of the Middle East, parts of Central Asia, and this is really a D-ISIS and a counterterrorism effort, is what it really boils down to. And so how do we develop policies and bring regional players together to address these threats of ISIS and counterterrorism?

[32] And we hosted I think what was a very successful coalition to defeat ISIS ministerial here at the State Department. I think there is a real renewed sense of energy and commitment to win this war against ISIS. We will; we are defeating ISIS in their caliphate in Syria and Iraq, but we know that ISIS exists more broadly than that. And so, as we said in that coalition effort, we've got to move beyond the battlefield, we've got to move into the cyberspace, we've got to move into the social communications space, and get inside of the messaging that allows them to recruit people around the world to their terrorism efforts.

[33] So there is a big effort underway with players in the region, most notably the Kingdom of Saudi Arabia, and working with other partners to get inside of this conversation that's going on within the Muslim community around what this is doing to the way the Muslim faith is understood by others in the world. And I would say it's a very open conversation we're having and a renewed commitment on the part of leaders in the Muslim world that want to take this on. So we're going to be leveraging on that as well.

[34] So as you're seeing this play out in the Middle East, still a lot of hard work to do to get coalition partners together around ceasefires and peace processes in Syria. How do we advance our interest in Afghanistan to a legitimate peace process is what we're pursuing in Afghanistan, and then keeping this terrorism network confined as it wants to spread itself through North Africa and Central Africa. So a lot of work ahead of us, and many of you are directly engaged in it already; many more of you are going to become engaged in it, I think you can expect.

[35] The next kind of area of priority is our re-engagement with Russia. Obviously, they are part of the engagement in Syria, but we have other issues with Russia, as you all well know, in Europe, and the situation in Ukraine. As I know many of you heard from my trip to Moscow, characterized to

President Putin that the relationship between our two nations was the lowest it's been since the Cold War. He did not disagree. He shrugged his shoulders and nodded in agreement. And I said it's spiraling down, it's getting worse. And my comment to him was you—we cannot have, the two greatest nuclear powers in the world cannot have this kind of relationship. We have to change it.

[36] And so we have a number of efforts underway to first stabilize the relationship. And Deputy Secretary—acting Deputy Secretary Shannon is leading a working group effort to see if we can address some of the things that are just irritating the relationship, that make it hard for us to talk to one another even in civil tones. So we're working hard on that and we're hoping to begin to solve some of that, while Foreign Minister Lavrov and I, under the direction of President Putin and now President Trump, coming out of the call yesterday are going to continue to see if we can work together on the first big area of cooperation, which would be Syria, and can we achieve a ceasefire that will hold long enough for us to get a peace process underway.

[37] I don't want to say we're off to a great start on this, because it's very early stages. I don't know where it will go. So I've got a bilateral with Foreign Minister Lavrov in Alaska next week on the margins of the Arctic Council. Both our presidents have charged us to take this further and see where we can go with it. So obviously, close coordination with the Department of Defense, with our intelligence agencies, and importantly our allies in the region, because we want them to always know what we're doing, because we're going to need their support as well.

[38] So a lot of work ahead of us on the Russia engagement—work some small things, can we work one big thing together. If we can find space for something we feel we can begin to rebuild some level of trust, because today there is almost no trust between us. Can we build some level of trust? We've got a long list of things to work on from our arms agreements and issues we have with our nuclear arms agreements, to obviously, getting to Ukraine, Crimea, and other places where Russia is not being particularly helpful today.

[39] So that's what we're hoping, is that we can begin to build a way in which we can learn how to work with one another. I don't know whether we can or not. We'll—we're going to find out.

[40] So quickly to other parts of the world that are really important to us as well—the continent of Africa is so important from the standpoint that first, from a national security view, we cannot let Africa become the next breeding ground for a re-emergence of a caliphate for ISIS. We also cannot allow the terrorist networks that weave their way through Africa to continue unabated.

[41] You can connect the dots between countries throughout the central part of Africa and northern part of Africa where the terrorist networks are connected. We've got to get into the middle of that and disrupt that to save those countries.

[42] But Africa is also a continent of enormous opportunity, and needs and will get and will continue to receive our attention to support stabilizing governments as they are emerging and continuing to develop their own institutional capacity, but also looking at Africa for potential economic and trading opportunities. It's a huge, I think, potential sitting out there, waiting for us to capture it, and then, obviously, a big focus of our health initiatives, because Africa still struggles with huge health challenges. And those are important to us and they're going to continue to get our attention.

[43] So we're going to—we're working—today we have some things we're working in North Africa relative to its relationship to the Middle East challenges and our ISIS challenges. We've got to step back and take a more comprehensive look at our approach to the entire continent, and that's out in front of us as well.

[44] And then lastly, I want to go to the Western Hemisphere. And in the Western Hemisphere, obviously, our neighbors are vitally important to us, Canada and Mexico. It's not as rocky as it looks sometimes, and I think, in fact, the relationships are quite good. Both of our neighbors understand we have to refresh some of the agreements that have governed our relationship, particularly in the areas of trade, and both countries are ready to engage in a good-faith effort with us as well.

[45] In particular, we're investing a lot of effort into Mexico because of the transmigration issues and organized crime. And so we have an initiative underway where the senior members of the Mexican Government will be coming up here on May the 18th to participate in an interagency process with us to see if we can get at transnational organized crime and begin

to break these organized crime units up. Not only are they a threat to us and to Mexico's stability and the scourge of drugs that just flow into this country, they also are part of the integrated terrorist financing networks as well. So this is vital to us for a number of reasons and we look forward to making some progress there.

[46] South of Mexico, we've got some initiatives underway to work with the Latin American countries, which are where a lot of the people are trying to leave to come up to the U.S., to continue economic development, security investments in Latin America, and working with the Department of Homeland Security. We're actually hosting an event in Miami to bring those leaders up so we can talk with them about how we get better organized to address these issues and how we can bring more private capital into investment opportunities in Central and Latin America.

[47] Southern cone, we have a lot of opportunity and some challenges down there. What we want to do is step back and develop a Western Hemisphere strategy that thinks about South America in its entirety and its relationship to Central America, but Cuba and the Caribbean as well. There are terrorist financing issues. There are terrorist networks that are beginning to emerge in parts of South America that have our attention. There are governance issues in certain countries—certainly all of you are following the situation in Venezuela; a real tragedy, but we're hopeful that working with others, including interventions by others in Europe, that we may be able to gain some traction in Venezuela. So we have a number of things in front of us yet to develop clear policies on how we want to go forward.

[48] So my view is that we want to look at these regions almost in their entirety first, because everything is interconnected. We can take a country and develop something, but if we don't have the perspective regionally, we're probably not going to be as effective. So we're trying to start out here, and then we'll bring it down to a country-by-country level so we can execute. So that's just to give you a little perspective on how we're approaching these things in policy planning, and then we try to get a big-picture view and then we bring the bureau people in, the experts in, and help us start developing, now, how do you execute something like this? How do you implement it?

[49] So for those of you that have participated in these early efforts, thank you. I feel quite good about the one—the pieces that have been completed

and are in execution, I feel good about those. I can tell you the White House feels good about it. The National Security Council really values the work that we provide in the interagency process. And I would share with you I hear that from them all the time, that the stuff that comes over from the State Department, we've done our homework. It's a complete piece of work, it's useful, we can use it, and that's not always the case from all of the other agencies. So thank you for the efforts you're putting into that in that regard.

"Deliver[ing] on Mission"

[50] So let me turn now quickly to the last thing I wanted to talk about, which is the future and where we're going. And I alluded to this a little bit when I was commenting about the post–Cold War era. And during the Cold War—and I've had this conversation with some of you in this room before in our interactions—in many respects the Cold War was a lot easier. Things were pretty clear, the Soviet Union had a lot of things contained, and I had a conversation with Secretary-General Guterres at the UN. He described it as during the Cold War, we froze history. History just stopped in its tracks because so many of the dynamics that existed for centuries were contained. They were contained with heavy authoritarianism. And when the Cold War ended and the Soviet Union broke up, we took all of that off and history regained its march. And the world got a whole lot more complicated. And I think that's what we see. It has become much more complicated in terms of old conflicts have renewed themselves because they're not contained now. So that's the world as it is and that's the world we have to engage with.

[51] And so I'm going to—I'm saying this as a preface to as we get into thinking about how we should deliver on mission is to be thinking about how the way we have been delivering was in many ways shaped and as a residual of the Cold War era. And in many respects, we've not yet transitioned ourselves to this new reality either. And I don't say that just about the State Department, I say that about institutions globally. In fact, this is the—this—I had this same conversation with Secretary Guterres about the United Nations, that there are many institutions—and you can see when we have our conversations with NATO, another example, but there are many institutions around the world that were created during a different era. And so they were set up to deal with certain conditions and their processes and

their organizations were set up, and as things have changed, we've not really fully adapted those. It's not that we've not recognized, but we've not fully adapted how we deliver on mission.

[52] So one of the things, as we get into this opportunity to look at how we get our work done, is to think about the world as it is today and to leave behind—we've been—well, we do it this way because we've been doing it this way for the last 30 years or 40 years or 50 years, because all of that was created in a different environment. And so I think—I guess what I'm inviting all of you to do is to approach this effort that we're going to undertake with no constraints to your thinking—with none.

[53] One of the great honors for me serving in this department, the Department of State, and all of you know, the Department of State, first cabinet created and chartered under the Constitution. Secretary of State, first cabinet position chartered and created under the Constitution. So we are part of a living history and we're going to get to carve our little piece of it, our increment, in that clock of time. We're going to carve our piece into that history.

[54] And I think the question is how we will do that and how effectively we will do that. And history is moving around us as we just spoke. And how do we adapt to that? And so I want to ask all of you to be very free in your thinking. So the process going forward, as you know we've just kicked off this listening exercise and I really encourage all of you to please go online and participate in the survey online. This is vital to how we understand where we want to go and I think we have about 300 individuals that we've selected to sit down face-to-face and do some interviews so we have a more fulsome understanding. We want to collect all of these—all this input and your thoughts and ideas, both here and at USAID, and that is going to guide how we approach both our organizational structure, but more importantly, our work process design: How do we actually deliver on mission? That's the real key. How do you deliver on mission?

[55] And really, the way I have found these things to be the most successful is I understand how to deliver on mission first, I understand how the work processes work, and then I'll put the boxes around it to make all that work. Most people like to start with the boxes and then try to design it. I'm—I do it the other way around. How do we get the work done? We'll then

put the organization structure in place to support that. So we need a lot of creative thinking. We need to hear from you. This is going to inform how this turns out. I want to emphasize to you we have no preconceived notions on the outcome. I didn't come with a solution in a box when I showed up. I came with a commitment to look at it and see if we can't improve it.

[56] And I know change like this is really stressful for a lot of people. There's nothing easy about it, and I don't want to diminish in any way the challenges I know this presents for individuals, it presents to families, it presents to organizations. I'm very well aware of all of that. All I can offer you on the other side of that equation is an opportunity to shape the future way in which we will deliver on mission, and I can almost promise you—because I have never been through one of these exercises where it wasn't true—that I can promise you that when this is all done, you're going to have a much more satisfying, fulfilling career, because you're going to feel better about what you're doing because of the impact of what you are doing. You will know exactly how what you do every day contributes to our delivery on mission, and that is when I find people are most satisfied with their professional careers. And you're going to have clear line of sight about what do you want for yourself in the future.

[57] So this is a—it's a big undertaking. This is a big department, between this and USAID, and we are including all of our missions, all of our embassies, all of our consular offices, because we all are part of how we deliver on mission. So we want to look at it in its entirety as to how we do that. So I appreciate your participating openly in this listening exercise, but importantly, I want to condition you to be ready to participate in the next phase, because that's when it'll become more challenging. But we're all on this boat, on this voyage—I'm not going to call it a cruise; it's not—may not be that much fun. (Laughter.) But we're on all this ship, on this voyage together. And so we're going to get on the ship and we're going to take this voyage, and when we get there, we're all going to get off the ship at wherever we arrive. But we're all going to get on and we're going to get off together. We don't intend to leave anybody out.

[58] So I appreciate your participation. I hope you will approach this with a level of excitement as to what it may hold for this State Department first and then for you as an individual and what it means for you. So we're asking all of you to do that.

[59] Let me lastly say that I do appreciate all of the work that you do. Believe it or not, I do read all these memos that come to me from—all the way from missions to the various bureaus. I appreciate those of you that get them on one page, because I'm not a fast reader. But they're extraordinarily helpful to me, and so keep sending me insights as to what you're doing, how you're doing it, and in particular the perspective on how we got to where we are. It is very valuable to me.

[60] I had the opportunity to address a group of young people yesterday—about 700 middle school, high school people—that were here participating in the model UN conference. We were hosting it here at the State Department. One of the—there's a few fun things you get to do in this job, and talking to young people is one of them. So I had a Q&A time, and a young lady—I think she was in middle school—asked a question. She said, "What inspires you as Secretary of State when you come to work every day?" And I told her it's quite easy. I said the men and women of the State Department inspire me, my colleagues—their professionalism, their commitment, their patriotism. And I said, then our partners over at the Department of Defense, the men and women in uniform, because it's really the State Department and the Defense Department that deliver our national security. I'm inspired by you, and I thank you for that, and I'm honored to serve alongside of you.

[61] We'll be talking again. Thank you. (Applause.)

Appendix B

Being a Christian Leader[1]

Michael R. Pompeo, Secretary of State
American Association of Christian Counselors
Gaylord Opryland Hotel, Nashville, Tennessee
October 11, 2019

[1] **SECRETARY POMPEO:** Good morning, everyone (Cheers). Good morning. Good morning, thank you. Thank you. Good morning. Good morning, everyone. Thank you, Dr. Clinton, for that kind introduction. It's great to be with you and your wife, Julie. It's a real privilege to be with you, and it's a heck of a deal to be out of Washington today. (Laughter.) I was going to give you some wisdom, said maybe you'll hold your conference there next year, but I thought about it and that'd be a bad idea. (Laughter.) But Washington could use your spirit and your love.

[2] And I want, too, to take just a moment to pass along—I spoke to the President yesterday, and I told him I was coming down here. He reminded me that Tennessee won the country. (Laughter.) I told him I knew that. But he said to send his regards and his love and his appreciation for what you do taking care of people all around the world.

[3] I did want to talk to you about why I'm here. I'm the Secretary of State. I spend most of my time traveling around the world, but I wanted to come here because I have a profound appreciation for your mission. And when I had a chance to talk to Tim about the opportunity to come speak with you, I was thrilled to get the chance.

191

[4] Look, we share some things in common. We talk to people through hard times. We find ourselves in the middle of disputes and we seek to mediate them and try and identify their root causes. We try to keep conflict minimized, at bay. And when you think about those missions, the missions that you all have, it sounds a lot like the diplomacy that me at the State Department and my team engage in every day.

[5] We're both in very people-intensive lines of work, and we're both appealing to the hearts and minds to change behaviors. As believers, we draw on the wisdom of God to help us get it right, to be a force for good in the life of human beings.

[6] Now, I know that even having just said that, I know some people in the media will break out the pitchforks when they hear that I ask God for direction in my work. (Applause.) But you should know, as much as I'd like to claim originality, it is not a new idea. (Laughter.) I love this quote from President Lincoln. He said that he—he said, quote, "I have been driven many times upon my knees by the overwhelming conviction that I had nowhere else to go." (Laughter.)

[7] And so with that in mind, I want to use my time today to think about what it means to be a Christian leader, a Christian leader in three areas:

[8] First is disposition. How is it that one carries oneself in the world? The second is dialogue, talking. How is it that we engage with others around the world? And third is decisions, decisions that we make. How do we make choices? Upon what basis? What do we use as our bedrock to get to those decisions? These are things that you face in your work every day. They are issues that the State Department and President Trump, each of us, must face.

[9] And my focus too, to be quite candid, is not just on being a leader. I learned how to lead at whatever level I'm blessed with during my time at West Point and other experiences, but I want to talk today about being a Christian leader. I learned that through a very different experience, an experience with God and my own personal faith in Christ.

[10] Like a lot of people—and you don't have to admit it today—but like a lot of people, I grew up going to church but with a relationship with God that wasn't especially important for me, because I was destined to be

in the NBA. (Laughter.) But as I grew older, when I started my time at the United States Military Academy, there were two young men—they were in the class ahead of me—who invited me to a Bible study. They were very intentional to me in explaining God's Word. And after some study and discipleship with them, they helped me begin my walk with Christ.

[11] And since then I've been privileged to have many different leadership roles. I was a captain in the United States Army in a cavalry unit. I was—I ran two small companies in my home state of Kansas. I served as a member of Congress trying to do my level best to represent the people of south-central Kansas. And then I served as CIA Director, and now I have the incredible privilege to serve President Trump as his 70th Secretary of State. I'm mindful he's the 45th president, so there's a lot more turnover in my job than in his. (Laughter.)

[12] But back—Susan and I have been—had Christ at the center of our lives. Back in my church in Wichita I was a deacon. She and I taught fifth grade Sunday School, which was a great, great lesson for my time as Secretary of State (Laughter and Applause). But we also saw in that, in our time serving in that, we saw how many challenging issues that you all address every single day.

[13] I've had the privilege to do it all alongside Susan, my wonderful Christian wife, and my son, Nick, who keeps me humble. Yeah, he reminded me. So I'm going to get off an airplane the other day at 3 o'clock in the morning, I forget where I was, and he texted me. It was a different time here on the East Coast. And he texted and said, "Dad, you almost fell down." And he was not worried about me; he was worried about America. (Laughter.) He did not want me to embarrass America. (Laughter.) There is absolutely no shortage of leadership wisdom gathered from raising a teenage boy, I can certainly tell you that. (Laughter.)

[14] And so my prayer today is that whatever understanding I've gained in these various opportunities that I've had, these blessings I've had to lead—some of which I've learned the hard way, for sure—I hope that I can share some of these with you today and it will bless you in your work as well.

[15] We all know this: Before you can help others, you need to have the right approach to yourself. This is where I get to the first point I wanted to

talk about, which is disposition. How—what's the attitude with which we approach each of these challenges, all the things that we see in the world? How you carry yourself is the first arena of Christian leadership.

[16] Scripture calls us to be "transformed by the renewing of [our] minds." And so I keep a Bible open on my desk, and I try every morning to try and get in a little bit of time with the Book. I need my mind renewed with truth each day. And part of that truth is, as my son reminds me, is to be humble. Proverbs says, "With the humble is wisdom."

[17] Every day, as Secretary of State, I get a real chance to be humble, because I get to see the great work that my team is doing. I, like many of you, am also confronted with highly complex problem sets, and I need wisdom to try and make the right calls. I need to admit what I don't know and try to learn it, to ask the questions that others might find obvious and be unembarrassed, and to accept conclusions when the facts are presented that might go against whatever preconceived notion that I might have had.

[18] Indeed, this disposition is my duty; it's my duty to the American people to pursue the outcomes based on an honest analysis of the facts as they present themselves. We know this, too—we see this in our lives: Pride can get in the way of that. But wisdom comes from a humble disposition.

[19] And one more point on disposition: forgiveness. I love the story of the prodigal son in the Scripture: the son comes homes with his tail between his legs, he knows he's messed up, and yet his father runs—runs—to welcome him back home.

[20] The people who work for me know this, too: I have high standards for excellence. I hold them accountable and give them authority. I hold myself to that high set of standards because there is so much riding on what we do to keep the American people safe that we can't accept anything less.

[21] But when there is failure, when the people close to me misfire, I don't strip away their responsibilities. I don't cut them out of meetings. I keep them in the fold. I keep giving them important work. That's what Christ does for us; we have an obligation to do the same.

[22] We should all remember—we should all remember that we are imperfect servants serving a perfect God who constantly forgives us each and every

day. He keeps using us—(applause)—he keeps using us to do a higher work. And my work at the State Department, as it is for those who work alongside of me, is to serve America each and every day.

[23] And that brings me to a second idea of the Christian leader: dialogue. How we speak, our speech, our dealings with others.

[24] For a moment, back to the Book of James: "Everyone should be quick to listen, and slow to speak."

[25] That's a lesson I learned in the Army from a guy named SFC Pretre, and I was reminded of it in an interview this morning (Laughter). I'll do better. (Laughter.) I was a brand new Second Lieutenant. I'd just arrived in Germany and I'd had my four years at West Point, and I was set to conquer the world. I went out to the field in a little tiny town in the far—then far-eastern stretches of West Germany, and there he was, a grizzled old soldier named Sergeant Pretre. And I walked up, he saluted me because I was the officer and he was the noncommissioned officer, and I greeted him, and he said, "Young man, you'll do really well if you just shut up for a while." (Laughter.) He actually had an adjective in there that I shall not use in polite company. (Laughter.)

[26] I listened to him then, and I continued to listen. Every day, too, I engage with foreign leaders who sit across the table from me, or sit in a room, and I try to understand what it is they want. What are their objectives for their people? How can the United States deliver to help them in a way that treats America, the people that I am responsible for keeping safe—puts America first and delivers on behalf of the American people?

[27] It reminds me, when I'm with them, that sound relationships abso- lutely depend on open ears. Good listening means more than just hearing; it means not rushing to judgment before you hear every side of a particular fact set. This comes through so clearly in Proverbs, which say, "The one who states his case first seems right, until the other comes and examines him."

[28] There's a lot of times members of my team will come into my office and they respectfully disagree. They'll have ideas that are different from mine or, in fact, often different from each other. I need to make sure that I listen, that I scrutinize each position before I say one is right or wrong, or that the truth is somewhere in between.

[29] I'm sure you all see that. I'm sure you all see that in your research, in your studies, in the counseling that you do when you counsel people wrestling over a disagreement, whether that's in their marriage or in a church matter or with their family. Let's make sure we understand the facts. When we have that, we can begin to move forward and heal and solve problems.

[30] After I've collected data, I feel like I have the seasoning to then be able to begin to speak fundamental basic, simple, small "t" truths. Colossians talks about this. It says, "Let your speech always be gracious, seasoned with salt, so that you may know how you ought to answer to each person." I know this is a critical part of what so many of you do, whether it's pointing those you counsel back to the truth of the Scripture, or giving them a hard wake-up call over their trespasses.

I've found this in life—truth telling isn't just a matter of private conversations for me. It's what I try to do publicly as we lay down President Trump's foreign policy to keep Americans safe and secure.

This administration has spoken to the truth in many ways that previous administrations haven't done (Applause). For example, on China's rule-breaking and authoritarianism; for example, on why the Islamic Republic of Iran is an aggressor, not a victim; for why, in fact, we know in our hearts that America is a force for good in the world. (Applause.)

[31] And I'm especially telling the truth about the dire condition of religious freedom around the world. America has a proud history of religious freedom, and we want jealously to guard it here. But around the world, more than 80% of mankind lives in areas where religious freedom is suppressed or denied in its entirety.

[32] The Chinese Communist Party—as we sit here today in the beautiful facility in Nashville, the Chinese Communist Party is detaining and abusing more than one million Uighur Muslims in internment camps in the Xinjiang. It's the western region of China. The pages of George Orwell's 1984 are coming to life there. I wish the NBA would acknowledge that. (Applause.)

[33] So Christian pastors today are being unlawfully arrested, beaten, detained inside the Islamic Republic of Iran. We need to speak about this.

[34] Christian areas in northern Iraq that I've had the privilege to visit have been ravaged by ISIS, part of a greater trend of Christian persecution all across the Middle East.

[35] And so the truth—for the past two years we've spoken the truth. We've hosted ministerials. We bring leaders from all around the world called the Ministerial on Religious Freedom at the State Department. We've told the world about these shortfalls and the success of nations when individuals are given their basic human dignity to practice their conscience, their faith, or to choose no faith if they so choose all around the world.

[36] We hosted the largest human rights conference ever at the United States Department of State just this past summer. It was truly remarkable. Faith leaders from all across the globe came together at our beautiful facility in the western party of Washington, D.C. to talk about the importance of religious freedom.

[37] Just this week, the United States made a decision. We put visa restrictions on those responsible for the some of the human rights violations that took place in China and that continue to take place today.

[38] And we've stopped American companies from exporting certain products to Chinese tech companies that are enabling these very human rights abuses. We did these things under President Trump's direction for the simple reason that we know Americans do not want their companies building the machinery of a totalitarian surveillance state.

[39] There's so much more work to do. I would ask you today to pray for my work in defending religious freedom. (Applause.)

[40] This is—look, I'll be straight up with you—I'm from Kansas—but this is not a popular conversation to raise in Washington, D.C. sometimes, and sometimes not with other leaders around the world as well. But the world needs to hear this truth. And with you all, or with you having your voices being raised for this purpose, I am confident that we can improve human dignity for individuals all across the world. (Applause.)

[41] Now for my final thought on Christian leadership. I want to talk about how it is we make decisions, individual decisions in our personal lives, in our family lives, and other decisions as well.

Let's start with some of the toughest decisions of all: those involving money. I know you all see this as Christian counselors. I'm willing to bet my organization's budget is a little bigger than yours. Although this is a big group. (Laughter.) But no matter whether it's your family's finances or you're responsible for protecting taxpayer funds and being a good steward, as I am today, the Bible calls us to be faithful in our stewardship of whatever it is that we have been privileged to hold onto, no matter how much or how little. We have to be faithful in every single circumstance.

[42] Think of that famous parable of the talents. The servant called "good and faithful" used what he had wisely.

[43] Last year—and I confront this with some frequency—last year, I had a group of folks in my office who came and said, "Mike, we have this project we want to work on. It's going to spend tens of millions of dollars. Here's how we're going to deliver that. Here's the end state that we're seeking." And just like you do in your life every day and each as you do in your—the faith part of your life as well, I asked a handful of simple questions about whether this would be a responsible use of the American people's money? Are we going to create value for the American people?

[44] In this particular case, I recall it was a close call. It was a difficult decision. I ultimately decided that spending these resources was appropriate and that we'd put in place a set of metrics that would ensure that we delivered a good outcome for the American people. I'm sure you—there are many pastors out here—you make decisions, too, about how to spend the money you're your [sic] flock has so generously contributed to the Lord. And I know you'll do the best for your congregation and for your church as well. And you'll do that remembering this important Christian leadership principle, this call for stewardship.

[45] Because we are mindful that decisions are a question of priorities, often. I just talked about one decision we made at the State Department. It meant that those resources couldn't be spent elsewhere. We were setting a priority. And I am grateful that my call as a Christian to protect human dignity overlaps with America's centuries-old commitment to the same mission in our foreign policy all across the world.

[46] My day is often scheduled into 15-minute increments. Every now and again I get a half hour, and every now and again I get to hear some of the beautiful worship music that I was able to sit with you for. I need to be intentional—we each need to be intentional—about carving out time to pursue the mission of defending human dignity.

[47] I'm proud to say that President Trump has let our State Department do that. Indeed, he has demanded that we do.

[48] International organizations will try, from time to time, to sneak language into their documents claiming that abortion is a human right. And we'll never accept that. (Applause and cheers.) We've worked diligently to find every dollar that might be going to that and we have worked tirelessly and successfully now to bring it nearly to an end.

[49] We also face situations around the world of human trafficking. We're exposing them. We're fighting them. (Applause and cheers.)

[50] Earlier this year, our Diplomatic Security Service came across a young woman and pulled her out of a human trafficking situation not too far from here in Dallas, Texas. This young woman was separated from her mother and she had been shipped off to the United States from Guinea when she was just a small child.

[51] She had been toiling for 12 to 16 hours a day, seven days a week, without pay: cooking and cleaning and caring for five children of a wealthy Texas family. She wasn't permitted to attend school. She didn't receive medical care. She wasn't allowed to play with the other children in the neighborhood.

[52] This young woman endured sheer misery for 16 years until, with the help of concerned neighbors, she escaped.

[53] The blessing in this story is that her case came to the attention of the United States Department of State. We became the lead investigator in the case, and one of our agents tracked down this young woman's mother, who had been desperate to see her again. (Applause.) We were able to fly her to Texas to testify at trial. She was there to vouch for the girl's identity, to say, "This is my daughter."

Ultimately, the perpetrators were put in prison for a good long time. And the girl is, today, working towards her GED and receiving counseling and living a wonderful life. (Applause.)

[54] These violations of the most fundamental freedoms, human dignity that I spoke about today—religious persecution, human trafficking, political repression—they leave deep scars.

[55] And I am sure that some of you—and especially our friends who have traveled here from overseas today—I'm sure you counsel folks who are healing from those kinds of traumas.

[56] My team and I at the State Department are out there every day, using our diplomacy to fix the very conditions that allowed these evils to fester.

[57] Others will confront these evils closer to home, where the emotional aftermath is no less terrible: vicious abuse, or the opioid epidemic, just to name a couple.

[58] But no matter what comes before you, I pray you'll help hurting people stay immersed in God's Word. By remaining humble. By showing forgiveness. By listening intently and carefully and thoughtfully. By not rushing to judgment in complicated matters. By being a faithful steward. By using your time with intentionally.

[59] And I pray you'll do these things not out of your own strength, but by relying on, as Paul says, "Him who is able to do immeasurably more than all we are able to ask or to imagine."

[60] You will all be in my prayers as you do God's work, and I covet yours as I lead American diplomacy.

[61] Thank you for joining me here today. God bless you. And may God bless the United States of America. Thank you, all. (Applause and cheers.)

Notes

Introduction

1. Andrew R. Flores, *Polarized Progress: Social Acceptance of LGBT People in 141 Countries*, Williams Institute, UCLA School of Law, 2019, https://williamsinstitute.law.ucla.edu/wp-content/uploads/Global-Acceptance-Index-LGBT-Oct-2019.pdf.

2. "Life Beyond Europe's Rainbow Curtain," Charlemagne, *Economist*, November 21, 2020, https://www.economist.com/europe/2020/11/21/life-beyond-europes-rainbow-curtain.

3. Kristopher Velasco, "Queering Global Norms, Rival Transnational Networks, and the Contested Case of LGBT Rights," Queer Politics webinar, July 23, 2020, https://www.queerpolitics.org/qp-webinar-2020.

4. Some proponents use sexual orientation and gender identity or expression, or SOGIE.

5. For a range of anti-LGBTQ techniques populist authoritarian leaders adopt to advance their interests, see Meredith L. Weiss and Michael J. Bosia, eds., *Global Homophobia: States, Movements, and the Politics of Oppression* (Urbana: University of Illinois Press, 2013).

6. Helena Andrews-Dyer, "Donald Trump Says Caitlyn Jenner Can Use Whatever Bathroom She Wants at Trump Tower," *Washington Post*, April 21, 2016, https://www.washingtonpost.com/news/reliable-source/wp/2016/04/21/donald-trump-says-caitlyn-jenner-can-use-whatever-bathroom-she-wants-at-trump-tower/.

7. Scott Lively and Kevin Abrams, *The Pink Swastika: Homosexuality in the Nazi Party* (Keiser, OR: Founders, 1995). The Lively and Abrams book can be read as an antigay counterpoint to Richard Plant, *The Pink Triangle: The Nazi War against Homosexuals* (New York: Holt Paperbacks, 1988).

8. Scott Lively, "Trump and the LGBT Agenda," December 9, 2016, https://barbwire.com/2016/12/09/trump-lgbt-agenda/. See also Brian Tashman, "Scott Lively: Trump Presidency Is the Beginning of the End of LGBT Movement," December 9, 2016, http://www.rightwingwatch.org/post/scott-lively-trump-presidency-is-the-beginning-of-the-end-of-lgbt-movement/.

9. Robert D. Benford and David A. Snow, "Framing Processes and Social Movements: An Overview and Assessment," *Annual Review of Sociology* 26 (2000): 614, 613.

10. I adapt the terminology of political economist Charles E. Lindblom, who posits that corporations occupy a "privileged position" among interest groups in the US. I don't argue that the Christian right occupied "the" privileged position, just "a" privileged position. See Charles E. Lindblom, *Politics and Markets: The World's Political-Economic Systems* (New York: Basic Books, 1977). For evidence on the privileged position of business, see Jason Webb Yackee and Susan Webb Yackee, "A Bias Toward Business? Assessing Interest Group Influence on the U.S. Bureaucracy," *Journal of Politics* 68, no. 1 (2006): 128–39.

11. Cynthia Burack, *Because We Are Human: Contesting US Support for Gender and Sexuality Human Rights Abroad* (New York: State University of New York Press, 2018), 38–41.

12. Phillip M. Ayoub, *When States Come Out: Europe's Sexual Minorities and the Politics of Visibility* (Cambridge: Cambridge University Press, 2016). For the "life cycle" of norms, see Elizabeth Baisley, "Reaching the Tipping Point? Emerging International Human Rights Norms Pertaining to Sexual Orientation and Gender Identity," *Human Rights Quarterly* 38, no. 1 (2016): 134–63.

13. Elise Carlson Rainer and Jacqueline Dufalla, "The Foreign Policy of LGBT Rights: Russia's Reaction and Resistance to US Policy," *Global Studies Journal* 9, no. 4(2016): 13.

14. Jack Donnelly, *International Human Rights*, 4th ed. (Boulder, CO: Westview, 2013), p. 51.

15. The latest attempt to document global spending on LGBTI rights is Global Philanthropy Project and Funders for LGBTQ Issues, *2017–2018 Global Resources Report: Government and Philanthropic Support for LGBTI Communities*, May 2020, https://globalresourcesreport.org/. Data on which the report relies aren't entirely reliable because of difficulties obtaining some information. The report underreports some governments' contributions to LGBTI human rights and overreports some funding for LGBTI by conflating support for human rights with funding for HIV/Aids.

16. Louise Diamond and John McDonald, *Multi-track Diplomacy: A Systems Approach to Peace*, 3rd ed. (West Hartford, CT: Kumarian, 1996).

17. Doris Buss and Didi Herman, *Globalizing Family Values: The Christian Right in International Politics* (Minneapolis: University of Minnesota Press); Clifford Bob, *The Global Right Wing and the Clash of World Politics* (Cambridge: Cambridge University Press, 2012).

18. Pew Research Center, "Faith and the 2016 Campaign," January 27, 2016, https://www.pewforum.org/2016/01/27/faith-and-the-2016-campaign/.

19. Sarah Eekhoff Zylstra, "Dobson Explains Why He Called Trump a 'Baby Christian,'" *Christianity Today*, August 4, 2016, https://www.christianitytoday.com/news/2016/august/james-dobson-explains-why-donald-trump-baby-christian.html.

20. Cynthia Burack, "How Christian Conservatives Learned to Love Donald Trump," *Huffington Post*, May 25, 2017, https://www.huffpost.com/entry/christian-conservatives-l_b_10101018.

21. Lance Wallnau, *God's Chaos Candidate: Donald J. Trump and the American Unraveling* (Keller, TX: Killer Sheep Media, 2016); Tara Isabella Burton, "The Biblical Story the Christian Right Uses to Defend Trump," *Vox*, March 5, 2018, https://www.vox.com/identities/2018/3/5/16796892/trump-cyrus-christian-right-bible-cbn-evangelical-propaganda.

22. Rebecca Barrett-Fox, "A King Cyrus President: How Donald Trump's Presidency Reasserts Conservative Christians' Right to Hegemony," *Humanity and Society* 42, no. 4 (2018): 502–22; Salena Zito and Brad Todd, *The Great Revolt: Inside the Populist Coalition Reshaping American Politics* (New York: Crown Forum, 2018).

23. Stephanie McCrummen, "Judgment Days," *Washington Post*, July 21, 2018, https://www.washingtonpost.com/news/national/wp/2018/07/21/feature/god-trump-and-the-meaning-of-morality/?utm_term=.59e0f3e02ec3&wpisrc=nl_evening&wpmm=1.

24. Trump attorney Michael Cohen paid Clifford for her silence, and the *National Enquirer* paid McDougal for her story about the affair, thereby "catching and killing" the story to benefit Trump's campaign.

25. In 2021, Barna joined the Family Research Council's new Center for Biblical Worldview as a senior research fellow.

26. George Barna, *The Day Christians Changed America: How Christian Conservatives Put Trump in the White House and Redirected America's Future* (Ventura, CA: Metaformation, 2017). The Metaformation imprint is a product of the Barna Group.

27. We don't know the exact number of David's wives and concubines, but 2 Samuel 5:13 tells us that in the course of David's successful military campaign to unite Israel under his rule he acquired "more" of both.

28. Sarah Pulliam Bailey, " 'I Am the Chosen One': Trump again Plays on Messianic Claims as He Embraces 'King of Israel' Title," *Washington Post*, August 21, 2019, https://www.washingtonpost.com/religion/2019/08/21/i-am-chosen-one-trump-again-plays-messianic-claims-he-embraces-king-israel-title/.

29. Elizabeth Bruenig, "In God's Country," *Washington Post*, August 14, 2019, https://www.washingtonpost.com/opinions/2019/08/14/evangelicals-view-trump-their-protector-will-they-stand-by-him/.

30. John Fea, *Believe Me: The Evangelical Road to Donald Trump* (Grand Rapids, MI: Eerdman's, 2018), 38–39; Thomas J. Main, *The Rise of the Alt-Right* (Washington, DC: Brookings Institution Press, 2018), 230.

31. Chip Berlet, ed., *Trumping Democracy: From Reagan to the Alt-Right* (New York: Routledge, 2019).

32. Nancy D. Wadsworth, *Ambivalent Miracles: Evangelicals and the Politics of Racial Healing* (Charlottesville: University of Virginia Press, 2014).

33. Fea, *Believe Me*.

34. George Schroeder, "Seminary Presidents Reaffirm BFM, Declare CRT Incompatible," *Baptist Press*, November 30, 2020, https://www.baptistpress.com/resource-library/news/seminary-presidents-reaffirm-bfm-declare-crt-incompatible/. The SBC has also been challenged in recent years over misogyny and covering up sexual abuse.

35. Sarah Posner, *Unholy: Why White Evangelicals Worship at the Altar of Donald Trump* (New York: Random House, 2020), 9.

36. Rachel Marie Blum and Christopher Sebastian Parker, "Trump-ing Foreign Affairs: Status Threat and Foreign Policy Preferences on the Right," *Perspectives on Politics* 17, no. 3 (2019): 737–54; Pippa Norris and Ronald Inglehart, *Cultural Backlash: Trump, Brexit, and Authoritarian Populism* (Cambridge: Cambridge University Press, 2019), 15–16.

37. For moral foundations and justificatory strategic reasoning that rationalizes moral worldviews, see Jonathan Haidt, *The Righteous Mind: Why Good People are Divided by Politics and Religion* (New York: Random House, 2012).

38. Andrew Koppelman, *Gay Rights vs. Religious Liberty? The Unnecessary Conflict* (Oxford: Oxford University Press, 2020), 2, 7, 8. See also William N. Eskridge, Jr., and Robin Fretwell Wilson, eds., *Religious Freedom, LGBT Rights, and the Prospects for Common Ground* (New York: Cambridge University Press, 2018); Nathan A. Berkeley, "Religious Freedom and LGBT Rights: Trading Zero Sum Approaches for Careful Distinctions and Genuine Pluralism," *Gonzaga Law Review* 50, no. 1 (2014–15): 1–28.

39. Frederick Clarkson, "Religious Freedom Is the Cornerstone of Our Democracy," Political Research Associates, February 28, 2018, https://www.politicalresearch.org/2018/02/28/religious-freedom-is-the-cornerstone-of-our-democracy.

40. For some of these interconnections between elites across the movement, see Katherine Stewart, *The Power Worshippers: Inside the Dangerous Rise of Religious Nationalism* (New York: Bloomsbury, 2019).

41. In its messaging, FRC boasts to its constituents about "shaping the narrative." As I prepared this book for publication, I received a subscriber email from FRC that explained what the organization does: "Every day our team of experts have the honor of representing you through discussions with policymakers, shaping the narrative through multimedia broadcasts, equipping pastors and ministry leaders to preach the Word of God without apology, educating parents and teachers on how to protect schoolchildren from leftist indoctrination, and encouraging believers to stand firm for biblical truth." Email to the author, Scott Hurley, "Free FRC Resources to Educate and Inspire," Family Research Council, July 8, 2021.

42. Family Research Council, "History of Family Research Council," accessed October 14, 2020, https://www.frc.org/historymission.

43. Family Research Council, "About FRC," accessed October 14, 2020, https://www.frc.org/.

44. Because of the Covid-19 pandemic, the 2020 summit was virtual. I've attended every Values Voter Summit from the inception of the meeting in 2006 to 2019.

45. Southern Poverty Law Center, "Family Research Council," accessed October 14, 2020, https://www.splcenter.org/fighting-hate/extremist-files/group/family-research-council.

46. For an official FRC response to the SPLC, see Rob Schwarzwalder, "Answering the Southern Poverty Law Center's Attacks upon Family Research Council," Family Research Council, August 20, 2012, https://www.frc.org/issue brief/answering-the-southern-poverty-law-centers-attacks-upon-family-research-council. For an overview of the scandal that enveloped the SPLC, see Bob Moser, "The Reckoning of Morris Dees and the Southern Poverty Law Center," *New Yorker*, March 21, 2019, https://www.newyorker.com/news/news-desk/the-reckoning-of-morris-dees-and-the-southern-poverty-law-center.

47. Fea, *Believe Me.*

48. Howard S. Becker, *Outsiders: Studies in the Sociology of Deviance* (New York: Free Press, 1963).

49. Eric Bradner, "Trump Blames Tony Perkins for '2 Corinthians,' " CNN, January 21, 2016, https://www.cnn.com/2016/01/20/politics/donald-trump-tony-perkins-sarah-palin/index.html.

50. Michael Gerson, "The Last Temptation," *Atlantic*, April 2018, https://www.theatlantic.com/magazine/archive/2018/04/the-last-temptation/554066/; Family Research Council, "A Gerson of Interest," March 12, 2018, http://www.frc.org/updatearticle/20180312/gersoninterest. By October 13, 2020, the link to "A Gerson of Interest" was broken, and the essay was no longer available at FRC.

51. See Bryan D. Jones and Frank R. Baumgartner, *The Politics of Attention: How Government Prioritizes Problems* (Chicago: University of Chicago Press, 2005).

52. Michael R. Pompeo, "Being a Christian Leader," October 14, 2019, https://www.state.gov/being-a-christian-leader/. I address the speech at greater length in chapter 3, and a full text can be found in appendix B.

53. Tony Perkins, "The Trump Administration's Not-So Closeted Christians," *Family Research Council*, October 22, 2019, https://www.frc.org/get.cfm?i=WA19J43&f=WU19J14.

54. Bob Eschliman, "Evangelical Women 'Speak Up' for Donald Trump," *Charisma News*, November 2, 2016, https://www.charismanews.com/politics/elections/60980-evangelical-women-speak-up-for-donald-trump.

55. John Hudson, "Ex-Palin Aide Lands Job at Trump's State Department," *Foreign Policy*, February 9, 2017, https://foreignpolicy.com/2017/02/09/ex-palin-aide-lands-job-at-trumps-state-department/.

56. Pam Pryor, "Upholding Religious Freedom as a Core American Value and Universal Human Right," *Dipnote: U.S. Department of State Official Blog*,

October 27, 2017, https://www.state.gov/upholding-religious-freedom-as-a-core-american-value-and-universal-human-right/.

57. Equity Forward, "Pam Pryor," accessed July 20, 2020, https://equityfwd.org/pam-pryor.

58. Tom LoBianco, "How Pence's Camp Persuaded Trump to Pick Their Guy as VP," *Politico*, September 11, 2019, https://www.politico.com/magazine/story/2019/09/11/mike-pence-donald-trump-vp-228059.

59. Andrew Kaczynski, "Mike Pence Argued Homosexuality Was 'a Choice' or 'Learned Behavior' during 1990's Fight against Gay Rights Ordinance," CNN, September 13, 2019, https://www.cnn.com/2019/09/13/politics/mike-pence-gay-rights-1990s/index.html.

60. Philip Oltermann, "New US Ambassador to Germany Under Fire for Rightwing Support," *Guardian*, June 4, 2018, https://www.theguardian.com/world/2018/jun/04/new-us-ambassador-to-germany-under-fire-for-rightwing-support. Thomas J. Main designates *Breitbart* as an "Alt-Lite" media outlet, which he defines as "the somewhat watered-down version of the Alt-Right's ideology" and a "hybrid of mainstream conservatism and the Alt-Right." See Thomas J. Main, *The Rise of the Alt-Right* (Washington, DC: Brookings Institution Press, 2018), 9, 213.

61. Edward Wong, Annie Karni, and Emily Cochrane, "Trump Administration Drops Proposal to Cut Foreign Aid after Intense Debate," *New York Times*, August 22, 2019, https://www.nytimes.com/2019/08/22/us/politics/trump-foreign-aid.html.

62. John Riley, "Mick Mulvaney, Trump's New Chief of Staff, Has an Anti-LGBTQ Record That Would Rival Mike Pence," *Metro Weekly*, December 18, 2018, https://www.metroweekly.com/2018/12/mick-mulvaney-trumps-new-chief-of-staff-has-an-anti-lgbtq-record-that-would-rival-mike-pence/.

63. BBC News, "Mick Mulvaney: Trump Replaces White House Chief of Staff," March 7, 2020, https://www.bbc.com/news/world-us-canada-51779902.

64. Julie Moreau, "Trump Taps LGBTQ-Rights Opponent Sam Brownback as Religious Freedom Ambassador," NBC News, July 31, 2017, https://www.nbcnews.com/feature/nbc-out/trump-taps-lgbtq-rights-opponent-sam-brownback-religious-freedom-ambassador-n788101.

65. Leigh Hartman, "U.S. Launches International Religious Freedom Alliance," *ShareAmerica*, US State Department, February 6, 2020, https://share.america.gov/u-s-launches-international-religious-freedom-alliance/; US State Department, "Declaration of Principles for the International Religious Freedom Alliance," February 5, 2020, https://www.state.gov/declaration-of-principles-for-the-international-religious-freedom-alliance/#:~:text=The%20Alliance%20is%20a%20network,based%20on%20religion%20or%20belief.

66. US State Department, "International Religious Freedom Fund," July 27, 2018, https://www.state.gov/remarks-and-releases-bureau-of-democracy-human-rights-and-labor/international-religious-freedom-fund/.

67. *New York Times*, "Senator Brownback and the Judge," December 22, 2006, https://www.nytimes.com/2006/12/22/opinion/senator-brownback-and-the-judge.html.

68. Brooke Sopelsa, "LGBTQ Groups Slam Confirmation of Brownback as Religious Freedom Ambassador," NBC News, January 26, 2018, https://www.nbcnews.com/feature/nbc-out/lgbtq-groups-slam-confirmation-brownback-religious-freedom-ambassador-n841481.

69. David Brody, " 'My Belief in Jesus Christ Makes a Real Difference': Mike Pompeo Says His Christian Faith Puts Everything in Perspective," CBN News, April 2, 2019, https://www1.cbn.com/cbnnews/politics/2019/april/my-belief-in-jesus-christ-makes-a-real-difference-mike-pompeo-says-his-christian-faith-puts-everything-in-perspective.

70. KSNT News, "Congressman Mike Pompeo Released This Statement," June 26, 2015, https://www.facebook.com/ksntnews/photos/congressman-mike-pompeo-released-this-statement-just-a-few-moments-agoi-am-deepl/1018839604793898/.

71. Eugene Scott, "Cory Booker Grills Mike Pompeo on Whether He Believes Being Gay Is a 'Perversion,' " *Washington Post*, April 12, 2018, https://www.washingtonpost.com/news/the-fix/wp/2018/04/12/cory-booker-grills-mike-pompeo-on-whether-he-believes-being-gay-is-a-perversion/.

72. Paul Musgrave, "The Slip That Revealed the Real Trump Doctrine," *Foreign Policy*, May 2, 2019, https://foreignpolicy.com/2019/05/02/the-slip-that-revealed-the-real-trump-doctrine/.

73. Nahal Toosi and Eliana Johnson, "Top State Department Advisor Fired Over 'Abusive' Management Style," *Politico*, August 2, 2019, https://www.politico.com/story/2019/08/02/top-state-department-adviser-fired-1444894.

74. US Department of State, "Bureau of Democracy, Human Rights, and Labor," US Government, accessed October 21, 2017, https://www.state.gov/j/drl/.

75. Michael Gordon and Tim Funk, "Should Catholic Churches, Schools Be Able to Fire Gay Employees Who Marry Their Partners?," *Charlotte Observer*, October 9, 2017, https://www.charlotteobserver.com/news/politics-government/article177426591.html.

76. GLAAD, "Robert Destro," accessed July 20, 2020, https://www.glaad.org/tap/robert-destro.

77. Center for Reproductive Rights, "Letter to Senators Risch and Menendez," March 22, 2019, https://www.reproductiverights.org/sites/crr.civicactions.net/files/documents/Civil-Society-Letter-Opposing-Robert-Destro-Nomination.pdf. More organizations dedicated to women's reproductive rights signed this letter than organizations representing LGBTQ or SOGI human rights.

78. Council for Global Equality, "Robert Destro Can't Credibly Lead America's Human Rights Policy," March 27, 2019, https://globalequality.wordpress.com/2019/03/27/robert-destro-cant-credibly-lead-americas-human-rights-policy/.

79. US Department of State, "Global Equality Fund," accessed February 16, 2021, https://www.state.gov/global-equality-fund/.

80. See Zein Murib, "Rethinking GLBT as a Political Category in U.S. Politics," in *LGBTQ Politics: A Critical Reader*, ed. Marla Brettschneider, Susan Burgess, and Christine Keating (New York: New York University Press, 2017).

81. At times, we see a variation that adds an "E" for gender expression: SOGIE. However, in 2021, SOGI remains most common.

82. Cynthia Burack, *Sin, Sex, and Democracy: Antigay Rhetoric and the Christian Right* (Albany: State University of New York Press, 2008), 3–4.

83. The most effective Christian conservative work to emerge from this recent attentiveness to transgender rights advocacy is Ryan T. Anderson, *When Harry Became Sally: Responding to the Transgender Moment* (New York: Encounter, 2018).

84. One possible exception is the clash that may proceed from the intersex movement's demand for an end to nonconsensual medical interventions on infants and children and the Christian right's firm support for parents' rights. It makes sense that these demands would conflict; however, I haven't seen specific rhetoric about such a conflict in Christian conservative political literature.

85. I analyze Trump speeches before the United Nations that refer to decriminalization of same-sex sexuality in chapter 4, when I discuss Ric Grenell's decriminalization initiative.

86. Elise Carlson Rainer, "Will Sexual Minority Rights Be Trumped? Assessing the Policy Sustainability of LGBTI Rights Diplomacy in American Foreign Policy," *Diplomacy and Statecraft* 30, no. 1 (2019): 148.

87. Readers who are primarily interested in the discourse of the Christian right on international LGBTI human rights can focus their attention on chapters 1, 2, and the afterword. Those who would benefit from a deep dive into the differences and similarities between the orientations toward human rights programs of Trump's two secretaries of state can find this analysis in chapter 3. Readers who are interested in how SOGI fared under Trump and how SOGI policy and programs work in a world of grassroots and international activism for LGBTI human rights can focus on chapters 4 and 5, and the afterword. However, the whole book tells a story.

Chapter 1

1. Brett M. Clifton, "Romancing the GOP: Assessing the Strategies Used by the Christian Coalition to Influence the Republican Party," *Party Politics* 10, no. 5 (2004): 475–98.

2. Dana Milbank, "Religious Right Finds Its Center in Oval Office," *Washington Post*, December 24, 2001, https://www.washingtonpost.com/archive/politics/2001/12/24/religious-right-finds-its-center-in-oval-office/21a47914-6e0e-4854-adff-085e0e750b13/.

3. Benjamin G. Bishin, *Tyranny of the Minority: the Subconstituency Politics Theory of Representation* (Philadelphia: Temple University Press, 2009).

4. See Michael Lienesch, "Right-Wing Religion: Christian Conservatism as a Political Movement," *Political Science Quarterly* 97, no. 3 (1982): 403–25; Clyde Wilcox and Carin Robinson, *Onward Christian Soldiers? The Religious Right in American Politics*, 4th ed. (New York: Routledge, 2018); Daniel K. Williams, *God's Own Party: The Making of the Christian Right* (Oxford: Oxford University Press, 2010).

5. AP-NORC Center for Public Affairs Research, "Same-Sex Marriage and Gay Rights: A Shift in Americans' Attitudes," http://www.apnorc.org/projects/Pages/HTML%20Reports/same-sex-marriage-and-gay-rights-a-shift-in-americans-attitudes0305-8272.aspx. Other polls identified this tipping point in 2011 and 2012.

6. Daniel C. Lewis, Andrew R. Flores, Donald P. Haider-Markel, Patrick R. Miller, Barry L. Tadlock, and Jami K. Taylor, "Degrees of Acceptance: Variation in Public Attitudes toward Segments of the LGBT Community," *Political Research Quarterly* 70, no. 4 (2017): 871. See also Anna Brown, "Republicans, Democrats Have Starkly Different Views on Transgender Issues," Pew Research Center, November 8, 2017, https://www.pewresearch.org/fact-tank/2017/11/08/transgender-issues-divide-republicans-and-democrats/; Gregory A. Smith, "Views of Transgender Issues Divide along Religious Lines," Pew Research Center, November 27, 2017, https://www.pewresearch.org/fact-tank/2017/11/27/views-of-transgender-issues-divide-along-religious-lines/.

7. John Stuart Mill, *On Liberty and Other Writings* (Cambridge: Cambridge University Press, 1994), 75–93. For an analysis of how the Christian right has employed something like a harm principle in making the case against freedom to engage in same-sex sexuality, see Cynthia Burack, *Sin, Sex, and Democracy: Antigay Rhetoric and the Christian Right* (Albany: State University of New York Press, 2008), 124–30.

8. See Cynthia Burack, *Tough Love: Sexuality, Compassion, and the Christian Right* (Albany: State University of New York Press, 2014); Burack, *Sin, Sex, and Democracy*, 28.

9. US House of Representatives Committee on Foreign Affairs, "Advancing and Protecting LGBTQI+ Rights Abroad," House Foreign Affairs Committee, streamed live, June 24, 2021, YouTube video, https://www.youtube.com/watch?v=cPzB7RgVPuE. This was the first hearing of the committee to be dedicated exclusively to the rights of gender and sexual minorities. During the hearing, Busby also affirmed the position of the Biden administration and the State Department that LGBTQI human rights and religious freedom, including the religious freedom of LGBTQI people, are not mutually exclusive.

10. White House, "President Biden Announces U.S. Special Envoy to Advance the Human Rights of LGBTQI+ Persons, White House, June 25, 2021, https://www.whitehouse.gov/briefing-room/statements-releases/2021/06/25/president-biden-announces-u-s-special-envoy-to-advance-the-human-rights-of-lgbtqi-persons/.

11. Benjamin G. Bishin, Thomas J. Hayes, Matthew B. Incantalupo, and Charles Anthony Smith, *Elite-Led Mobilization and Gay Rights: Dispelling the Myth of Mass Opinion Backlash* (Ann Arbor: University of Michigan Press, 2021).

12. The examples I use are formally attributed to Tony Perkins but note that articles are written by Perkins "with the aid of FRC senior writers." Just as presidential speeches are attributed to the presidents who deliver them regardless of authorship, I record Perkins as the authors of these FRC missives.

13. Melani McAlister, *The Kingdom Has No Borders: A Global History of American Evangelicals* (New York: Oxford University Press, 2018).

14. FRC Action, "Rainbow Blight: Obama's LGBT Legacy," October 31, 2016, https://www.frcaction.org/updatearticle/20161031/rainbow-blight.

15. Nahal Toosi, "Gay Diplomats Cling to Signs of Hope under Trump," *Politico*, January 9, 2017, https://www.politico.com/story/2017/01/trump-lgbt-diplomats-state-233369.

16. News reports about the statement contain a broken link to FRC. Michael K. Lavers, "Tony Perkins to Trump: Remove 'Activists' from State Department," *Washington Blade*, December 16, 2016, https://www.washingtonblade.com/2016/12/16/tony-perkins-urges-trump-remove-activists-state-dept/.

17. The high-water mark for FRC messaging on religious freedom/persecution abroad, the problem of SOGI human rights, and the linkage between the two (the SOGI human rights vs. religious freedom frame) came in 2018.

18. Tony Perkins, "U.S. Gets Off on the Wrong Foote with Zambia," FRC Action, January 6, 2020, https://www.frcaction.org/get.cfm?i=WA20A02&f=WU20A01.

19. The phrase, "Hillary Clinton's State Department" links to Igor Volsky and Zack Ford, "Sec. Clinton to UN: 'Gay Rights Are Human Rights and Human Rights Are Gay Rights,'" *Think Progress*, December 6, 2011, https://thinkprogress.org/sec-clinton-to-un-gay-rights-are-human-rights-and-human-rights-are-gay-rights-2b2653e32ed1/.

20. Tony Perkins, "Show and Intel: Spy Chief Acts on LGBT Views," Family Research Council, April 24, 2020, https://www.frc.org/get.cfm?i=WA20D61&f=WU20D18.

21. Jennifer Agiesta, "Misperceptions Persisist about Obama's Faith, but Aren't So Widespread," Washington Post, September 14, 2015, https://www.cnn.com/2015/09/13/politics/barack-obama-religion-christian-misperceptions/index.html; CNN/ORC International, "Poll 9," September 18, 2015, http://i2.cdn.turner.com/cnn/2015/images/09/12/iranpoll.pdf.

22. Arielle Del Turco, "Amidst Election Uncertainties, The State Department Continues to Press for Human Rights," Family Research Council, November 11, 2020, https://www.frc.org/get.cfm?i=WA20K17&f=WU20K04.

23. For a more complete discussion and analysis of this charge from the political right and left, see Cynthia Burack, *Because We Are Human: Contesting US Support for Gender and Sexuality Human Rights Abroad* (New York: State University

of New York Press, 2018), ch. 2, on critiques of Hillary Clinton's announcement of US SOGI advocacy.

24. Daniel Davis, "Cory Booker's Inquisition into Marriage Views Is about Keeping You Silent," *Daily Signal,* April 13, 2018, https://www.dailysignal.com/2018/04/13/cory-bookers-inquisition-into-marriage-views-is-about-keeping-you-silent/.

25. Michael R. Pompeo, "Secretary Michael R. Pompeo with Tony Perkins of Washington Watch," US Department of State, January 24, 2020, https://www.state.gov/secretary-michael-r-pompeo-with-tony-perkins-of-washington-watch-with-tony-perkins/.

26. Elise Harris, "New Skepticism Targets Right to Religious Freedom, Expert Says," *Crux,* November 19, 2018, https://cruxnow.com/church-in-the-usa/2018/11/new-skepticism-targets-right-to-religious-freedom-expert-says/.

27. Jan-Werner Müller, *What Is Populism?* (Philadelphia: University of Pennsylvania Press, 2016), 22, 19, 4.

28. Cynthia Burack, "Let Death Seize Upon Them: Populism in Political Prayers of Imprecation," *Politics and Religion* 13, no. 3 (2020): 492–516.

29. Margaret E. Keck and Kathryn Sikkink, *Activists beyond Borders: Advocacy Networks in International Politics* (Ithaca, NY: Cornell University Press, 1998), 36.

30. Roger Ross Williams, "*God Loves Uganda*: Director's Statement," 2014, accessed October 16, 2020, https://www.godlovesuganda.com/film/directors-statement/.

31. See, for example, Kapya J. Kaoma, "The Marriage of Convenience: The U.S. Christian Right, African Christianity, and Postcolonial Politics of Sexual Identity," in *Global Homophobia: States, Movements, and the Politics of Oppression,* ed. Meredith L. Weiss and Michael J. Bosia (Urbana: University of Illinois Press, 2013), 91–93; Cynthia Burack, "Christian Right Leader Lauds Homophobic Ugandan Dictator," *Salon,* December 7, 2012, https://www.salon.com/2012/12/07/christian_right_leader_lauds_homophobic_ugandan_dictator/.

32. See several chapters in *Global Homophobia.* In particular, Weiss theorizes and provides examples of "anticipatory homophobia" in Meredith L. Weiss, "Prejudice before Pride," *Global Homophobia: States, Movements, and the Politics of Oppression,* ed. Meredith L. Weiss and Michael J. Bosia (Urbana: University of Illinois Press, 2013), 149–73.

33. Peter Montgomery, "Anti-Gay Activism Trumps Religious Freedom at UN 'Family' Event," Right Wing Watch, May 18, 2016, http://www.rightwingwatch.org/content/anti-gay-activism-trumps-religious-freedom-un-family-event.

34. Group of Friends of the Family, "Uniting Nations for a Family Friendly World," 2019, accessed September 7, 2020, https://unitingnationsforthefamily.org/background-2/organisers/.

35. United States Commission on International Religious Freedom, *Annual Report 2020,* April 2020, https://www.uscirf.gov/sites/default/files/USCIRF%202020%20Annual%20Report_Final_42920.pdf.

36. Francis A. Schaeffer, *Plan for Action: An Action Alternative Handbook for "Whatever Happened to the Human Race?"* (Grand Rapids, MI: Fleming H. Revell, 1980), 68.

37. See the Global Acceptance Index in Andrew R. Flores, *Social Acceptance of LGBT People in 174 Countries: 1981–2017*, Williams Institute, October 2019, https://williamsinstitute.law.ucla.edu/wp-content/uploads/Global-Acceptance-Index-LGBT-Oct-2019.pdf.

38. Sam Brownback, "Ambassador Sam Brownback and Wajahat Ali: International Religious Freedom," *Faith Angle*, January 1, 2020, podcast, https://faithangle.podbean.com/e/amb-sam-brownback-and-wajahat-ali-international-religious-freedom/. Transcribed by the author, emphases added.

39. Mike Lofgren, "Essay: Anatomy of the 'Deep State,'" *Moyers and Company*, February 21, 2014, https://billmoyers.com/2014/02/21/anatomy-of-the-deep-state/. See also Mike Lofgren, *The "Deep State": The Fall of the Constitution and the Rise of a Shadow Government* (New York: Penguin, 2016).

40. Angelia R. Wilson and Cynthia Burack, "'Where Liberty Reigns and God Is Supreme': The Christian Right and the Tea Party Movement," *New Political Science* 34, no. 2 (2012): 172–90. This advocacy took many forms. For one example, see a book that was distributed to all attendees at the 2009 Values Voter Summit in Washington, DC: Heritage Foundation, *Indivisible: Social and Economic Foundations of American Liberty* (Washington, DC: Heritage Foundation, 2009), https://thf_media.s3.amazonaws.com/2013/pdf/Indivisible_Revised.pdf.

41. The former George W. Bush administration speechwriter has repudiated the racial politics of the Trump administration in many articles, but see especially Michael Gerson, "We Can't Rest from Trump's Racism and Dehumanization," *Washington Post*, July 15, 2019, https://www.washingtonpost.com/opinions/trump-never-takes-a-vacation-from-provocation/2019/07/15/3377696c-a724-11e9-a3a6-ab670962db05_story.html; "Ignoring Trump's Racism Betrays Our Country's Victims," *Washington Post*, August 1, 2019, https://www.washingtonpost.com/opinions/ignoring-trumps-racism-betrays-our-countrys-victims/2019/08/01/78b9d0e6-b471-11e9-8949-5f36ff92706e_story.html. For an analysis of the Christian right's racial politics in the Trump era, see Sarah Posner, *Unholy: Why White Evangelicals Worship at the Altar of Donald Trump* (New York: Random House, 2020).

42. Andrew Rudalevige, "Trump and the 'Deep State': A Love Story," paper presented at the annual meeting of the Southern Political Science Association, San Juan, Puerto Rico, January 2020. Trump also attested to having fallen in love with another adversary: the president of North Korea, Kim Jong-un.

43. White House, "Fact Sheet: Promoting and Protecting Religious Freedom around the Globe," August 10, 2016, https://obamawhitehouse.archives.gov/the-press-office/2016/08/10/fact-sheet-promoting-and-protecting-religious-freedom-around-globe.

44. Frank R. Wolf International Religious Freedom Act, 2016, 22 USC § 6401, https://www.congress.gov/bill/114th-congress/house-bill/1150.

45. Theda Skocpol and Vanessa Williamson, *The Tea Party and the Remaking of Republican Conservatism* (Oxford: Oxford University Press, 2012), 6.

46. Stefano Gennarini, "Is the Trump Administration Serious about Refusing to Promote the LGBT Agenda?," *LifeSiteNews*, September 27, 2018, https://www.lifesitenews.com/news/is-the-trump-administration-serious-about-refusing-to-promote-the-lgbt-agen.

47. United Nations LGBTI Core Group, "History," accessed August 30, 2020, https://unlgbticoregroup.org/history/.

48. United Nations, "Violence against LGBTI Individuals: Extrajudicial, Summary or Arbitrary Executions," UN Web TV, September 25, 2018, http://webtv.un.org/search/violence-against-lgbti-individuals-extrajudicial-summary-or-arbitrary-executions/5840089676001/?term=&lan=english&page=6.

Chapter 2

1. The majority of these references are culled from public speeches. For "my Wilbur," see Cliff Sims, *Team of Vipers: My 500 Extraordinary Days in the Trump White House* (New York: St. Martin's Press, 2019), 129.

2. Joanna Walters and Sam Morris, "Trump's Evangelical Panel Remains Intact as Others Disband: Here Are His Religious Cheerleaders," *Guardian*, August 19, 2017, https://www.theguardian.com/us-news/2017/aug/18/donald-trump-evangelicals-charlottesville.

3. The third Ministerial to Advance Freedom of Religion or Belief was virtual, held November 16–17, 2020. Sponsored by the Polish Ministry of Foreign Affairs, the conference featured Mike Pompeo, Sam Brownback, and the Potomac Declaration.

4. Religious Freedom and Business Foundation, "Virtual International Religious Freedom (IRF) Roundtable," November 12, 2020, https://religiousfreedomandbusiness.org/2/post/2020/11/virtual-international-religious-freedom-irf-roundtable.html.

5. Angelia R. Wilson and Paul A. Djupe, "Communicating in Good Faith? Dynamics of the Christian Right Agenda," *Politics and Religion* 13, no. 2 (2020): 385–414.

6. Material for this discussion is from Cynthia Burack, field notes, Ministerial to Advance Religious Freedom, US State Department, Washington, DC, July 24, 2018, and other sources.

7. US State Department, "About the Ministerial to Advance Religious Freedom," July 19, 2018, https://www.state.gov/ministerial-to-advance-religious-freedom/about-the-ministerial-to-advance-religious-freedom/.

8. US State Department, "Ministerial to Advance Religious Freedom," accessed January 9, 2019, https://www.state.gov/j/drl/irf/religiousfreedom/index.htm.

9. US State Department, "Ministerial to Advance Religious Freedom Potomac Declaration," July 24, 2018, https://www.state.gov/ministerial-to-advance-religious-freedom-potomac-declaration/.

10. US State Department, "Ministerial to Advance Religious Freedom Potomac Plan of Action," July 24, 2018, https://www.state.gov/ministerial-to-advance-religious-freedom-potomac-plan-of-action/.

11. BBC News, "US Imposes Sanctions on Uganda for Anti-Gay Law," June 19, 2014, https://www.bbc.com/news/world-us-canada-27933051.

12. Mick Mulvaney, "Mulvaney: Ministerial to Advance Religious Freedom; 7-24-18," posted July 24, 2018, YouTube video, https://www.youtube.com/watch?v=f5PGq5y3Z34. Transcribed by the author.

13. US Department of State, "DRL Programs," accessed March 13, 2019, https://www.state.gov/j/drl/p/.

14. US Department of State, "DRL Programs: Human Rights and Democracy Fund," accessed August 19, 2019, https://2009-2017.state.gov/j/drl/p/index.htm.

15. US Department of State, *2016 Report on International Religious Freedom*, accessed June 28, 2020, https://www.state.gov/reports/2016-report-on-international-religious-freedom/.

16. US Department of State, Introduction to *2009 Country Reports on Human Rights Practices*, March 11, 2010, http://www.state.gov/j/drl/rls/hrrpt/2009/frontmatter/135936.htm.

17. Michael A. Weber, "Global Human Rights: International Religious Freedom Policy," *In Focus*, Congressional Research Service, May 5, 2020, https://fas.org/sgp/crs/row/IF10803.pdf.

18. Rachel Augustine Potter, Andrew Rudalevige, Sharece Thrower, and Adam L. Warber, "Continuity Trumps Change: The First Year of Trump's Administrative Presidency," *PS: Political Science and Politics* 52, no. 4 (2019): 613–19.

19. Material for this discussion is from Cynthia Burack, field notes, Ministerial to Advance Religious Freedom, US State Department, Washington, DC, July 16–17, 2019, and other sources.

20. United Nations Population Fund, "Human Rights Principles," 2005, https://www.unfpa.org/resources/human-rights-principles#.

21. David S. Gutterman and Andrew R. Murphy, *Political Religion and Religious Politics: Navigating Identities in the United States* (New York: Routledge, 2016).

22. Virginia Villa, "Religiously Unaffiliated People Face Harassment in a Growing Number of Countries," Pew Research Center, August 12, 2019, https://www.pewresearch.org/fact-tank/2019/08/12/religiously-unaffiliated-people-face-harassment-in-a-growing-number-of-countries/?utm_source=Pew+Research+Center&utm_campaign=6aa9753245-EMAIL_CAMPAIGN_2019_08_16_02_41&utm_medium=email&utm_term=0_3e953b9b70-6aa9753245-399484645.

23. It is beyond the scope of my analysis, but Mark Green also praised the Trump administration's policy of supporting refugees in the Middle East using Jesus's teaching (Luke 3:11) about giving the stranger without a tunic one of our tunics. Green delivered the same speech to the Values Voter Summit in the fall of 2019.

24. See, for example, Michael L. Brown, *Can You Be Gay and Christian? Responding with Love and Truth to Questions about Homosexuality* (Lake Mary, FL: Charisma House, 2014).

25. See Clifford Bob, *The Global Right Wing and the Clash of World Politics* (Cambridge: Cambridge University Press, 2012).

26. The Joshua Fund, "Our Story," accessed July 27, 2020, https://www.joshuafund.com/about/our-story.

27. Katayoun Kishi, "Christians Faced Widespread Harassment in 2015, but Mostly in Christian-Majority Countries," Pew Research Center, June 9, 2017, https://www.pewresearch.org/fact-tank/2017/06/09/christians-faced-widespread-harassment-in-2015-but-mostly-in-christian-majority-countries/.

28. Pew Research Center, *Global Uptick in Government Restrictions on Religion in 2016*, 2018, https://www.pewforum.org/2018/06/21/global-uptick-in-government-restrictions-on-religion-in-2016/.

29. Pew Research Center, *A Closer Look at How Religious Restrictions Have Risen around the World*, 2019, https://www.pewforum.org/2019/07/15/a-closer-look-at-how-religious-restrictions-have-risen-around-the-world/.

30. Colby Itkowitz, "A Yazidi Woman from Iraq Told Trump that ISIS Killed Her Family: 'Where Are They Now?' He Asked," *Washington Post*, July 19, 2019, https://www.washingtonpost.com/politics/a-yazidi-woman-from-iraq-told-trump-that-isis-killed-her-family-where-are-they-now-he-asked/2019/07/19/cc0c83e0-aa2d-11e9-a3a6-ab670962db05_story.html.

31. Nobel Prize, "Nadia Murad," 2020, https://www.nobelprize.org/prizes/peace/2018/murad/facts/.

32. Michael R. Pompeo, "Unalienable Rights and U.S. Foreign Policy," *Wall Street Journal*, July 7, 2019, https://www.wsj.com/articles/unalienable-rights-and-u-s-foreign-policy-11562526448.

33. US General Services Administration, "The Federal Advisory Committee Act," accessed April 18, 2020, https://www.gsa.gov/policy-regulations/policy/federal-advisory-committee-management/legislation-and-regulations/the-federal-advisory-committee-act.

34. Department of State Commission on Unalienable Rights, Public Notice 10777, 84 FR 25109, https://www.federalregister.gov/documents/2019/05/30/2019-11300/department-of-state-commission-on-unalienable-rights; Nahal Toosi, "State Department to Launch New Human Rights Panel Stressing 'Natural Law,'" *Politico*, May 30, 2019, https://www.politico.com/story/2019/05/30/human-rights-state-department-1348014?wpisrc=nl_daily202&wpmm=1.

35. Elise Harris, "New Skepticism Targets Right to Religious Freedom, Expert Says," *Crux*, November 19, 2018, https://cruxnow.com/church-in-the-usa/2018/11/new-skepticism-targets-right-to-religious-freedom-expert-says/.

36. David D. Kirkpatrick, "The Conservative-Christian Big Thinker," *New York Times*, December 16, 2009, https://www.nytimes.com/2009/12/20/magazine/20george-t.html.

37. Robert George, Timothy George, and Chuck Colson, *Manhattan Declaration: A Call of Christian Conscience*, October 20, 2009, https://www.manhattan-declaration.org/.

38. James E. Fleming and Linda C. McClain, *Ordered Liberty: Rights, Responsibilities, and Virtues* (Cambridge, MA: Harvard University Press, 2013), 170–72.

39. Peter C. Myers, *From Natural Rights to Human Rights—and Beyond*, Special Report 197 (Washington, DC: Heritage Foundation, 2017), https://www.heritage.org/node/1705172/print-display.

40. For an account of this meeting, see Sarah Posner, *Unholy: Why White Evangelicals Worship at the Altar of Donald Trump* (New York: Random House, 2020), 240; Heritage Foundation, "How to Protect International Religious Freedom from the Politicization of Human Rights," video, July 26, 2018, https://www.heritage.org/event/how-protect-international-religious-freedom-the-politicization-human-rights.

41. Pompeo, "Unalienable Rights and U.S. Foreign Policy."

42. "Trump Should Focus More on Defending Human Rights Than Redefining Them," editorial, *Washington Post*, June 2, 2019, https://www.washingtonpost.com/opinions/global-opinions/trump-should-focus-more-on-defending-human-rights-than-redefining-them/2019/06/02/39eba7fc-83c7-11e9-bce7-40b4105f7ca0_story.html.

43. "Why Redefine U.S. Policy on Human Rights?," editorial, *Washington Post*, August, 23, 2019, https://www.washingtonpost.com/opinions/global-opinions/why-redefine-us-policy-on-human-rights/2019/08/23/d570aadc-a33f-11e9-b732-41a79c2551bf_story.html.

44. Rob Berschinski and Andréa Worden, "Pompeo's Commission on Unalienable Rights Looks to Be a 'Win-Win' for China," *Just Security*, March 23, 2020, https://www.justsecurity.org/69323/pompeos-commission-on-unalienable-rights-looks-to-be-a-win-win-for-china/.

45. Eliot L. Engel, et al., "Letter to the Honorable Mike Pompeo," U.S. House of Representatives Committee on Foreign Affairs, July 18, 2019, https://foreignaffairs.house.gov/_cache/files/2/9/294cc9ed-3391-4fa2-968a-424f8e687dac/6B92FE10FE738FAEB3A6FB2BB7E69BC9.doc139.pdf.

46. Cynthia Burack, field notes, Human Rights Campaign National Headquarters, Washington, DC, July 17, 2019.

47. Cynthia Burack, field notes, US Department of State, Washington, DC, December 11, 2019; US Department of State, "U.S. Department of State Commission on Unalienable Rights Meeting, December 11, 2019, Featuring Michael Abramowitz," video, https://video.state.gov/detail/video/6166908217001.

48. Martha Minow, "Remarks Before the Commission on Unalienable Rights," February 21, 2020, https://www.state.gov/wp-content/uploads/2020/04/Remarks-Before-the-Commission-on-Unalienable-Rights-by-Martha-Minow-Harvard-University.pdf.

49. Diane Winston, "The History of the National Prayer Breakfast," *Smithsonian Magazine*, February 2, 2017, https://www.smithsonianmag.com/history/national-prayer-breakfast-what-does-its-history-reveal-180962017/.

50. Jeff Sharlet, *The Family: The Secret Fundamentalism at the Heart of American Power* (New York: HarperCollins, 2009), 7, 22, 24. Reflections on the difference between "privacy" and "secrecy" can be found at 397n11.

51. Cal Thomas, "It Might Be Time to Suspend the National Prayer Breakfast," Washington Post, February 7, 2020, https://www.washingtonpost.com/religion/2020/02/07/it-might-be-time-suspend-national-prayer-breakfast/.

52. Arthur Brooks, "America's Crisis of Contempt," *Washington Post*, February 7, 2020, https://www.washingtonpost.com/opinions/2020/02/07/arthur-brooks-national-prayer-breakfast-speech/?arc404=true.

53. Donald J. Trump, "Remarks: 68th Annual National Prayer Breakfast," WhiteHouse.gov, February 6, 2020, https://www.whitehouse.gov/briefings-statements/remarks-president-trump-68th-annual-national-prayer-breakfast/. Denotations of "laughter" and "applause" in reaction to Trump's remarks are in the posted transcript.

54. US Department of State, *Declaration of Principles for the International Religious Freedom Alliance*, February 5, 2020, https://www.state.gov/declaration-of-principles-for-the-international-religious-freedom-alliance/.

55. Cal Thomas, "It Might Be Time to Suspend the National Prayer Breakfast," *Washington Post*, February 7, 2020, https://www.washingtonpost.com/religion/2020/02/07/it-might-be-time-suspend-national-prayer-breakfast/. For Thomas's critique of the Christian right political movement he helped to create, see Cal Thomas and Ed Dobson, *Blinded by Might: Why the Religious Right Can't Save America* (Nashville, TN: Zonderan, 2000).

56. Democracy Forward, "Fmr. Sec. Pompeo's 'Commission on Unalienable Rights' Cannot Evade Accountability after Breaking Federal Law," press release, February 2, 2021, https://democracyforward.org/press/pompeo-commission-on-unalienable-rights-cannot-evade-accountability-after-breaking-federal-law/.

57. Robert F. Kennedy Center for Justice and Human Rights v. Pompeo (1:20-cv-02002) District Court, S.D. New York (filed March 6, 2020), pp. 1–51, https://democracyforward.org/wp-content/uploads/2020/03/Complaint-As-Filed.pdf.

58. Austin Ruse, "Organized Gays and Feminists Sue State Department over Human Rights Commission," Center for Family and Human Rights, March 26, 2020, https://c-fam.org/friday_fax/organized-gays-feminists-sue-state-department-over-human-rights-commission/.

59. Trump's approval of Chinese violations against Uighurs was first reported by John Bolton in *The Room Where It Happened* (New York: Simon and Schuster,

2020); see "Trump Said He Avoided Punishing China over Uighur Camps," *New York Times*, June 21, 2020, https://www.nytimes.com/2020/06/21/us/politics/trump-uighurs-china-trade.html.

60. Michael R. Pompeo, "Unalienable Rights and the Securing of Freedom," US Department of State, July 16, 2020, https://www.state.gov/unalienable-rights-and-the-securing-of-freedom/.

61. This paragraph contains a comment I left on the commission's website during the comment period following the public launch of the draft report. While Trump was in office, comments could be found at https://www.state.gov/draft-report-of-the-commission-on-unalienable-rights-public-comment/. The conclusion of my comment, not included here, reads, "Just as autocrats and corrupt regimes around the world have found solace in the president's lack of interest in human rights, I'm sure these same actors will quickly learn how to manipulate the conception of human rights you've endorsed for their own ends."

62. Shane Phelan, *Sexual Strangers: Gays, Lesbians, and Dilemmas of Citizenship* (Philadelphia, PA: Temple University Press, 2001).

63. US State Department, Report of the Commission on Unalienable Rights, August 2020, p. 11, https://www.state.gov/wp-content/uploads/2020/07/Draft-Report-of-the-Commission-on-Unalienable-Rights.pdf.

64. Tony Perkins, "America Finds Its Mr. Rights," Family Research Council, July 17, 2020, https://www.frc.org/get.cfm?i=WA20G29&f=WU20G11.

65. Helene Cooper, "U.S. to Aid Gay Rights Abroad, Obama and Clinton Say," *New York Times*, December 6, 2011, https://www.nytimes.com/2011/12/07/world/united-states-to-use-aid-to-promote-gay-rights-abroad.html?ref=global-home.

66. Tony Perkins, "Mike Pompeo: In His Own Words," Family Research Council, July 21, 2020, https://www.frcaction.org/get.cfm?i=WA20G36&f=WU20G02.

67. Mike Pompeo, "Secretary Mike Pompeo Speaks with Pastors about Their Essential Role Protecting Human Rights," Family Research Council, July 21, 2020, audio, https://soundcloud.com/family-research-council/sec-pompeo-unalienable-rights.

68. Daniel Nexon, "Sebastian Gorka May Be a Far-Right Nativist, but for Sure He's a Terrible Scholar," *Foreign Policy*, March 17, 2017, https://foreignpolicy.com/2017/03/17/dr-sebastian-gorka-may-be-a-far-right-nativist-but-for-sure-hes-a-terrible-scholar-trump-radical-islam/.

69. Ms. Gorka may also have received a poor civics education. The Roanoke (North Carolina) colony, whose disappearance has never been explained, was established in the late sixteenth century during the reign of Elizabeth I, but that settlement wasn't founded as a haven from religious persecution. The first permanent British colony, at Jamestown (Virginia), was founded in 1607, and the Mayflower arrived at Plymouth Rock (Massachusetts) in 1620.

70. David J. Kramer, "Mike Pompeo Has Given Up Being Secretary of State," *Bulwark*, July 21, 2020, https://thebulwark.com/mike-pompeo-has-given-up-being-secretary-of-state/?utm_source=afternoon-newsletter&utm_medium=email&utm_source=The+Bulwark+Newsletter&utm_campaign=4afeb10198-EMAIL_

CAMPAIGN_2020_07_21_09_09&utm_medium=email&utm_term=0_f4bd64ac2e-4afeb10198-80937206 (accessed July 21, 2020).

Chapter 3

1. David E. Sanger and Matt Flegenheimer, "In Rocky Hearing, Tillerson Tries to Separate from Trump," *New York Times*, January 11, 2017, https://www.nytimes.com/2017/01/11/us/rex-tillerson-confirmation-hearings.html.

2. Martin Pengelly, Sabrina Siddiqui, and David Smith, "Trump Challenges Tillerson to 'Compare IQ Tests' after Reported 'Moron' Dig," Guardian, October 10, 2017, https://www.theguardian.com/us-news/2017/oct/10/donald-trump-forbes-rex-tillerson-moron. The story was confirmed and expanded in Philip Rucker and Carol Leonnig, *A Very Stable Genius: Donald J. Trump's Testing of America* (New York: Penguin, 2020).

3. Rex Tillerson, "Remarks to U.S. Department of State Employees," US State Department, May 3, 2017, https://www.state.gov/secretary/remarks/2017/05/270620.htm. The video and full text of Tillerson's "Remarks" was originally posted to the State Department website. This official transcript can be found in appendix A and continues to be available at Wikisource, https://en.wikisource.org/wiki/Rex_Tillerson%27s_Remarks_to_U.S._Department_of_State_Employees.

4. Eugene Scott, "Cory Booker Grills Mike Pompeo on Whether He Believes That Being Gay Is a 'Perversion,'" *Washington Post*, April 12, 2018, https://www.washingtonpost.com/news/the-fix/wp/2018/04/12/cory-booker-grills-mike-pompeo-on-whether-he-believes-being-gay-is-a-perversion/?noredirect=on&utm_term=.0b8c8e1dc342.

5. Josh Lederman, "Watch Live: Mike Pompeo to Deliver Brief Speech to State Department Employees," May 1, 2018, https://www.pbs.org/newshour/politics/watch-live-mike-pompeo-to-deliver-brief-speech-to-state-department-employees.

6. Michael Pompeo, "Being a Christian Leader," US Department of State, October 11, 2019, https://2017-2021.state.gov/being-a-christian-leader/index.html. The full text of the speech is available in appendix B.

7. Laura Koran, "Tillerson Skips Release of the Annual Human Rights Report," CNN, March 3, 2017, http://www.cnn.com/2017/03/03/politics/rex-tillerson-state-department-human-rights-report/index.html.

8. US Congress, Congressional Budget Justification, "Foreign Assistance: Supplementary Tables, Fiscal Year 2018," US State Department, p. 102, accessed October 4, 2017, https://www.state.gov/documents/organization/271014.pdf.

9. David Gibson, "Trump's Pick of Rex Tillerson as Secretary of State Upsets Religious Right Leader," *Washington Post*, December 13, 2016, https://www.washingtonpost.com/news/acts-of-faith/wp/2016/12/13/trumps-pick-of-rex-tillerson-as-secretary-of-state-upsets-religious-right-leaders/.

10. Tillerson, "Remarks to U.S. Department of State Employees."

11. *The Shepherd of Hermas*, trans. Alexander Roberts and James Donaldson, Early Christian Writings, n.d., http://www.earlychristianwritings.com/text/shepherd.html. The material quoted here is found in book 2, commandment 6.

12. An early Christian book that teaches this conception of the self as riven with capacities for virtue and vice is the allegorical early Christian text *The Psychomachia of Prudentius: Text, Commentary, and Glossary*, trans. Aaron Pelttari (Norman: University of Oklahoma Press, 2019).

13. John Landis, dir., *Animal House* (Universal Pictures, 1978). See "Animal House (1978) Red Band Clip: Angel VS Devil," Trailer Addict video, posted March 23, 2009, https://www.traileraddict.com/animal-house/red-band-clip-angel-vs-devil.

14. For example, in one episode, Peter's shoulder devil appears suddenly and urges him, "Lie to her! It's ok to lie to women because they're not people like us." When Peter, expecting an angel to rebut the devil, glances to his other shoulder, he finds it empty. His shoulder angel is stuck in traffic on a highway overpass. When the angel finally arrives, the angel's own shoulder devil manifests to encourage Peter's angel to advise him to lie.

15. See Robert Hertz, "The Pre-eminence of the Right Hand: A Study in Religious Polarity," *HAU: Journal of Ethnographic Theory* 3, no. 2 (2013): 335–57.

16. Thomas Koch and Thomas Zerback, "Helpful or Harmful? How Frequent Repetition Affects Perceived Statement Credibility," *Journal of Communication* 63, no. 6 (2013): 993–1010.

17. Hillary Clinton, "Remarks in Recognition of International Human Rights Day," US Department of State, December 6, 2011, https://2009-2017.state.gov/secretary/20092013clinton/rm/2011/12/178368.htm.

18. Tony Perkins, "Mike Pompeo, Religious Freedom and a Safer World—How are These Three Things Connected?," Family Research Council, May 9, 2018, https://www.frc.org/op-eds/mike-pompeo-religious-freedom-and-a-safer-world-how-are-these-three-things-connected; Abigail Tracy, " 'Be Careful What You Wish For': How Mike Pompeo Trumpified the State Department," *Vanity Fair*, June 25, 2018, https://www.vanityfair.com/news/2018/06/how-mike-pompeo-trumpified-the-state-department.

19. Cynthia Burack, "Sexual Orientation and Gender Identity Human Rights Assistance in the Time of Trump," *Politics and Gender* 14, no. 4 (2018): 561–80.

20. Randall Balmer, *Thy Kingdom Come: How the Religious Right Distorts the Faith and Threatens America* (New York: Basic Books, 2006), 8.

21. Alan Cooperman, "Bush's References to God Defended by Speechwriter," *Washington Post*, December 12, 2004, http://www.washingtonpost.com/wp-dyn/articles/A57915-2004Dec11.html.

22. Mike Pompeo, "Secretary of State Mike Pompeo Addresses State Department Employees," US Department of State, posted May 1, 2018, YouTube Video, https://www.youtube.com/watch?v=mFWWwVGMLJY.

23. Reuters, "Mike Pompeo Nearly Doubles Promotions of Top Diplomats as He Seeks to Restore Ties with Alienated US Diplomats," CNBC, September 17,

2018, https://www.cnbc.com/2018/09/17/us-secretary-of-state-mike-pompeo-has-nearly-doubled-promotions.html.

24. Stormie Omartian, *The Power of a Praying Nation* (Eugene, OR: Harvest House, 2002), 24.

25. Stormie Omartian, "Standing in the Gap for Our Nation," Facebook, October 5, 2017, https://af-za.facebook.com/stormieomartianofficial/posts/standing-in-the-gap-for-our-nationalmighty-god-i-lift-up-my-nation-to-you-with-a/193284 9580098959/.

26. American Pastors Network, "About," accessed November 23, 2019, https://americanpastorsnetwork.net/about/.

27. Michele Bachmann, "Stand Up: God's at Work!," *Stand in the Gap Today*, July 22, 2019, podcast, https://subsplash.com/americanpastors/lb/mi/+fm3s43s. Cynthia Burack, field notes, October 11, 2019, Values Voter Summit, Omni Shoreham Hotel, Washington, DC.

28. Family Research Council, "Family Research Council Statement on the Nomination of Mike Pompeo for Secretary of State," Cision PR Newswire, March 13, 2018, https://www.prnewswire.com/news-releases/family-research-council-statement-on-the-nomination-of-mike-pompeo-for-secretary-of-state-300613288.html.

29. Mike Pompeo, "Secretary Pompeo Delivers Remarks at 13th Annual Values Voter Summit," US Department of State, posted September 21, 2018, YouTube video, https://www.youtube.com/watch?v=04u3I0V9rlw. Cynthia Burack, field notes, September 21, 2018, Omni Shoreham Hotel, Washington, DC.

30. Merriam-Webster, s.v. "hide one's light under a bushel," https://www.merriam-webster.com/dictionary/hide one%27s light under a bushel.

31. "This Little Light of Mine," Hymnary.org, https://hymnary.org/text/this_little_light_of_mine_im_gonna_let (accessed December 2, 2019).

32. Stephen Schwartz, composer, "Light of the World," track 8 on *Godspell*, Bell Records, 1971.

33. Sara Diamond, *Spiritual Warfare: The Politics of the Christian Right* (Boston: South End Press, 1989), 136–37.

34. Julie Ingersoll, *Building God's Kingdom: Inside the World of Christian Reconstruction* (Oxford: Oxford University Press, 2015).

35. American Pastors Network, "About."

36. Cynthia Burack, "The Politics of a Praying Nation: The Presidential Prayer Team and Christian Right Sexual Morality," *Journal of Religion and Popular Culture* 26, no. 2 (2014): 215–29.

37. Salt and Light Council, "Start a Salt and Light Biblical Citizenship Ministry," 2018, https://saltandlightcouncil.org/start-a-slc-ministry-2019.

38. Mike Pompeo, "Secretary Pompeo Delivers Remarks at 13th Annual Values Voter Summit," US Department of State, posted September 21, 2018, YouTube video, https://www.youtube.com/watch?v=04u3I0V9rlw. Transcribed by author. Cynthia Burack, field notes, September 21, 2018, Omni Shoreham

Hotel, Washington, DC. The emphasis is added to reflect the words emphasized in delivery.

39. David Brody, "Secretary of State Pompeo to CBN News: God May Have Raised Up Trump Like He Raised Up Queen Esther," CBN News, March 21, 2019, https://www1.cbn.com/cbnnews/israel/2019/march/exclusive-secretary-of-state-pompeo-to-news-god-raised-up-trump-like-he-raised-up-queen-esther.

40. Edward Wong, "The Rapture and the Real World: Mike Pompeo Blends Belief and Policy," *New York Times*, March 20, 2019, https://www.nytimes.com/2019/03/30/us/politics/pompeo-christian-policy.html; Dana Milbank, "Holy Moses, Mike Pompeo Thinks Trump Is Queen Esther," *Washington Post*, March 27, 2019, https://www.washingtonpost.com/opinions/this-is-trumps-year-of-living-biblically/2019/03/27/e3d00802-50c9-11e9-8d28-f5149e5a2fda_story.html.

41. Steven Waldman, "Heaven Sent: Does God Endorse George Bush," September 13, 2004, https://slate.com/human-interest/2004/09/does-god-endorse-bush.html.

42. For a partial literature on these identifications, see Salena Zito and Brad Todd, *The Great Revolt: Inside the Populist Coalition Reshaping American Politics* (New York: Crown Forum, 2018); Rebecca Barrett-Fox, "A King Cyrus President: How Donald Trump's Presidency Reasserts Conservative Christians' Right to Hegemony," *Humanity and Society* 42, no. 4 (2018): 502–22; Lance Wallnau, *God's Chaos Candidate: Donald J. Trump and the American Unraveling* (Keller, TX: Killer Sheep Media).

43. Mary R. Jackman, *The Velvet Glove: Paternalism and Conflict in Gender, Class, and Race Relations* (Berkeley: University of California Press, 1994), 120.

44. Michael R. Pompeo, "Being a Christian Leader."

45. James C. Scott, *Domination and the Arts of Resistance: Hidden Transcripts* (New Haven, CT: Yale University Press, 1990).

46. Brittany Shammas, "NPR Reporter Says Pompeo Cursed at Her, Told Her to Point to Ukraine on Map," *Washington Post*, January 25, 2020, https://www.washingtonpost.com/national-security/2020/01/25/pompeo-npr-reporter-ukraine/.

47. Senate Committee on Foreign Relations, Robert Menendez, Ranking Member, "Letter to the Honorable Mike Pompeo," United States Senate, October 10, 2019, https://www.foreign.senate.gov/imo/media/doc/10-10-19%20Yovanovitch%20letter%20signed.pdf.

48. Michael LaForgia and Walt Bogdanich, "Why Bombs Made in America Have Been Killing Civilians in Yeman," *New York Times*, May 17, 2020, https://www.nytimes.com/2020/05/16/us/arms-deals-raytheon-yemen.html.

49. Kevin Breuninger, "Democrats Demand Reinstatement of State Department Inspector General Fired by Trump," CNBC, May 21, 2020, https://www.cnbc.com/2020/05/21/democrats-demand-reinstatement-of-state-department-inspector-general-fired-by-trump.html.

50. Elise Carlson Rainer, "Will Sexual Minority Rights Be Trumped? Assessing the Policy Sustainability of LGBTI Rights Diplomacy in American Foreign Policy," *Diplomacy and Statecraft* 30, no. 1 (2019): 147–63.

51. Burack, "Sexual Orientation and Gender Identity Human Rights Assistance in the Time of Trump."

52. Craig Kallendorf and Carol Kallendorf, "The Figures of Speech, Ethos, and Aristotle: Notes toward a Rhetoric of Business Communication," *International Journal of Business Communication* 22, no. 1 (1985): 42–43.

53. "Now We Know What Pompeo's 'Swagger' at the State Department was Really About," editorial, *Washington Post*, April 20, 2021, https://www.washingtonpost.com/opinions/global-opinions/an-investigation-reveals-mike-pompeos-petty-tyranny-at-the-state-department/2021/04/19/80666b6c-a12b-11eb-a774-7b47ceb36ee8_story.html.

54. Ülkü D. Demirdöğen, "The Roots of Research in (Political) Persuasion: Ethos, Pathos, Logos, and the Yale Studies of Persuasive Communications," *International Journal of Social Inquiry* 3, no. 1 (2010): 189–201.

55. US Congress, Senate, Committee on Appropriations, Department of State, "Foreign Operations, and Related Programs Appropriations Bill," 2019, June 28, 2018, 115 Cong., 2nd sess. S. Rept., 5.

56. Michael R. Pompeo, "Unalienable Rights and U.S. Foreign Policy," *Wall Street Journal*, July 7, 2019, https://www.wsj.com/articles/unalienable-rights-and-u-s-foreign-policy-11562526448.

57. Dana Milbank, "Religious Right Finds Its Center in Oval Office: Bush Emerges as Movement's Leader after Robertson Leaves Christian Coalition," *Washington Post*, December 24, 2001, A2.

58. Max Boot, "Mike Pompeo Talks as If Obama Is Still President," *Washington Post*, July 14, 2020, https://www.washingtonpost.com/opinions/2020/07/14/credibility-gap-between-mike-pompeos-pronouncements-trumps-reality/.

59. See Cynthia Burack, *Because We Are Human: Contesting US Support for Gender and Sexuality Human Rights Abroad* (New York: State University of New York Press, 2018), 160–88.

60. Ingersoll, *Building God's Kingdom*, 64.

Chapter 4

1. On a list of participant biographies distributed to attendees, the subtitle of the event was "A Pride Panel Discussion." More provocative was the full title listed on the ticket for the event: "U.S. Support for Global LGBT Equality, Obama to Trump: What Has Been Lost?"

2. James Hohmann, "The Daily 202: Five Overshadowed Stories Spotlight Trump's Domestic Priorities," *Washington Post*, May 8, 2018, https://www.washingtonpost.com/news/powerpost/paloma/daily-202/2018/05/08/daily-202-five-overshadowed-stories-spotlight-trump-s-domestic-priorities/5af0daaf30fb042db579739f/?utm_term=.9c79e58b07c3.

3. John M. Donnelly, "GOP Congress Tries to Rein in Trump on Foreign Policy," *Roll Call*, August 6, 2018, https://www.rollcall.com/2018/08/06/gop-congress-tries-to-rein-in-trump-on-foreign-policy/.

4. Hans N. Tuch, *Communicating with the World: U.S. Public Diplomacy Overseas* (New York: St. Martin's, 1990), 3–4.

5. See Seong-hun Yun, "Toward Public Relations Theory-Based Study of Public Diplomacy: Testing the Applicability of the Excellence Study," *Journal of Public Relations Research* 18, no. 4 (2006): 287–312; Guy J. Golan, Sung-un Yang, and Dennis F. Kinsey, eds., *International Public Relations and Public Diplomacy: Communication and Engagement* (Bern: Peter Lang, 2014).

6. Josh Rogin, "State Department Considers Scrubbing Democracy Promotion from Its Mission," *Washington Post*, August 1, 2017, https://www.washingtonpost.com/news/josh-rogin/wp/2017/08/01/state-department-considers-scrubbing-democracy-promotion-from-its-mission/?utm_term=.b2fb76a9e3de; Will Racke, "State Department Looks to Strip Democracy Promotion from Mission Statement," *Daily Caller*, August 1, 2017, http://dailycaller.com/2017/08/01/state-department-might-remove-democracy-promotion-from-mission-statement/.

7. US Department of State, "Mission," accessed October, 22, 2017,https://www.state.gov/s/d/rm/rls/dosstrat/2004/23503.htm.

8. US Department of State, "The Department of State's Accomplishments Promoting the Human Rights of Lesbian, Gay, Bisexual, and Transgender People," press release, December 6, 2011, http://www.state.gov/r/pa/prs/ps/2011/12/178341.htm.

9. Some examples and controversies over SOGI embassy engagement can be found in Cynthia Burack, *Because We Are Human: Contesting US Support for Gender and Sexuality Human Rights Abroad* (New York: State University of New York Press, 2018), 100–104.

10. Josh Lederman, "Trump Admin Tells U.S. Embassies They Can't Fly Pride Flag on Flagpoles," NBC News, June 7, 2019, https://www.nbcnews.com/politics/national-security/trump-admin-tells-u-s-embassies-they-can-t-fly-n1015236.

11. Tal Axelrod, "Some US Embassies Fly Rainbow Flag Despite Rejected Request from Trump Admin," *The Hill*, June 8, 2019, https://thehill.com/home-news/administration/447595-some-us-embassies-fly-rainbow-flag-despite-rejected-requests-from.

12. Joseph Wilkinson, "Vladimir Putin Trashes U.S. Embassy for Flying Rainbow Flag During Pride Month," *New York Daily News*, July 4, 2020, https://www.nydailynews.com/news/world/ny-vladimir-putin-us-embassy-rainbow-flag-moscow-20200704-aphmjndwdzdxrd2m2qd3yufhme-story.html.

13. Rex Tillerson, "2017 Lesbian, Gay, Bisexual, Transgender and Intersex (LGBTI) Pride Month," US Department of State, June 7, 2017, https://www.state.gov/secretary/remarks/2017/06/271626.htm. Emphasis added.

14. Mike Pompeo, "Statement by Secretary Pompeo: LGBTI Pride Month," US Department of State, June 1, 2018, https://www.state.gov/secretary/remarks/2018/06/282908.htm.

15. United States Mission to the United Nations, "Statement by Ambassador Haley on LGBTI Pride Month," US Department of State, June 6, 2018, https://usun.state.gov/remarks/8468.

16. Cynthia Burack, field notes, Pride @ State, US Department of State, Washington, DC, June 5, 2018.

17. Cynthia Burack, field notes, Pride @ State, US Department of State, Washington, DC, June 19, 2013.

18. Cynthia Burack, field notes, Pride @ State, US Department of State, Washington, DC, June 3, 2019.

19. Chris Johnson, "Key LGBT Groups Not Invited to Trump Summit on Decriminalizing Homosexuality," *Washington Blade*, February 19, 2019, https://www.washingtonblade.com/2019/02/19/key-lgbt-groups-not-invited-to-trump-summit-on-decriminalizing-homosexuality/.

20. Melissa Eddy and Rick Gladstone, "A U.S. Ambassador Announces a Global Push to Decriminalize Homosexuality," *New York Times*, February 20, 2019, https://www.nytimes.com/2019/02/20/world/europe/grenell-homosexuality-decriminalize-.html.

21. Josh Lederman, "Trump Administration Launches Global Effort to End Criminalization of Homosexuality," NBC News, February 19, 2019, https://www.nbcnews.com/politics/national-security/trump-administration-launches-global-effort-end-criminalization-homosexuality-n973081.

22. Michael Gerson, "Trump's Speech Was Nasty, Brutish and Interminable," *Washington Post*, August 28, 2020, https://www.washingtonpost.com/opinions/trumps-speech-was-nasty-brutish-and-interminable/2020/08/28/d3a0ff96-e947-11ea-97e0-94d2e46e759b_story.html.

23. Donald J. Trump, "Remarks by President Trump to the 74th Session of the United Nations General Assembly," White House, September 25, 2019, https://www.whitehouse.gov/briefings-statements/remarks-president-trump-74th-session-united-nations-general-assembly/.

24. Hillary Rodham Clinton, "Remarks in Recognition of International Human Rights Day," US State Department, December 11, 2011, https://2009-2017.state.gov/secretary/20092013clinton/rm/2011/12/178368.htm.

25. Donald J. Trump, "Remarks by President Trump to the 75th Session of the United Nations General Assembly," White House, September 22, 2020, https://www.whitehouse.gov/briefings-statements/remarks-president-trump-75th-session-united-nations-general-assembly/.

26. United States Mission to the United Nations, "Decriminalizing Sexual Orientation," media note, December 19, 2019, https://usun.usmission.gov/media-note-decriminalizing-sexual-orientation/.

27. Michael K. Lavers, "U.S. Embassy in Germany Hosts Meeting with LGBTI Activists," *Washington Blade*, July 31, 2019, https://www.washingtonblade.com/2019/07/31/u-s-embassy-in-germany-hosts-meeting-with-lgbti-activists/; Ursula Perano, "U.S. May Cut Intelligence Sharing with Countries That Ban Homosexuality,"

Axios, April 22, 2020, https://www.axios.com/grenell-intelligence-sharing-homosex-uality-737d222a-3ea9-446a-b90c-1d77af434db3.html.

28. Perano, "U.S. May Cut Intelligence Sharing with Countries That Ban Homosexuality."

29. Barack Obama, "Presidential Memorandum—International Initiatives to Advance the Human Rights of Lesbian, Gay, Bisexual, and Transgender Persons," White House, December 6, 2011, https://obamawhitehouse.archives.gov/the-press-office/2011/12/06/presidential-memorandum-international-initiatives-advance-human-rights-l.

30. I refer here to interviews and conversations with US government officials between 2013 and 2016.

31. Scott Bixby, "Ric Grenell's Claim Trump Helped Legalize Homosexual-ity Worldwide Is a Lie, Activists Say," *Daily Beast*, August 26, 2020, https://www.thedailybeast.com/smoke-and-mirrors-grenell-claim-trump-helped-legalize-homosex-uality-worldwide-is-fake-news-activists-say.

32. Dan Spinelli, "'There's Nothing': Trump's LGBTQ Campaign Is a Whole Lot of Smoke and Mirrors," Mother Jones, October 9, 2019, https://www.mother-jones.com/politics/2019/10/trump-decriminalization-homosexuality-lgbtq-richard-grenell-state-department/.

33. See Edward Marks, "Defining Diplomacy: Speaking Out," American Foreign Service Association, 2019, https://www.afsa.org/defining-diplomacy.

34. Jeremy Shapiro and Philip H. Gordon, "Trump and the Rise of Sadistic Diplomacy," *Foreign Policy*, August 17, 2020, https://foreignpolicy.com/2020/08/17/trump-the-death-of-the-deal/.

35. See David F. Schmitz and Vanessa Walker, "Jimmy Carter and the Foreign Policy of Human Rights: The Development of a Post-Cold War Foreign Policy," *Diplomatic History* 28, no. 1 (2004): 113–43.

36. Debra Liang-Fenton, "Conclusion: What Works?," in *Implementing U.S. Human Rights Policy*, ed. Debra Liang-Fenton (Washington, DC: United States Institute of Peace Press, 2004), 440.

37. Nahal Toosi, "State Department Report Will Trim Language on Women's Rights, Discrimination," *Politico*, February 21, 2018, https://www.politico.com/story/2018/02/21/department-women-rights-abortion-420361.

38. John J. Sullivan, "Remarks on the Release of the 2017 Country Reports on Human Rights Practices," US Department of State, April 20, 2018, https://www.state.gov/s/d/2018/280666.htm.

39. US Congress, Senate, Committee on Appropriations, Department of State, "Foreign Operations, and Related Programs Appropriations Bill," 2019, June 28, 2018, 115 Cong., 2nd sess. S. Rept., 56.

40. The LGBTI category in the 2019 reports reorders these terms: "Acts of Violence, Discrimination, and Other Abuses Based on Sexual Orientation and Gender Identity." An online feature debuted in 2017 that allowed users to compile

their own tailored human rights report. From a main webpage, users could select "Build a Custom Report" and then follow the steps to (1) select sections of the reports they wish to view (such as those that focus on gender and sexual minorities); (2) select regions and countries; and (3) create the customized report. Thus, citizens and CSOs could quickly isolate instances and discern patterns of human rights violations against LGBTI persons or members of other marginalized groups outside the US. By 2020, this feature only permitted users to curate a report by region, not by a focus on marginalized groups.

41. US Department of State, "2019 Country Reports on Human Rights Practices, Foreign Press Centers Briefing," March 11, 2020, https://www.state.gov/2019-country-reports-on-human-rights-practices/.

42. Michael K. Lavers, "State Department: Chechnya Extrajudicial Killings Are 'Troubling,'" *Washington Blade*, July 11, 2017, http://www.washingtonblade.com/2017/07/11/state-department-chechnya-extrajudicial-killings-troubling/.

43. Michael K. Lavers, "State Department Expresses Concern over Egypt, Azerbaijan Crackdowns," *Washington Blade*, October 3, 2017, http://www.washingtonblade.com/2017/10/03/state-department-expresses-concern-egypt-azerbaijan-anti-lgbt-crackdowns/.

44. BBC News, "US Imposes Sanctions on Uganda for Anti-Gay Law," June 19, 2014, http://www.bbc.com/news/world-us-canada-27933051.

45. Mike Pompeo, "On the International Day Against Homophobia, Transphobia, and Biphobia," US Department of State, May 17, 2018, https://www.state.gov/secretary/remarks/2018/05/282185.htm.

46. *Foreign Policy* editors, "U.S. Ambassador Puts Zambia on Notice," *Foreign Policy*, December 6, 2019, https://foreignpolicy.com/2019/12/06/american-ambassador-zambia-foote-criticizes-human-rights-lgbtq-abuse-corruption/.

47. Daniel L. Foote, "Press Statement from U.S. Ambassador Daniel L. Foote," US Embassy in Zambia, December 2, 2019, https://zm.usembassy.gov/press-statement-from-u-s-ambassador-daniel-l-foote/.

48. Michael Conte and Kylie Atwood, "US Ambassador Recalled after Dispute with Zambian Government over Gay Rights and Corruption," CNN, December 25, 2019, https://www.cnn.com/2019/12/25/politics/daniel-foote-zambia-ambassador/index.html.

49. Randy Berry, interview by the author, US State Department, Washington, DC, December 22, 2016.

50. US Congress, Senate, Committee on Appropriations, "A Bill Making Appropriations for the Department of State, Foreign Operations, and Related Programs for the Fiscal Year Ending September 30, 2018, and for Other Purposes," September 7, 2017, 115 Cong., 1st sess. S. 1780, 347–48.

51. Rex Tillerson, "Letter to Honorable Bob Corker, Chairman, Senate Committee on Foreign Relations," n.d., accessed October 8, 2017, https://www.documentcloud.org/documents/3982871-State-Letter.html#document/p1.

52. US Congress, Senate, Committee on Appropriations, Department of State, "Foreign Operations, and Related Programs Appropriations Bill," 2019, June 28, 2018, 115 Cong., 2nd sess. S. Rept., 16.

53. Scott Busby, "Public Hearing on the Human Rights of LGBTI People Outside the EU and Implementation of the EU Guidelines on the Topic," US Department of State, September 25, 2017, https://www.state.gov/j/drl/rls/rm/2017/274413.htm.

54. United Nations General Assembly, "The Question of the Death Penalty," UN Doc. A/HRC/36/L.6 (September 22, 2017), http://ilga.org/downloads/HRC36_resolution_question_death_penalty.pdf.

55. Rick Gladstone, "U.S. Vetoes UN Resolution on Gaza, Fails to Win Second Vote on Its Own Measure," New York Times, June 1, 2018, https://www.nytimes.com/2018/06/01/world/middleeast/gaza-israel-palestinians-.html.

56. Carol Morello, "U.S. Withdraws from U.N. Human Rights Council over Perceived Bias against Israel," Washington Post, June 19, 2018, https://www.washingtonpost.com/world/national-security/us-expected-to-back-away-from-un-human-rights-council/2018/06/19/a49c2d0c-733c-11e8-b4b7-308400242c2e_story.html?utm_term=.e11112a50144.

57. UN Human Rights Council, "Discriminatory Laws and Practices and Acts of Violence against Individuals Based on Their Sexual Orientation and Gender Identity," accessed July 12, 2013, https://www.ohchr.org/documents/issues/discrimination/a.hrc.19.41_english.pdf.

58. US Department of the Treasury, "Publication of Magnitsky Act Sanctions Regulations; Magnitsky Act-Related Designations," December 20, 2017, https://www.treasury.gov/resource-center/sanctions/OFAC-Enforcement/Pages/20171220_33.aspx; Mike Eckel, "U.S. Sanctions Chechen Leader Kadyrov, Four Others under Magnitsky Act," Radio Free Europe, December 20, 2017, https://www.rferl.org/a/us-sanctions-kadyrov-four-others-magnitsky-act/28929548.html.

59. Michael R. Pompeo, "Public Designation of Russian National Ramzan Kadyrov Due to Involvement in Gross Violations of Human Rights," US State Department, July 20, 2020, https://www.state.gov/public-designation-of-russian-national-ramzan-kadyrov-due-to-involvement-in-gross-violations-of-human-rights/.

60. For reporting about the 2014 meeting in DC, see Burack, Because We Are Human, 108–11.

61. "Equal Rights Coalition: Founding Principles," LGBTI Montevideo, July 13, 2016, http://www.lgbtimontevideo2016.org/admin/files/lgbtimontevideo2016/upload/files/Equal%20Rights%20Coalition%20-%20Founding%20Principles%20ENG.pdf; "Equal Rights Coalition: Fact Sheet," LGBTI Montevideo, accessed July 30, 2016, http://www.lgbtimontevideo2016.org/admin/files/lgbtimontevideo2016/upload/files/Factsheet%20Equal%20Rights%20Coalition%20ENG.pdf.

62. "Equal Rights Coalition," Government of Canada, May 25, 2018, http://international.gc.ca/world-monde/issues_development-enjeux_developpement/human_rights-droits_homme/coalition-equal-rights-droits-egaux.aspx?lang=eng.

63. Kailie Annetts, "Here Are All the Photos of Justin Trudeau's Surprise Appearance at Vancouver's Pride Parade," *Narcity*, August, 2018, https://www.narcity.com/news/prime-minister-justin-trudeau-just-surprised-vancouver-to-walk-in-the-pride-parade.

64. Michael K. Lavers, "US Officials Take Part in Global LGBTI Rights Conference," *Washington Blade*, August 8, 2018, https://www.washingtonblade.com/2018/08/08/us-officials-take-part-in-global-lgbti-rights-conference/.

65. Government of the United Kingdom, "Equal Rights Coalition," September 30, 2019, https://www.gov.uk/government/collections/equal-rights-coalition; Andrew Slinn, "Global LGBT+ Conference in London Confirmed for May 2020," Global Equality Caucus, November 16, 2019, https://equalitycaucus.org/news000000/lgbt-conference-may2020.

66. Equal Rights Coalition, "ERC Statement on Covid-19 and the Human Rights of LGBTI Persons," May 17, 2020, https://www.government.nl/documents/diplomatic-statements/2020/05/17/erc-statement-on-covid-19-and-the-human-rights-of-lgbti-persons.

67. Daniel W. Drezner, "Let's Grade the Commission on Unalienable Rights!," *Washington Post*, July 20, 2020, https://www.washingtonpost.com/outlook/2020/07/20/lets-grade-commission-unalienable-rights/.

68. Commission on Unalienable Rights, *Report of the Commission on Unalienable Rights*.

69. Carol Morello, "Pompeo Urges Other Countries to Join Alternative U.S. View on Human Rights," *Washington Post*, September 23, 2020, https://www.washingtonpost.com/national-security/pompeo-human-rights-un/2020/09/23/f34a4d2c-fdc2-11ea-830c-a160b331ca62_story.html.

70. Michael R. Pompeo, "Protecting and Promoting Human Rights: A Re-dedication to the Universal Declaration of Human Rights," US State Department, September 23, 2020, https://2017-2021.state.gov/promoting-and-protecting-human-rights-a-re-dedication-to-the-universal-declaration-of-human-rights/index.html.

71. Pompeo, "Protecting and Promoting Human Rights."

72. US Department of State, "Framework for U.S. Foreign Assistance," January 20, 2009, https://2001-2009.state.gov/f/c23053.htm.

73. US Department of State, "About Us: Office of Foreign Assistance," accessed September 5, 2020, https://www.state.gov/about-us-office-of-foreign-assistance/.

74. The Trump administration didn't withdraw or threaten to withdraw from only high-profile international bodies and agreements. One example of a less prominent body the administration threatened to withdraw from was the Universal Postal Union, the specialized agency of the UN that coordinates the international postal system and postal policies among member nations.

75. Although it doesn't provide a full picture of GEF funding to grantees and implementing partners, the best and most recent resource for LGBTI movement funding is Global Philanthropy Project and Funders for LGBTQ Issues, *2017–2018*

Global Resources Report: Government and Philanthropic Support for LGBTI Communities, https://globalresourcesreport.org/.

76. US Department of State, "Global Equality Fund," March 18, 2019, https://www.state.gov/global-equality-fund/.

77. fundsforNGOs, "Global Equality Fund: Strengthening Legal Protection for LGBTI Persons," 2017, https://www2.fundsforngos.org/latest-funds-for-ngos/global-equality-fund-strengthening-legal-protection-lgbti-persons/.

78. Burack, *Because We Are Human*, 147.

79. Freedom House, "About Us," accessed June 27, 2015, https://freedomhouse.org/about-us#.VZA-w0Z9l-w.

80. Freedom House, "Dignity for All: LGBTI Assistance Program," 2018, https://freedomhouse.org/program/dignity-all-lgbti-assistance-program.

81. Cynthia Burack, field notes, Donor Preconference, ILGA World conference, Bangkok, Thailand, November 29, 2016.

82. Human Rights Campaign, Twitter post, November 1, 2017, 2:48 pm, https://twitter.com/HRC/status/925842118068916228.

83. German Federal Foreign Office, "Together for LGBTI Human Rights," October 12, 2018, https://www.auswaertiges-amt.de/en/aussenpolitik/themen/menschenrechte/07-lgbti/roth-global-equality-fund/2148584.

84. Cynthia Burack, field notes, Global Equality Fund meeting and reception, Berlin, Federal Republic of Germany, October 12–13, 2018.

85. Norwegian Ministry of Foreign Affairs, calendar: "Statssekretær Hagen held ei innleiing på møte i Global Equality Fund," October 16–17, 2019, https://www.regjeringen.no/en/aktuelt/Calendar/id1330/?from=17.10.2019.

86. US State Department, "DRL FY2020: Global Equality Fund Programs in East Asia," December 30, 2020, https://www.state.gov/statements-of-interest-requests-for-proposals-and-notices-of-funding-opportunity/drl-fy2020-global-equality-fund-programs-in-east-asia/.

87. US State Department, "Global Equality Fund," 2021, https://www.state.gov/global-equality-fund/.

88. Alex Lockie, "Mattis Once Said That If State Department Funding Gets Cut 'Then I Need to Buy More Ammunition,'" *Business Insider*, February 27, 2017, https://www.businessinsider.com/mattis-state-department-funding-need-to-buy-more-ammunition-2017-2. Trump's first secretary of defense, Mattis resigned his position and, later, denounced Trump for using the military to attack peaceful protesters outside the White House. See Jeffrey Goldberg, "James Mattis Denounces President Trump, Describes Him as a Threat to the Constitution," *Atlantic*, June 3, 2020, https://www.theatlantic.com/politics/archive/2020/06/james-mattis-denounces-trump-protests-militarization/612640/.

89. Cynthia Burack, "Sexual Orientation and Gender Identity Human Rights Assistance in the Time of Trump," *Politics and Gender* 14, no. 4 (2018): 561–80; Elise Carlson Rainer, "Will Sexual Minority Rights Be Trumped? Assessing the Policy

Sustainability of LGBTI Rights Diplomacy in American Foreign Policy," *Diplomacy and Statecraft* 30, no. 1 (2019): 147–63.

Chapter 5

1. Naa Hammond, Lyle Matthew Kan, and Ben Francisco Maulbeck, *2013–2014 Global Resources Report: Government and Philanthropic Support for Lesbian, Gay, Bisexual, Transgender, and Intersex Communities*, Global Philanthropy Project and Funders for LGBTQ Issues, 2016, https://www.aidsdatahub.org/sites/default/files/resource/2013-2014-global-resources-report-govt-philanthropic-support-lesbian-gay-bisexual-transgender.pdf.

2. Robbie Corey-Boulet. "The Trump Effect: Elections at Home and Abroad Dampen Liberia's Gay-Rights Revival," *World Policy Journal* 34, no. 3 (2017): 86.

3. Meredith L. Weiss and Michael J. Bosia, eds., "Political Homophobia in Comparative Perspective," in *Global Homophobia: States, Movements, and the Politics of Oppression*, ed. Meredith L. Weiss and Michael J. Bosia (Urbana: University of Illinois Press, 2013), 1–29.

4. US Department of State, "Marking Policy," accessed July 9, 2015, https://www.statebuy.state.gov/fa/Pages/MarkingPolicy.aspx.

5. Cynthia Burack, field notes, ASOGIHRO conference, Africa, 2015.

6. The foregoing account of the 2015 ASOGIHRO conference relies on the case study in *Because We Are Human: Contesting US Support for Gender and Sexuality Human Rights Abroad* (New York: State University of New York Press, 2018), 114–19.

7. Marla Brettschneider, Susan Burgess, and Christine Keating, eds., *LGBTQ Politics: A Critical Reader* (New York: New York University Press, 2017).

8. Cynthia Burack, "Top Down, Bottom Up, or Meeting in the Middle? A SOGI Human Rights Case Study," in Brettschneider, Burgess, and Keating, *LGBTQ Politics: A Critical Reader*, 477–92; Burack, *Because We Are Human*.

9. Cynthia Burack, field notes, ASOGIHRO conference, Africa, 2019.

10. See Burack, *Because We Are Human*, 194–97.

11. See, e.g., Joyce K. Fletcher, *Disappearing Acts: Gender, Power, and Relational Practice at Work* (Cambridge, MA: MIT Press); Laura Morgan Roberts, Anthony J. Mayo, and David A. Thomas, eds., *Race, Work, and Leadership: New Perspectives on the Black Experience* (Boston, MA: Harvard Business Review Press, 2019).

12. African Women's Development Fund, *Charter of Feminist Principles for African Feminists* [African Feminist Charter], 2016, http://awdf.org/wp-content/uploads/AFF-Feminist-Charter-Digital-â%C2%80%C2%93-English.pdf.

13. Sarah Gunther and Mihika Srivastava, *Feminist Funding Principles*, Astraea Lesbian Foundation for Justice, 2019, https://astraeafoundation.org/microsites/feminist-funding-principles/. Contributors include J. Bob Alotta, Miriam Gagoshashvili, Bridget de Gersigny, Kim Kaletsky, Lame Olebile, Cara Page, and Sabrina Rich.

14. Regions Refocus, *Intersecting Movements Resisting Authoritarianisms: Feminist and Progressive Analysis and Tactics*, Regions Refocus, 2018, https://regions refocus.org/app/uploads/2020/05/RegionsRefocus_IntersectingMovementsResisting Authoritarianisms.pdf.

15. African Women's Development Fund, *Charter of Feminist Principles for African Feminists*, 5.

16. Ibid., 7.

17. I nod here to D. W. Winnicott's concept of the "good enough mother" in Winnicott, *The Child, the Family, and the Outside World* (New York: Penguin, 1973). The concept has been applied to other objects, including "good enough enemies": Howard F. Stein, *Developmental Time, Cultural Space: Studies in Psychogeography* (Norman: University of Oklahoma Press, 1987), 188–89.

18. Anna Marie Smith, *New Right Discourse on Race and Sexuality: Britain, 1968–1990* (Cambridge: Cambridge University Press, 1994), 204–5.

Conclusion

1. The phrase is Eric Hoffer's, but I gesture here to a groupish worldview that goes beyond his work. See Eric Hoffer, *The True Believer: Thoughts on the Nature of Mass Movements* (New York: Harper Perennial, 2002). For "groupishness," see Wilfred R. Bion, *Experiences in Groups and Other Papers* (London: Routledge, 1989); Cynthia Burack, *Healing Identities: Black Feminist Thought and the Politics of Groups* (Ithaca, NY: Cornell University Press, 2004); Jonathan Haidt, *The Righteous Mind: Why Good People Are Divided by Politics and Religion* (New York: Vintage, 2012).

2. Yascha Mounk, "Trump's Speech Was Too Effective for Comfort," *Slate*, January 8, 2019, https://slate.com/news-and-politics/2019/01/trumps-immigra-tion-speech-wall-effective.html. Mounk seems to revise, or at least update, his estimate of the danger associated with Trump's incompetence in Kristy Parker and Yascha Mounk, "Authoritarian Populists Have Six Classic Moves; Trump's Response to Covid-19 Uses Five of Them," *Atlantic*, April 2, 2020, https://www.theatlantic.com/ideas/archive/2020/04/trumps-authoritarian-covid/609304/.

3. Scott Lively, "Trump and the LGBT Agenda," December 9, 2016, https://barbwire.com/2016/12/09/trump-lgbt-agenda/.

4. See Meredith L. Weiss and Michael J. Bosia, *Global Homophobia: States, Movements, and the Politics of Oppression* (Urbana: University of Illinois Press, 2013).

5. Peter Baker, Michael M. Grynbaum, Maggie Haberman, Annie Karni, and Russ Buettner, "Trump Employs an Old Tactic: Using Race for Gain," *New York Times*, July 20, 2019, https://www.nytimes.com/2019/07/20/us/politics/trump-race-record.html; Ritu Prasad, "How Trump Talks about Women—and Does It Matter?," BBC News, November 29, 2019, https://www.bbc.com/news/world-us-canada-50563106.

6. Ayesha Rascoe, "'Low IQ,' 'SPECTACULAR,' 'Dog': How Trump Tweets about African-Americans," NPR, September 10, 2018, https://www.npr.org/2018/09/10/645594393/low-iq-spectacular-dog-how-trump-tweets-about-african-americans. For analyses of the history of the negative stereotype, see Steven Fraser, ed., *The Bell Curve Wars: Race, Intelligence, and the Future of America* (New York: Basic Books, 1995).

7. See Amber Ruffin, "Amber Ruffin Shares What Trump Has Done for Black America," Late Night with Seth Meyers, posted August 12, 2020, YouTube video, https://www.youtube.com/watch?v=iKgfgSch8BU; Amber Ruffin, "Amber Ruffin Shares What Trump Has Done for Women," Late Night with Seth Meyers, posted August 18, 2020, YouTube video, https://www.youtube.com/watch?v=b-cFVXEJKchw&utm_campaign=wp_the_daily_202&utm_medium=email&utm_source=newsletter&wpisrc=nl_daily202.

8. Mary L. Trump, *Too Much and Never Enough: How My Family Created the World's Most Dangerous Man* (New York: Simon and Schuster, 2020); Bill Eddy, *Why We Elect Narcissists and Sociopaths—and How We Can Stop* (Oakland, CA: Berrett-Koehler Publishers, 2019).

9. Bob Altemeyer, *The Authoritarians* (2006), access options listed at https://theauthoritarians.org/options-for-getting-the-book/. Altemeyer's essay on applying the analysis of *The Authoritarians* to Trump is "Why Do Trump's Supporters Stand by Him, No Matter What?," August 23, 2018, https://www.theauthoritarians.org/48-2/.

10. Thomas J. Main, *The Rise of the Alt-Right* (Washington, DC: Brookings Institution Press, 2018), 230.

11. Jim Sidanius and Felicia Pratto, *Social Dominance: An Intergroup Theory of Social Hierarchy and Oppression* (Cambridge: Cambridge University Press, 1999), 48.

12. John W. Dean and Bob Altemeyer, *Authoritarian Nightmare: Trump and His Followers* (New York: Penguin Random House, 2020).

13. Altemeyer, *The Authoritarians*, 169.

14. Sidanius and Pratto, *Social Dominance*, 36–37.

15. Woody Allen, dir., *Annie Hall* (Rollins-Joffe Productions, 1977). In one scene, Allen tells a college audience that he was expelled from NYU for cheating on his metaphysics final by "look[ing] within the soul of the boy sitting next to" him.

16. Cynthia Burack, *Sin, Sex, and Democracy: Antigay Rhetoric and the Christian Right* (Albany: State University of New York Press, 2008), 109–15.

17. Sam Brownback, "Ambassador Sam Brownback and Wajahat Ali: International Religious Freedom," *Faith Angle*, January 1, 2020, podcast, https://faithangle.podbean.com/e/amb-sam-brownback-and-wajahat-ali-international-religious-freedom/. Transcribed by the author, emphasis added.

18. Family Research Council, email to the author, "Join FRC at This Year's IRF Summit!," June 15, 2021. Like other emails I receive from Christian conservative organizations, the email was addressed to me personally, beginning, "Dear Cindy."

19. Arielle Del Turco, "Promoting Religious Freedom Even When the Government Doesn't," Family Research Council, July 9, 2021, https://www.frc.org/get.cfm?i=WA21G16&f=WU21G06.

20. International Religious Freedom Roundtable, "Purpose and Overview Statement," 2020, https://www.irfroundtable.org/blank-page.

21. Robert Seiple founded the Institute for Global Engagement, a 501(c)(3) nonprofit with which his son and several IRF Roundtable regional working group chairs are also affiliated.

22. At the summit, Simran Singh Stuelpnagel was also introduced as a cochair of the IRF Roundtable.

23. Cynthia Burack, field notes, International Religious Freedom Summit, Omni Shoreham Hotel, Washington, DC, July 13–15, 2021.

24. Greg Mitchell, "Advocacy Coalitions and Legislative Lobbying for International Religious Freedom," *Review of Faith and International Affairs* 10, no. 3 (2012): 51–57.

25. The formats of the IRF summit and the ministerials have a number of elements in common: their timing (midsummer); a program that alternates speeches and panels with testimonies from survivors of religious persecution perpetrated outside the US; and bipartisan support. In other respects, the IRF format reflects the FRC's annual Values Voter Summits: the meeting was held in the same Washington, DC, hotel that hosts the FRC's summits; unlike the ministerials, a number of young people, most associated with US Christian conservative organizations, attended; and an exhibits room was staffed by members of religious organizations (at the IRF summit, these included Falun Gong and Scientology).

26. In reporting on the summit, *Christianity Today* stressed the reluctance of Democrats to endorse the meeting and inaccurately reported that Blinken "had a keynote address from the stage." Jayson Caspar, "Summit Produces a 'Pentecost' Moment for International Religious Freedom," *Christianity Today*, July 19, 2021, https://www.christianitytoday.com/news/2021/july/irf-summit-religious-freedom-ambassador-brownback-democrats.html.

27. For an analysis of the ways in which the US Christian right has exported American culture wars see Kapya J. Kaoma, "The Marriage of Convenience: The U.S. Christian Right, African Christianity, and Postcolonial Politics of Sexual Identity," in Weiss and Bosia, *Global Homophobia*, 75–102.

28. Mike Pompeo, "LIVE: International Religious Freedom Summit Featuring Mike Pompeo," NTD News, posted July 14, 2021, YouTube video, https://www.youtube.com/watch?v=dAD_B9YnKuY. Several speakers appear in the video; Pompeo's speech begins at 50:10.

29. Human Rights Watch, "Guatemala: Events of 2020," 2021, https://www.hrw.org/world-report/2021/country-chapters/guatemala; Neela Ghoshal, *"It's What Happens When You Look Like This": Violence and Discrimination against LGBT People in Guatemala*, Human Rights Watch, March, 2021, https://www.hrw.org/sites/

default/files/media_2021/03/%E2%80%9CIt%E2%80%99s What Happens When You Look Like This%E2%80%9D_0.pdf.

30. Jorge Contessa, "The Inter-American Court of Human Rights' Advisory Opinion on Gender Identity and Same-Sex Marriage," *American Society of International Law* 22, no. 9 (July 26, 2018).

31. Human Rights Watch, "Guatemala: Free Press under Attack," February 18, 2021, https://www.hrw.org/news/2021/02/18/guatemala-free-press-under-attack.

32. Alejandro Giammattei, "The President of Guatemala, Alejandro Giammattei Addressed the IRF Summit," Facebook, July 20, 2021, https://www.facebook.com/watch/?v=372758184198306.

33. Elise Carlson Rainer, "Will Sexual Minority Rights Be Trumped? Assessing the Policy Sustainability of LGBTI Rights Diplomacy in American Foreign Policy," *Diplomacy and Statecraft* 30, no. 1 (2019): 147–63. Also see Elise Carlson Rainer, *From Pariah to Priority: How LGBTI Rights Became a Pillar of American and Swedish Foreign Policy* (Albany: State University of New York Press, 2021).

Appendix A

1. The video and full text of Tillerson's "Remarks" were originally posted to the State Department website. Rex Tillerson, "Remarks to U.S. Department of State Employees," US State Department, May 3, 2017, https://www.state.gov/secretary/remarks/2017/05/270620.htm. This transcript continues to be available at Wikisource, https://en.wikisource.org/wiki/Rex_Tillerson%27s_Remarks_to_U.S._Department_of_State_Employees. To assist the reader, I have added subheads, bracketed paragraph numbers, and a few bracketed references to Tillerson's gestures to the transcript.

Appendix B

1. Michael Pompeo, "Being a Christian Leader," US Department of State, October 11, 2019, https://2017-2021.state.gov/being-a-christian-leader/index.html. To assist the reader, I have added bracketed paragraph numbers to the original transcript.

Index

CPSIA information can be obtained
at www.ICGtesting.com
Printed in the USA
BVHW070934310123
657511BV00012B/57

During the Obama administration, Christian conservatives insisted that securing human rights for LGBTI people abroad diminished human rights protections for people of faith. During the 2016 presidential election, the Christian right backed Donald Trump and demanded an end to sexual orientation and gender identity (SOGI) foreign policy. Did the Trump administration move to terminate US advocacy for SOGI human rights? Did Christian conservative US officials and elites do everything in their power to publicize, curb, defund, and undermine US support for SOGI? If not—spoiler alert: they did not—why not? Analyzing SOGI human rights and religious freedom foreign policy, *How Trump and the Christian Right Saved LGBTI Human Rights* reveals the indifference, mendacity, and political interests at play in Trump's alliance with Christian right elites.

"Burack's insight into the Christian conservative takeover of the Republican party, in state legislatures and presidencies, is profoundly disturbing. Trump made this takeover easier yet since one thing and one thing only defined who he considered qualified for top-level policy and cabinet positions: loyalty. Christian conservatives played that card easily and 'for the higher purposes' of carrying out God's plan on earth. More frightening is the belief that transforming our democracy into a theocracy is not enough. The 'end time' when believers will meet their savior must be global. The infiltration of international human rights policy by Christian conservative moral entrepreneurs is an essential, perhaps final, move—yet one that never materialized. This book methodically investigates the mystery of how and why US SOGI rights support survived under the Trump administration."
— Franke Wilmer, author of *Breaking Cycles of Violence in Israel and Palestine: Empathy and Peacemaking in the Middle East*

Cynthia Burack is Professor of Women's, Gender and Sexuality Studies at the Ohio State University. Her many books include *Because We Are Human: Contesting US Support for Gender and Sexuality Human Rights Abroad*, also published by SUNY Press.

A volume in the SUNY series in Queer Politics and Cultures
Cynthia Burack and Jyl J. Josephson, editors

SUNY
PRESS
STATE UNIVERSITY OF NEW YORK PRESS
www.sunypress.edu

ISBN: 978-1-4384-8882-0

9 781438 488820